the **NEW** edition

New Headway

Upper-Intermediate Student's Book

Liz and John Soars

OXFORD
UNIVERSITY PRESS

CONTENTS

LISTENING	SPEAKING	EVERYDAY ENGLISH	WRITING
'Things I miss from home' – people describe what they miss when they travel abroad p14	Exchanging information about people who live abroad p10 Discussion – the pros and cons of living abroad p11	Social expressions *Great to see you!* *Don't I know you from somewhere?* p15	Applying for a job A CV and a covering letter p110
An interview with Tashi Wheeler about her travels as a child with her parents, who founded the *Lonely Planet* guides p24	Information gap and roleplay – Tony and Maureen Wheeler p18 Dreams come true – things to do before you die p22	Exclamations *Wow! That's unbelievable!* *How amazing!* *What a brilliant idea!* *What rubbish!* p25	Informal letters Correcting mistakes p112
The money jigsaw – a news item from the BBC's Radio 4 *Today* programme p32	Retelling a news story Responding to a news story p28 Talking about your favourite book or film p29	Showing interest and surprise Echo questions *A new boyfriend?* Reply questions *'He lives in a castle.' 'Does he?'* p33	Narrative writing 1 Using adverbs in narratives *I used to go skiing frequently in winter.* p113
'My most memorable lie!' – people confess to untruths p37	Discussion – good and bad lies p37 Exchanging information about conspiracy theories p38	Being polite *I'm sorry to bother you.* *Could you possibly change a ten-pound note?* p43	Linking ideas Conjunctions *whenever, so that, even though* p114
Arranging to meet – three friends decide a time and a place to get together (jigsaw) p52	Future possibilities in your life p47 Exchanging information about people arranging to meet p52	Telephone conversations Beginning a call Ending a call Roleplay p53	Writing emails Emailing friends *Sorry, can't make next Sat.* p115
Radio advertisements – what's the product? What's the selling point? p57	A lifestyle survey p56 Writing an advert p57 Exchanging information about famous brands p58 A business maze – opening a restaurant p60	Business expressions *Bear with me.* *I'll email the information as an attachment.* Numbers, fractions, decimals, dates, time, phone numbers, sports scores p61	A consumer survey Report writing *FAO: The Managing Director* p116

Phonetic symbols

1

No place like home

TEST YOUR GRAMMAR

1 Which time expressions from the box can be used with the sentences below?

1 My parents met in Paris.
2 They travel abroad.
3 They were working in Canada.
4 I was born in Montreal.
5 My grandparents have lived in Ireland.
6 I wrote to my grandmother.
7 I'm going to work in the US.
8 My brother's flying to Argentina on business.
9 He's been learning Spanish.
10 I'll see you.

> when I was born   never   in the 1970s
> tonight   frequently   for ages   ages ago
> the other day   in a fortnight's time
> recently   during a snowstorm   for a year
> since I was a child   later   sometimes

2 Talk to a partner about yourself and your family using some of the time expressions.

WRITING HOME
Tense revision and informal language

1 Read the letter. Who is writing? Who to? Where is he? What is he complaining about? How old do you think the writer is?

2 Complete the questions. Then ask and answer them with a partner.

1 'How long _____ Max _____ at summer camp?'
  'Just _____.'

2 '_____ he _____ a good time?'
  'No, not really. He _____ very homesick.'

3 'Is this his first time at summer camp?'
  'No, it _____ . He _____ once before. Last year he _____ to Pine Trees.'

4 '_____ he like it at Pine Trees?'
  'Oh, yes, he _____ , very much.'

5 'Why was that?'
  'Because _____.'

6 'What _____ tomorrow?'
  'He _____ pancakes.'

7 'Why _____ his cell phone?'
  'Because _____.'

3 〔 T 1.1 〕 Listen and check your answers.

Tuesday, 9.00pm

Hi Mom, Hi Dad!

   Been here two days but seems like FOREVER – it's kind of boring and I'm feeling very homesick – more homesick than last year 'cause at Pine Trees we had more exciting stuff to do. Here we have an activity called 'extreme sun tanning', where you sit outside for two hours and do nothing. We also have an activity called 'sitting around playing cards'. Last year we did stuff like archery and mountain biking. I'm still hanging in there, though. Got to go to sleep now. We're making chocolate chip pancakes for breakfast tomorrow.

Love you lots,

   Max xxxxx

   P.S. Could you send me more money? Oh, and my cell phone. ALL the other kids have their cell phones!

GROVE HILL SUMMER CAMP
MONMOUTH COUNTY

4 Read Sophie's email. What is it about? What do you learn about Sophie's likes and dislikes? Who is Rob? Who do you think Catherine is? Ask and answer the questions with a partner.

1 How long/Sophie/New Zealand?
2 How long/she/Australia?
3 Who/travel/with?
4 Why/like New Zealand?
5 Why/like Kangaroo Island?
6 What/their car like?
7 Which wildlife/already?
8 Where/next?
9 Why/photos?

5 **T 1.2** Listen and check your answers.

LANGUAGE FOCUS

1 Which tenses can you identify in the questions and answers in exercises 2 and 4? Why are they used?

2 **Informal writing** often has lots of colloquial language and words missed out.

kind of boring	= quite boring
Been here two days but seems like FOREVER	= I've been here two days but it seems like forever.
'cause (US), 'cos (UK)	= because

3 Work with a partner. Read the letter and email again.

1 What do 'stuff' and 'hanging in there' mean in Max's letter? Find colloquial words in Sophie's email and express them less colloquially.

2 Find examples where words are missing. Which words?

▶▶ **Grammar Reference pp140–141**

From:	**Sophie Beasely** <sophie.beas@yoohoo.com>
Date:	Wed 16 March, 10.36 am
To:	Robert Elliman
Subject:	New Zealand and missing you.

Hello again Rob!

Nearly two-thirds of the way through the trip now. Still having a great time but missing you like crazy! Been in New Zealand nearly a week and have met up with Catherine at last. Like it lots here. It has many advantages over Australia, the main ones being that it's smaller and cooler. Still, 3 weeks in Oz had its good points, despite the 44 degree heat! Kangaroo Island (near Adelaide) was my favourite place – loads of wildlife – did I tell you I'd seen some platypus there?

Here in New Zealand, first thing we did was buy a car. Went to the classy sounding 'Del's Cars' and, using our extensive mechanical knowledge (ha! ha!), chose a car and gave it a thorough examination (i.e. checked the lights worked & the glove box could hold 8 large bars of chocolate). It's going OK so far, but sometimes makes strange noises! We're taking things nice and slowly now. Have already seen dolphins, whales, and enormous albatrosses.

So – that's it for now. We're heading up the west coast next. Thanks for all your emails – it's great to get news from home. Can't wait to see you. I'm sending you some photos so you won't forget what I look like!

Love you. Wish, wish, wish you were here!

Sophie xxxxx (Catherine sends love too)

PRACTICE

Identifying the tenses

1 Complete the tense charts. Use the verb *work* for the active and *make* for the passive.

ACTIVE	Simple	Continuous
Present	he **works**	we **are working**
Past	she	I
Future	they	you
Present Perfect	we	she
Past Perfect	**I had worked**	you
Future Perfect	they	he **will have been working**

PASSIVE	Simple	Continuous
Present	it **is made**	they **are being made**
Past	it	it
Future	they	
Present Perfect	they	
Past Perfect	it	
Future Perfect	they **will have been made**	

2 **T 1.3** Listen to the lines of conversation and discuss what the context might be. Listen again and identify the tenses. Which lines have contractions?

He's been working such long hours recently. He never sees the children.

– Could be a wife talking about her husband.

– Present Perfect Continuous, Present Simple.

– He's (He has) been working ...

Discussing grammar

3 Compare the meaning in the pairs of sentences. Which tenses are used? Why?

1 Klaus **comes** from Berlin.
Klaus **is coming** from Berlin.

2 You**'re** very kind. Thank you.
You**'re being** very kind. What do you want?

3 What **were** you **doing** when the accident happened?
What **did** you **do** when the accident happened?

4 I**'ve lived** in Singapore for five years.
I **lived** in Singapore for five years.

5 When we arrived, he **tidied** the flat.
When we arrived, he**'d tidied** the flat.

6 We**'ll have** dinner at 8.00, shall we?
Don't call at 8.00. We**'ll be having** dinner.

7 How much **are** you **paying** to have the house painted?
How much **are** you **being paid** to paint the house?

8 How **do you do**?
How **are you doing**?

Talking about you

4 Complete these sentences with your ideas.

1 At weekends I often ...
2 My parents have never ...
3 I don't think I'll ever ...
4 I was saying to a friend just the other day that ...
5 I hate Mondays because ...
6 I'd just arrived home last night when ...
7 I was just getting ready to go out this morning when ...
8 I've been told that our teacher ...
9 In my very first English lesson I was taught ...
10 The reason I'm learning English is because ...

T 1.4 Listen and compare. What are the responses?

5 Work with a partner. Listen to each other's sentences and respond.

SPOKEN ENGLISH Missing words out

Which words are missing in these lines from conversations?

1 Heard about Jane and John splitting up?
2 Leaving already? What's wrong?
3 Failed again? How many times is that?
4 Sorry I'm late. Been waiting long?
5 Doing anything interesting this weekend?
6 Like the car! When did you get it?
7 Bye Jo! See you later.
8 Just coming! Hang on!
9 Want a lift? Hop in.
10 Seen Jim lately?

Read the lines aloud to your partner and make suitable responses.

T 1.5 Listen and compare.

A long-distance phone call

6 Read through these lines of a phone conversation. Kirsty is calling her father. Where do you think she is? Why is she there? Where is he? Work with a partner to complete her father's lines in the conversation.

D ...

K Dad! It's me, Kirsty.

D ...

K I'm fine, but still a bit jet-lagged.

D ...

K It's nine hours ahead. I just can't get used to it. Last night I lay awake all night, and then today I nearly fell asleep at work in the middle of a meeting.

D ...

K It's early days but I think it's going to be really good. It's a big company but everybody's being so kind and helpful. I've been trying to find out how everything works.

D ...

K I've seen a bit. It just seems such a big, busy city. I don't see how I'll ever find my way round it.

D ...

K No, it's nothing like London. It's like nowhere else I've ever been – masses of huge buildings, underground shopping centres, lots of taxis and people – so many people – but it's so clean. No litter on the streets or anything.

D ...

K Well, for the time being I've been given a tiny apartment, but it's in a great part of town.

D ...

K That's right. I won't be living here for long. I'll be offered a bigger place as soon as one becomes available, which is good 'cos this one really is tiny, but at least it's near to where I'm working.

D ...

K Walk! You're kidding! It's not *that* close. It's a short subway ride away. And the trains come so regularly – it's a really easy journey, which is good 'cos I start work very early in the morning.

D ...

K Again it's too early to say. I think I really will be enjoying it all soon. I'm sure it's going to be a great experience. It's just that I miss everyone at home so much.

D ...

K I will. I promise. And you email me back with all your news. I just love getting news from home. Give everyone my love. Bye.

D ...

T 1.6 Listen and compare. Identify some of the tenses used in the conversation.

▶▶ **WRITING** Applying for a job **p110**

READING AND SPEAKING
A home from home

1 Why do people go to live abroad? Make a list of reasons and discuss with your class.

2 You are going to read about Ian Walker-Smith, who moved to Chile, and Thomas Creed, who moved to Korea.

Which of these lines from the articles do you think are about Chile (**C**) and which about Korea (**K**)?

1. ☐ As we're 2,600 m above sea level, I easily get puffed when I'm exercising.
2. ☐ Soccer is a really big deal here ever since they hosted the 2002 World Cup.
3. ☐ … we converse in what we call 'Espanglish' …
4. ☐ … learning Chinese characters stinks.
5. ☐ … its surrounding mines are said to make more money than any other city.
6. ☐ I can eat spicy food like *kimchee* …
7. ☐ It's also normal to roll out mattresses and sleep on the floor.
8. ☐ We now have a pleasant walkway along the seafront.

3 Divide into two groups.

Group A Read about Ian on this page.
Group B Read about Thomas on p12.

Check your answers to exercise 2.

4 Answer the questions about Ian or Thomas.

1. Where did he go to live abroad? Why?
2. How long has he been there?
3. What does he do there?
4. What do you learn about his family?
5. What is the new home town like?
6. Have there been any difficulties?
7. In what ways is he 'in the middle of nowhere'?
8. Does he feel at home in his new home?
9. What does he like and dislike about his new life?
10. What does he miss?

5 Find a partner from the other group. Compare your answers. Who do you think is happier about the move? Which new home would you prefer?

Expat tales

IAN WALKER-SMITH IN CHILE

Ian Walker-Smith comes from Crewe, England, but now lives and works in Chile. He's married to a Chilean woman,
05 Andrea, and works for a European astronomical agency in the town of Paranal.

Ian says: ❝ I work shifts of eight days in Paranal, and get six to rest at home – in my case, the mining town of Antofagasta, a harrowing
10 two-hour drive away on the coast. It takes a real toll, being so far from Andrea. I miss her when I'm away.

Where he works

I work at Paranal Observatory, where every night the boundaries of our universe are probed by four of the world's largest telescopes. I'm part of a 12-strong I.T. team which looks after everything from
15 satellite ground stations to desktop support. My role is to make sure the computers run 24/7. As Paranal is in the middle of nowhere – up a mountain in the desert – the sky is truly amazing. As we're 2,600 m above sea level, I easily get puffed when I'm exercising and each time I arrive for a week on shift, I can't think straight or fast for the first
20 day or so.

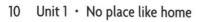

Why he moved

I decided to move to Chile four years ago when I was a 25-year-old with itchy feet (and wanted to get out of the way of an ex-girlfriend!). I was working for Littlewoods Home Shopping Group, and one day a colleague pointed out this job in Chile. We both thought it would be
25 a good idea, but I was the one who put a CV together.

Life in Chile

Landing at Santiago airport was my first experience of language being such a barrier. I couldn't speak more than a handful of words in Spanish, and would you believe that my baggage had got lost! So my first couple of hours in Chile were spent trying to locate my missing
30 possessions. Today I can order food in restaurants and argue with mechanics about my car, but I can't really make myself understood on any deeper level. I can't get my thoughts across as a native speaker could. Andrea speaks pretty good English, and we converse in what we call 'Espanglish' – at least we can understand each other.

35 Antofagasta, the town where we have made our home, was once described in a Chilean advertising campaign as the 'Pearl of the North'. Let's just say that it's hardly a tourist destination (which is pretty much what you'd say about my home town, Crewe!). Antofagasta and its surrounding mines are said to make more money
40 for Chile than any other city. During my time here, some money has been put back into the city. The municipal beach has been much improved. We now have a pleasant walkway along the seafront.

What he misses

Even after four years, I don't feel I belong. Over Christmas I went back to the UK for a month's holiday – on landing at Heathrow, I felt at home
45 straight away. What I miss most is greenery. My own culture still fits me like the winter gloves I left behind when I came to work in the desert sun. Shame I can't say the same of my old winter trousers … ,

Language work

Study the texts again and answer the questions about these expressions. Explain the meanings to a partner who read the other text.

Ian in Chile
1 *It takes a real toll, …* l.10
   What takes a toll? On what or who?
2 *… the computers run 24/7.* l.16
   How long do the computers operate?
3 *I easily get puffed …* l.18
   When and why does he get puffed?
4 *… itchy feet …* l.24
   Why did he get itchy feet?
5 *… winter gloves …* l.48
   What still fits him like winter gloves?

Thomas in Korea
1 *… I'm really into soccer.* l.07
   Is he a soccer fan?
2 *… a really big deal …* l.08
   What is a really big deal? Why?
3 *… doesn't get it.* l.09
   Who doesn't get what? Why not?
4 *… a big shot.* l.17
   Who is a big shot? What makes him a big shot?
5 *… the bad guy is beating him up.* l.53
   Who is the bad guy beating up?

Express all the lines marked with an asterisk (*) in more formal English.

What do you think?

Work in groups.

- Close your eyes and think about your country. What would you miss most if you went to live abroad? Compare ideas.

- Make a list of the disadvantages of moving abroad. Then for every disadvantage (−) try to find an advantage (+).

  ⊖ The language barrier – maybe you don't speak the language.

  ⊕ But this is an opportunity to learn a new language.

- Have any of your friends or family gone to live in a foreign country? Why?

- Do you know anyone who has come to live in your country from another country? Why? Do they have any problems?

- Which other countries would you like to live in for a while? Why?

Expat tales

'I'm part of the group now. The only difference is I have brown hair and blue eyes,' says Thomas Creed, an eleven-year-old originally from Boston, Massachusetts.

Thomas says: ❛These days I'm really into soccer. Soccer is a really big deal here ever since they hosted the 2002 World Cup. But Dad doesn't get it. I wasn't a soccer fan
10 either when I first came to Seoul six years ago. Like my dad, I was a big basketball fan – still am – watching all the games Dad taped, cheering for the Celtics. But now, me and my friends play soccer all the time. It's hard not to get addicted! My best friend Dong-won and I cut out photos
15 of David Beckham and trade them like baseball cards.

Why he moved

My dad's an officer in the US Army, but he wasn't always such a big shot. He had 'tours of duty', which means he's had to move around whether he liked it or not. He's lived in places like Germany, Vietnam, and Saudi Arabia.
20 My mom and I always stayed back in Boston. She's a scientist. But then my dad and my big brother Patrick both got transferred to Korea – Patrick's ten years older than me, and he's in the Army, too. So our whole family moved over. Seoul's cool. There are millions of places
25 called 'PC rooms' where you can play tons of Internet games. The city's a lot bigger than Boston, too, and way more crowded and busy. I didn't like that at first. I couldn't understand what anyone was saying, and people here don't always
30 smile at strangers like they do back in the US. I felt lonely, like I was in the middle of nowhere.

Life in Korea

Life's different here. Most homes don't have radiators –
35 the heat comes up through the floor instead. It's done like this because most Koreans eat cross-legged on floor mats. It's easier than using chairs but it gives my father leg cramps. It's also normal to roll out mattresses and sleep on the floor. That's how I sleep over at Dong-
40 won's house. Dong-won's great and helped me a lot when I first started elementary school here. I was five and didn't know anything or anybody and was pretty scared. I even made my dad wait for me in the next room. Now I can speak Korean fluently, but learning
45 Chinese characters stinks. I always do badly on those tests. I can eat spicy foods like kimchee, and I've read a lot of Korean books and stories, which I like.

What he misses

What I miss most are American comics. I know it's
50 stupid 'cause there are lots of comics here, but they're different. They don't have superheroes like Spiderman, who always has something cool to say, even when the bad guy is beating him up. Also, I wish basketball was more popular. I love soccer but no one understands
55 how *awesome a *'slam dunk' can be.

But I like living here. The people are really nice, and maybe I'll be a translator one day … or even better, a great soccer player like David Beckham.❜

* incredible
* when a basketball player jumps up above the basket and pushes the ball down into it

12

VOCABULARY AND PRONUNCIATION
House and home

> ### Compound nouns and adjectives
>
> Words can combine to make new words.
>
> **1** Look at the examples. Which are nouns and which are adjectives?
>
> **life**   *lifestyle   lifelong   life-size
> life expectancy   life insurance*
>
> Your dictionary can tell you when to use hyphens and spaces.
>
> **2** Read the compounds aloud. Which words are stressed?
>
> **3** Look at the texts on pp10–12 and find some compound nouns and adjectives.

1 How many new words can you make by combining a word on the left with a word on the right? Which are nouns and which are adjectives?

home
house

work	made	wife	sick	proud
page	plant	town	coming	
less	grown	bound	warming	

2 **T 1.7** Listen to the conversations. After each one, discuss these questions. Who is talking to who? What about? Which compounds from exercise 1 are used?

3 Complete these lines from the conversations.

1 I'm going away for two weeks. Do you think you could possibly water my _____ for me?

2 Don't worry, I know how _____ you are. I'll make sure everything stays clean and tidy.

3 Let's give her a spectacular _____ party when she gets back from New York.

4 Me? I'm just a _____. Four kids, _____ cakes, and _____ vegetables!

5 We're having a _____ party on the 12th. Can you come? I'll give you our new address.

6 Mind you, with it being much bigger, there's much more _____ to do!

7 Her grandmother's sick and _____, so they have to go and help.

'Please turn it down – Daddy's trying to do your homework.'

4 **T 1.8** Practise saying the lines in exercise 3 with correct stress and intonation. Listen and check. Try to remember more of each conversation and act some of them out with a partner.

5 Work in groups. Make compounds by combining words from one of the boxes in **A** with as many words as possible from **B**. Use your dictionary to help.

A

book	tea
computer	sleeping
air	door
junk	open
food	fire
word	head

B

pill line mail way case bell

light air house bag software

escape office processor

poisoning pot step rest

alarm shelf program food

Share your words with a different group and explain the meanings.

▶▶ **SONG** *Don't leave home* Teacher's Book *p143*

LISTENING AND SPEAKING
Things I miss from home

1 When have you spent time away from home? Where did you go? Why? Did you have a good time? What did you miss from home?

2 Write down one thing that you missed on a piece of paper, and give it to your teacher. You will use these later.

3 **T 1.9** Listen to some people talking about the things they miss most when they are away from home. Take notes and compare them in groups.

	What they miss	Other information
Andrew		
Helen		
Gabriele		
Paul		
Sylvia		
Chris		

4 **T 1.9** Read the lines below. Then listen again. Who is speaking? What do the words in *italics* refer to?

1 That sounds very silly but I like to see *them* from time to time.

2 I can't bear to wake up in the morning and be without *them* …

3 … *it*'s all very reassuring, even if *he*'s telling something dreadful.

4 And I am there, waving *the aerial* around and twiddling *the knob* …

5 *They* can be quite wonderful because you don't need to worry about traffic …

6 … and spend … a large part of *the day* just sitting around reading the paper …

5 Read aloud the things that were written down in exercise 2. Guess who wrote them. Whose is the funniest? The most interesting?

EVERYDAY ENGLISH
Social expressions and the music of English

1 Work with a partner. Match a line in **A** with a line in **B**.

A		B	
1	Great to see you. Come on in.	a	Let me see. No, actually, I don't think I'll bother with dessert.
2	Excuse me, don't I know you from somewhere?	b	I was just passing and thought I'd drop in.
3	What d'you mean you're not coming?	c	Really! That's a drag. I was hoping to meet her.
4	I think I'll have the chocolate mousse. What about you?	d	No, I don't think so.
5	My flatmate can't make it to your party.	e	Well, I just don't feel up to going out tonight.
6	How come you're not having a holiday this year?	f	Fantastic! I knew you'd swing it for us.
7	You'll make yourself ill if you carry on working at that pace.	g	We just can't afford it.
8	I've got you the last two tickets for the show.	h	That's as maybe but I have to get this finished by Friday.

T 1.10 Listen and check. Pay particular attention to the stress and intonation. Practise the lines with your partner.

> ### Music *of* English ♫♪
>
> **T 1.11** The 'music' of a language is made up of three things.
>
> 1 Intonation – the up and down of the voice:
>
> *Excuse me!* *Really?*
>
> 2 Stress – the accented syllables in individual words:
>
> *chocolate* *fantastic* *dessert*
>
> 3 Rhythm – the stressed syllables over a group of words:
>
> *What d'you mean you're not coming?*

2 **T 1.12** Listen to the conversation and concentrate on the 'music'. Who are the people? Do they know each other? Where are they?

3 Work with a partner. Look at the conversation on p153. Take the roles of **A** and **B** and read the conversation aloud, using the stress shading to help you.

T 1.12 Listen again and repeat the lines one by one. Practise the conversation again with your partner.

4 The stressed words are given in these conversations. Try to complete the lines. Practise saying them as you go.

1

A Excuse ... , ... know you ... somewhere?
B Actually, ... think so.
A ... Gavin's party last week?
B Not me. ... don't know anyone ... Gavin.
A Well, someone ... looked just like ... there.
B Well, that's ... maybe ... certainly wasn't me.
A ... am sorry!

2

A Tony! Hi! Great ... see ...!
B Well, ... just passing ... drop in ... 'hello'.
A ... in! Have ... drink!
B ... sure? ... too busy?
A Never ... busy ... talk ... you.
B Thanks, Jo. ... really nice ... chat.
A Fantastic! Let ... coat.

5 **T 1.13** Listen and compare your ideas and pronunciation.

2 Been there, done that!

Present Perfect · Simple and continuous · Hot verbs – *make*, *do* · Exclamations

TEST YOUR GRAMMAR

1 What is strange about these sentences? What should they be?

1. Columbus has discovered America.
2. Man first walked on the moon.
3. I travelled all my life. I went everywhere.
4. I've learnt English.
5. I've been losing my passport.

2 Which of these verb forms can change from simple to continuous or vice versa? What is the change in meaning?

1. What do you do in New York?
2. I know you don't like my boyfriend.
3. I had a cup of tea at 8.00.
4. Someone's eaten my sandwich.
5. I'm hot because I've been running.

EXPLORERS AND TRAVELLERS
Present Perfect

1 Look at the pictures. Why did people go exploring hundreds of years ago? Why do young people go travelling these days?

2 Read the first and last paragraphs of two articles about Marco Polo and Tommy Willis. Then match the sentences with the correct person. Put **MP** or **TW** in the boxes.

1. ☐ He was born in Venice, the son of a merchant. When he was 17, he set off for China. The journey took four years.
2. ☐ He's visited royal palaces and national parks in South Korea, and climbed to the summit of Mount Fuji in Japan.
3. ☐ He's been staying in cheap hostels, along with a lot of other young people.
4. ☐ His route led him through Persia and Afghanistan.
5. ☐ He was met by the emperor Kublai Khan. He was one of the first Europeans to visit the territory, and he travelled extensively.
6. ☐ 'I've had diarrhoea a few times.' Apart from that, his only worry is the insects. He's been stung all over his body.
7. ☐ He stayed in China for seventeen years. When he left, he took back a fortune in gold and jewellery.
8. ☐ He's been travelling mainly by public transport.

T 2.1 Listen and check. What other information do you learn about the two travellers?

MARCO POLO 1254–1324

MARCO POLO was the first person to travel the entire 8,000 kilometre length of the Silk Route, the main trade link between Cathay (China) and the West for over two thousand years.

He wrote a book called *The Travels of Marco Polo*, which gave Europeans their first information about China and the Far East.

3 Match a line in **A** with a line in **B**. Practise saying them. Pay attention to contracted forms and weak forms.

A	B
He's been stung	in cheap hostels.
He's visited	all over his body.
He's been staying	a lot of really great people.
I've been	to Vietnam and Japan.
I've met	pickpocketed and mugged.
He's been	royal palaces.

T 2.2 Listen and check.

TOMMY WILLIS backpacker in Asia

Tommy Willis is in Fiji. He's on a nine-month backpacking trip round south-east Asia. He flew into Bangkok five months ago. Since then, he's been to Vietnam, Hong Kong, South Korea, and Japan.

He's looking forward to taking things easy for another week, then setting off again for Australia. 'Once you've got the travel bug, it becomes very hard to stay in the same place for too long,' he said.

LANGUAGE FOCUS

1 What is the main tense used in the sentences about Marco Polo? Why?

What are the main tenses used in the sentences about Tommy Willis? Why?

2 Compare the use of tenses in these sentences.

1 I've read that book. It's good.
   I've been reading a great book. I'll lend it to you when I've finished.
   I've been reading a lot about Orwell recently. I've just finished his biography.

2 She's been writing since she was 16.
   She's written three novels.

3 He's played tennis since he was a kid.
   He's been playing tennis since he was a kid.

▶▶ **Grammar Reference pp141–142**

PRACTICE

Questions and answers

1 Read the pairs of questions. First decide who each question is about, Marco Polo or Tommy Willis. Then ask and answer the questions.

1 Where did he go?
   Where has he been?

2 How long has he been travelling?
   How long did he travel?

3 How did he travel?
   How has he been travelling?

4 Who has he met?
   Who did he meet?

5 Did he have any problems?
   Has he had any problems?

2 Here are the answers to some questions. Write the questions.

About Marco Polo
1 In 1254 in Venice.
2 Four years.
3 For seventeen years.
4 Gold and jewellery.
5 *The Travels of Marco Polo.*

About Tommy Willis
6 For five months. **How long ... away from home?**
7 Thailand, Vietnam, Hong Kong, South Korea, and Japan. **Which ...?**
8 In cheap hostels.
9 A few times. **How many ...?**
10 Yes, once. **Has ...?**

T 2.3 Listen and check your answers.

Discussing grammar

3 Put the verb in the correct tense.

1 Charles Dickens _____ (write) *Oliver Twist* in 1837.
I _____ (write) two best-selling crime stories.
She _____ (write) her autobiography for the past eighteen months.

2 _____ you ever _____ (try) Mexican food?
_____ you _____ (try) *chiles rellenos* when you were in Mexico?

3 How many times _____ you _____ (marry)?
How many times _____ Henry VIII _____ (marry)?

4 I _____ (live) in the same house since I was born.
He _____ (live) with his brother for the past week.

5 Cinda's very pleased with herself. She _____ finally _____ (give up) smoking. She _____ (try) to give up for years.

Simple and continuous

> **LANGUAGE FOCUS**
>
> **1** Simple verb forms see actions as a complete whole.
> *He **works** for IBM.   It **rained** all day yesterday.   **I've lost** my passport.*
>
> **2** Continuous verb forms see actions in progress, with a beginning and an end.
> *I'm **working** with Jim for a couple of days.*
> *It **was raining** when I woke up.*
> *The company **has been losing** money for years.*
>
> **3** State verbs don't tend to be used in the continuous.
> *I **know** Peter well.   I've always **liked** him.*
> *I **don't understand** what you're saying.*
>
> Do you know more verbs like these?
>
> ▶▶ **Grammar Reference pp140–141**

4 Match a line in **A** with a line in **B**. Write 1 or 2 in the box.

A	B
a ☐ Peter comes	1 from Switzerland.
b ☐ Peter is coming	2 round at 8.00 tonight.
c ☐ I wrote a report this morning.	1 I'll finish it this afternoon.
d ☐ I was writing a report this morning.	2 I sent it off this afternoon.
e ☐ I heard her scream	1 when she saw a mouse.
f ☐ I heard the baby screaming	2 all night long.
g ☐ What have you done	1 since I last saw you?
h ☐ What have you been doing	2 with my dictionary? I can't find it.
i ☐ I've had	1 a headache all day.
j ☐ I've been having	2 second thoughts about the new job.
k ☐ I've known	1 my new neighbours.
l ☐ I've been getting to know	2 Anna for over ten years.
m ☐ I've cut	1 my finger. It hurts.
n ☐ I've been cutting	2 wood all morning.

▶▶ **WRITING** Informal letters – Correcting mistakes *p112*

Exchanging information

5 Tony and Maureen Wheeler are the founders of the *Lonely Planet* travel guides. There are now over 650 books in the series.

Work with a partner. You each have different information. Ask and answer questions.

Student A Look at p153.
Student B Look at p154.

READING AND SPEAKING
Paradise Lost

1 Look at the pictures of tourist destinations in the world. Where are they? Have you been to any of them?

6 Work in groups to prepare an interview with Tony Wheeler. One half of the class will be the interviewers (look at the ideas below), and the other half Tony Wheeler (look at the ideas on p154).

Interviewers

BACKGROUND
Where ... grow up?
What ... father do?

EDUCATION
Where ... school?
Which university ...?

WORK
What work ... after university?

FAMILY
How many children ...?

HOLIDAYS
What ... like doing ...?

LONELY PLANET GUIDES
When ... the first guide book come out?
Where ... idea come from?
What ... the best and worst moment?
What ... secret of your success?
How ... get into travel writing?

FUTURE
Where would you like ...?

2 What are the most important tourist spots in your country? Does tourism cause any problems there?

3 What are the main problems associated with the tourist industry in the world?

Turn to p21.

Paradise lost

What can be done to stop tourism destroying the object of its affection? Maurice Chandler reports on the boom in world travel.

On the sun-soaked Mediterranean island of Majorca, the locals are angry. Too late. In the last quarter of the twentieth century, they cashed in on foreign nationals, mainly Germans, wanting to buy up property on their idyllic island. Suddenly it occurred to Majorcans that the island no longer belonged to them. They don't deny tourism's vital contribution to the local economy. The industry has transformed Majorca from one of Spain's poorest parts to the richest in per capita income. But the island's 630,000 inhabitants are increasingly convinced that the 14 million foreign visitors a year are far too much of a good thing. Water is rationed, pollution is worsening, and there is no affordable housing left for them to buy.

On the other side of the world, 250 Filipinos were recently evicted from their homes. Their lake-shore village of Ambulong was cleared by hundreds of police, who demolished 24 houses. The intention of the authorities was to make way for a major business venture – not oil, logging, or mining, but an environmentally-friendly holiday resort.

A growth industry

Tourism is the world's largest and fastest growing industry. In 1950, 25m people travelled abroad; last year it was 750m. The World Tourism Organization estimates that by 2020 1.6bn people will travel each year, spending over two trillion US dollars.

The effects of tourism

To millions of tourists, foreign destinations are exotic paradises, unspoilt, idyllic, and full of local charm. But many of the world's resorts are struggling to cope with relentless waves of tourists, whose demands for ever more swimming pools and golf courses are sucking them dry.

'The issue is massive and global,' says Tricia Barnett, director of Tourism Concern, a charity which campaigns for more responsible approaches to travel. 'Tourists in Africa will be having a shower and then will see a local woman with a pot of water on her head, and they are not making the connection. Sometimes you'll see a village with a single tap, when each hotel has taps and showers in every room.'

The problem is that tourists demand so much water. It has been calculated that a tourist in Spain uses up 880 litres of water a day, compared with 250 litres by a local. An 18-hole golf course in a dry country can consume as much water as a town of 10,000 people. In the Caribbean, hundreds of thousands of people go without piped water during the high tourist season, as springs are piped to hotels.

In 1950, 25m people travelled abroad; last year it was 750m.

Winners and losers

The host country may not see many benefits. In Thailand, 60% of the $4bn annual tourism revenue leaves the country. Low-end package tourists tend to stay at big foreign-owned hotels, cooped up in the hotel compound, buying few local products, and having no contact with the local community other than with the waiters and chambermaids employed by the hotel. 'Mass tourism usually leaves little money inside the country,' says Tricia Barnett. 'Most of the money ends up with the airlines, the tour operators, and the foreign hotel owners.'

These days the industry's most urgent question may be how to keep the crowds at bay. A prime example of this is Italy, where great cultural centres like Florence and Venice can't handle all the tourists they get every summer. In Florence, where the city's half-million or so inhabitants have to live with the pollution, gridlock, and crime generated by 11 million visitors a year, there's talk not only of boosting hotel taxes, but even of charging admission to some public squares. The idea is to discourage at least some visitors, as well as to pay for cleaning up the mess.

The future

For many poorer countries, tourism may still offer the best hope for development. 'The Vietnamese are doing their best to open up their country,' says Patrick Duffey of the World Tourism Organization. 'Iran is working on a master plan for their tourism. Libya has paid $1 million for a study. They all want tourists. And people like to discover ever new parts of the world, they are tired of mass tourism. Even if a country doesn't have beaches, it can offer mountains and deserts and unique cultures.'

Yet if something isn't done, tourism seems destined to become the victim of its own success. Its impact on the environment is a major concern. In hindsight, tourist organizations might have second thoughts about what exactly they were trying to sell.

As Steve McGuire, a tourist consultant, says, 'Tourism more often than not ruins the very assets it seeks to exploit, and having done the damage, simply moves off elsewhere.'

For poorer countries, tourism may still offer the best hope for development.

Reading

4 Read the title and the quotes in the article. What do you think the article will be about?

5 Read the article. Answer the questions.
  1 Which of the places in the pictures on p19 are mentioned?
  2 What is said about them?
  3 What other places are mentioned?
  4 Does the article talk about any of the problems you discussed?
  5 The author asks 'What can be done to stop tourism destroying the object of its affection?' What would Steve McGuire's answer be?

6 In groups, discuss these questions.
  1 How is tourism destroying the object of its affection in Majorca and the Philippines?
  2 What are the statistics of the global tourist industry?
  3 What are the effects of tourism?
  4 Who are the winners and losers?
  5 What are possible future developments?

What do you think?

1 Give your personal reactions to the text using these phrases.

I didn't know/I already knew that ...	What surprised me was ...
It must be really difficult for ...	It's hard to believe that ...
I wonder what can be done to ...	It's a shame that ...

2 In groups, think of more questions to ask the other groups. Use the prompts if you want.

Who ...?	Why ...?	In what way ...?
What is meant by ...?	How many ...?	
What exactly ...?	What are some of the problems ...?	

Who has bought nearly all the property on the island of Majorca?

Vocabulary work

1 Work with a partner. Discuss the meaning of the words highlighted in the article.

2 Match a line in **A** with a line in **B**. Can you remember the contexts?

A	B
the boom	destinations
tourism's vital	venture
per capita	for development
a major business	income
foreign	example
consume	in world travel
a prime	as much water
the best hope	contribution to the economy

SPEAKING AND LISTENING
Dreams come true

1 20,000 people were asked what they most wanted to do before they die. Here are the top fifteen activities.

What are your top five? Number them 1–5. Which ones don't interest you at all? Put an **X**.

- ☐ go whale-watching
- ☐ see the Northern Lights
- ☐ visit Machu Picchu
- ☐ escape to a paradise island
- ☐ go white-water rafting
- ☐ fly in a fighter plane
- ☐ fly in a hot-air balloon
- ☐ climb Sydney Harbour Bridge
- ☐ swim with dolphins
- ☐ walk the Great Wall of China
- ☐ go on safari
- ☐ go skydiving
- ☐ dive with sharks
- ☐ drive a Formula 1 car
- ☐ go scuba diving on the Great Barrier Reef

Compare your lists in groups.

2 You can read the actual results of the poll on p155. Does anything surprise you? What do you think is missing from the list?

3 Do you know anyone who has done any of these things? What was it like?

4 **T 2.4** Listen to three people describing their experience of one of these activities. Which one are they talking about? What do they say about it?

VOCABULARY
Hot verbs – *make, do*

1 There are many expressions with *make* and *do*. Look at these examples from the text on p20.

- They wanted … to *make way* for a holiday resort.
- They aren't *making the connection*.
- The Vietnamese are *doing their best* to open up their country.
- Tourism, having *done the damage*, moves off elsewhere.

2 Put the words in the right box.

| a good impression   business   arrangements   a decision   a difference research   a profit/a loss   your best   a start/a move   sth clear a good job   a degree   an effort   sb a favour   a suggestion |

MAKE	DO

3 Complete the sentences with some of the expressions in exercise 2.

1 When you go for a job interview, it's important to _____.
2 I think we're all getting tired. Can I _____? How about a break?
3 A lot of _____ has been _____ into the causes of cancer.
4 I think the director is basically _____. He's reliable, he's honest, and he gets results.
5 I'd like to _____ right now that I am totally opposed to this idea.
6 Right. I think we should _____ and get down to business.
7 I don't mind if we go now or later. It _____ no _____ to me.
8 Could you _____ me _____ and lend me some money till tomorrow?

T 2.5 Listen and check.

4 Match an expression in **A** with a line in **B**. Underline the expression with *make* or *do*.

A	B
1 She's made the big time as an actress.	'She's an accountant.'
2 We'll never make the airport in time.	'I can make myself understood.'
3 'What does she do for a living?'	'Yeah. It really made my day.'
4 'You'll all have to do more overtime and work weekends.'	The traffic's too bad.
5 'How much do you want to borrow? £20?'	She can command $20 million a movie.
6 'How much Spanish do you speak?'	'Great. That'll do fine.'
7 'I hear the boss said you'd done really well.'	'That does it! I'm going to look for another job!'

Phrasal verbs

5 Complete the sentences with a phrasal verb with *do*.

| do away with sth   do without sth could do with sth   do sth up |

'I'm tired of wondering what I'd do without you, … I want to find out for sure.'

1 I'm so thirsty. I _____ a cup of tea.
2 We've bought an old flat. We're going to _____ it _____ over the next few years.
3 I think we should _____ the monarchy. They're all useless. And expensive.
4 I could never _____ my personal assistant. She organizes everything for me.

T 2.6 Listen and check.

6 Do the same with these phrasal verbs with *make*.

| make sth up   make up for sth make sth of sb   make off with sth |

1 Thieves broke into the castle and _____ jewellery and antique paintings.
2 Jake's parents buy him loads of toys. They're trying to _____ always being at work.
3 What do you _____ the new boss? I quite like him.
4 You didn't believe his story, did you? He _____ the whole thing _____.

T 2.7 Listen and check.

LISTENING AND SPEAKING
Tashi Wheeler – girl on the move

1 What are some of your earliest memories of holidays and travelling as a child? Tell the class, and show any photos you have brought.

2 Look at the photographs of Tashi Wheeler, the daughter of Tony and Maureen (p18). In each photo …
- How old is she?
- Where do you think she is –
  Mexico, Singapore, Kenya (x2), US (Arizona), or Peru?
- What is she doing?

3 Tashi began travelling when she was eight months old. What questions would you like to ask her?

What was the first foreign country you went to?
What are your earliest memories?
Which countries have you been to?

4 **T 2.8** Listen to part one of an interview with Tashi. Does she answer any of your questions?

What memories does she have of …?
- transport
- being on safari
- her mother
- trekking in Nepal

5 **T 2.9** Listen to part two. Correct the wrong information.

> On holiday, the Wheeler family are very relaxed. They get up late and go to bed early. They spend a lot of time on the beach. Tony Wheeler reads the paper. They go to the same restaurant every day. Tashi and her brother spend a lot of time watching movies. She doesn't feel that travel broadens the mind.

6 **T 2.10** Listen to part three and answer the questions.
1 How did her attitude to travel change as she got older?
2 What did she find difficult socially?
3 Why was 'adjusting back and forth' difficult?
4 What did the kids at school have that she didn't? What did she have that they didn't?
5 Where does she feel comfortable? Where does she feel uncomfortable?
6 What are Tashi's final bits of advice for future travellers?
7 'I get very itchy-footed.' Which phrase with a similar meaning did Tommy Willis use on p17?

SPOKEN ENGLISH Fillers

When we speak (in any language!), we can be vague and imprecise. We also use fillers, which don't mean very much, but fill the gaps!

Tashi	And Galapagos Islands, Philippines, *and stuff like that*. … monkeys swinging off the rear-view mirrors, *and things*. The getting up at *like* four in the morning …
Interviewer	And when you were on these travels, *I mean*, did your dad *sort of* have a notebook, and he'd be *sort of* stopping everywhere …?

Look at the tapescript on p126. Find more examples of imprecise language and fillers.

EVERYDAY ENGLISH
Exclamations

1 Look at these examples of exclamations. When do we use *What a(n) ...!*, *What ...!*, and *How...!*?

What an exciting experience!   What nonsense!   How horrible!

2 Match an exclamation in **B** with a line in **C**.

A	B	C
1	**Mmm!**	How interesting!
	Wow!	That's disgusting!
	Hey, Peter!	That's unbelievable! How amazing!
	Oh, really?	Sorry about that! I dropped it!
	Ah!	It's absolutely delicious!
	Ouch!	That's nonsense! What a stupid thing to say!
	Yuk!	What a shame!
	Uh?	That really hurt!
	Phew!	Come over here and sit with us.
	Whoops!	What a relief! Thank goodness for that!

3 **T 2.11** Listen to ten lines of conversation. Reply to each one using an exclamation in **B** and its matching line in **C**. Write the number of the conversation 1–10 in column **A**.

4 What is the next line in each conversation? Put a number 1–10 next to the correct line.

> **A** How's your steak? Is it OK?
> **B** Mmm! It's absolutely delicious! **Just the way I like it.**

	Don't worry. I'll get you a new one.
	Triplets! That'll keep them busy!
	You must be so disappointed!
1	Just the way I like it.
	I hadn't done any revising for it at all.
	You wouldn't catch me eating that!
	I told you! Well, it isn't bleeding, but you'll have a nice bruise.
	Let's have a chat.
	You know it's not true.
	I haven't seen her for ages. How is she?

T 2.12 Listen and check. Practise the conversations, paying special attention to intonation. You could act some of them out and make them longer!

Music *of* English ♪♫

With exclamations using *What ...!* and *How ...!*, your intonation should rise and fall on both the adjective and noun:

What awful shoes!   *What a fantastic view!*   *How amazing!*

T 2.13 Listen and repeat.

---

5 Put *What ...*, *What a ...*, or *How ...* to complete the exclamations.

1 _____ silly mistake!
2 _____ brilliant idea!
3 _____ utterly ridiculous!
4 _____ dreadful weather!
5 _____ rubbish!
6 _____ mess!
7 _____ awful!
8 _____ wonderful!
9 _____ relief!
10 _____ terrible thing to happen!

Which are positive reactions? Which are negative?

6 **T 2.14** Listen to some situations. Respond to them, using one of the exclamations in exercise 5.

7 Write a dialogue with a partner. Use some of the exclamations on this page. You could ask about a party, a meal, a holiday, or a sports event.

Begin with a question.

> **What was the ... like?**
> **Well, it was ...**

Act out your conversations to the class.

3 What a story!

TEST YOUR GRAMMAR

Read the story. Put the events into chronological order. What happened first? What happened last?

Burglar arrested

▶ A COUPLE came home at midnight to find their house had been burgled. Bob and Janet Gilbreath had left their house at six o'clock to go to the theatre. When they got home, the back door had been smashed, and money and jewellery stolen. A neighbour said that she had heard a loud noise at about eight o'clock. Mr and Mrs Gilbreath, who moved to the house five years ago, told police that they had seen a man who had been acting suspiciously for several days before the robbery, and were able to give a description. A man answering the description was later arrested.

WHAT'S IN THE NEWS?

Narrative tenses

1 Look at the newspaper headlines. What do you think is the whole story?

2 What would you like to know? Write some more questions.

> *Did he mean to fall over?*
> *Where was she climbing?*
> *How did he manage to hack into their systems?*

3 **T 3.1** Listen to three conversations about the stories. Which of your questions were answered?

4 Here are the answers to some questions. What are the questions?

1 Just ordinary clothes.
2 For a dare.
3 Three hours.
4 In a shelter.
5 His own software program.
6 To download from the Internet.

5 Match lines in A and B. Practise saying them with contracted and weak forms.

A	B
He was wearing	with a partner.
He'd been talking	he wouldn't do it.
His friends had bet him	the next night.
She was climbing	about doing it for ages.
They were rescued	ordinary clothes.

T 3.2 Listen and check.

Man survives plunge over Niagara Falls

180ft drop

Climber saved by

From: Rachel
Need heli rescue off
north ridge of piz Bad
ile. Switzerland

The nerd who hacked into US Defence systems

text plea to friend

LANGUAGE FOCUS

1 Complete the chart using the verb in brackets.

Past Simple	Past Continuous
(fall)	(read)
Past Perfect	**Past Perfect Continuous**
(hear)	(act)
Past Simple passive	**Past Perfect passive**
(arrest)	(burgle)

Look at tapescript T 3.1 on p127. Find an example of each tense. When do we use the Past Perfect? When do we use continuous tenses?

2 Why are different tenses used in these paragraphs?

John cooked a lovely meal. His guests had a good time. They left at midnight.

Just after midnight, John was looking at the mess. His guests had just left. He'd cooked a lovely meal, and everyone had had a good time.

▶▶ **Grammar Reference pp142–143**

PRACTICE

Discussing grammar

1 Compare the use of tenses in these sentences. Say which tense is used and why.

1	*I read* *I was reading*	a book on the plane.

2 When Alice arrived,	*I made a cake.* *I was making a cake.* *I had made a cake.*

3	*The film started* *The film had started*	when we got to the cinema.

4 He was sacked because	*he had stolen some money.* *he had been stealing money for years.*

5 When I got to the garage, my car	*was being repaired.* *had been repaired.*

Writing narratives

2 Rewrite the sentences as one sentence, beginning with the part in **bold**.

She won £2,000 in a competition. **Last night Sally was celebrating.**
Last night Sally was celebrating because she'd won £2,000 in a competition.

1 He got up at dawn. He was driving for ten hours. **Peter was tired when he arrived home.**
2 I parked my car on a yellow line. It was towed away. **I went to get my car, but it wasn't there.** (*When ...*)
3 He wasn't always poor. He had a successful business. Unfortunately, it went bust. **Mick was a homeless beggar.**
4 They were shopping all day. They spent all their money on clothes. **Jane and Peter arrived home.** They were broke. (*When ...*)
5 He saw a house in Scotland. He first saw it while he was driving on holiday. **Last week John moved to the house.**

The news

3 **T 3.3** Listen to the first story. Correct the mistakes in the sentences.

1 Ten workers have died.
2 They'd been trapped up a mountain.
3 They'd been building a new road.
4 There was an avalanche.
5 Sixteen men managed to escape.
6 Ten were fatally injured.
7 The men were recovering at home.
8 The cause of the accident is known.

4 **T 3.4** Listen to the second news item. Here are the answers to some questions. Write the questions.

1 For two days.
2 After school on Wednesday.
3 Their photographs.
4 Nearby houses.
5 A neighbour.
6 In a garden shed.
7 No, they hadn't. (*... realized ...?*)

SPOKEN ENGLISH News and responses

When we tell a story, we use certain expressions. When we listen to a story, we respond with different expressions. Put **G** (giving news), **R** (reacting to news), or **A** (asking for more information) after each expression.

1	☐	Did you read that story about ... ?
2	☐	What happened to him?
3	☐	That's amazing!
4	☐	What did he do it for?
5	☐	Apparently ...
6	☐	What a crazy guy!
7	☐	You're kidding!
8	☐	Then what happened?
9	☐	Actually, ...
10	☐	I don't get it.

Work with a partner. You are going to read and discuss two news stories.

Student A Read the story on p155.
Student B Read the story on p156.

When you've read your story, tell your partner about it. Try to use some of the phrases for giving and responding to news.

▶▶ **WRITING** Narrative writing 1 – Using adverbs in narratives *p113*

VOCABULARY AND SPEAKING
Books and films

1 We usually want to know some things about a book before we start reading it. Here are some answers. Write in the questions.

1 <u>Who wrote it</u>   ?
Charles Dickens/Jane Austen.

2 _____?
It's a romantic novel/It's a thriller/It's a biography.

3 _____?
It's about a tragic marriage/It's about politics and corruption.

4 <u>Where and</u> _____?
In India in the last century/In New York in the 80s.

5 _____?
A lawyer called Potts and his client, Lady Jane /A detective called Blunket.

6 _____?
Yes, it has. It came out quite a few years ago and starred Johnny Depp.

7 _____?
It ends really tragically/It's frustrating because we don't really know/They all live happily ever after.

8 _____?
I thought it was great/I couldn't put it down/I didn't want it to end/It was OK but I skipped the boring bits.

9 _____?
Yes, I would. It's great if you like a good love story/It's a terrific holiday read.

2 Which questions could also be asked about a film? Some might have to change. What extra questions can be asked about a film?

3 **T 3.5** Listen to two people, one talking about a film and the other a book. Take notes under these headings.

Title	Setting	Characters	Plot	Personal opinion

4 Work with a partner. Ask and answer the questions in exercise 1 about your favourite book or film.

5 Look at the front and back covers of *The Blind Assassin*. Which of the questions in exercise 1 can you answer?

FICTION/LITERATURE

INTERNATIONAL BESTSELLER

The BLIND ASSASSIN
A NOVEL

"The first great novel of the new millennium." —*Newsday*

WINNER OF THE BOOKER PRIZE

MARGARET ATWOOD

'Grand storytelling on a grand scale . . . . Sheerly enjoyable.'
The Washington Post Book World

The Booker Prize-winning sensation from the incomparable Margaret Atwood — a novel that combines elements of gothic drama, romantic suspense, and science fiction fantasy in a spellbinding narrative.
The Blind Assassin opens with these simple resonant words: "Ten days after the war ended, my sister Laura drove a car off a bridge." They are spoken by Iris Chase Griffen, sole surviving descendant of a once rich and influential Ontario family, whose terse account of her sister's death in 1945 is followed by an inquest report proclaiming the death accidental. But just as the reader expects to settle into Laura's story, Atwood introduces a novel-within-a-novel. Entitled *The Blind Assassin*, it is a science fiction story improvised by two unnamed lovers who meet in dingy backstreet rooms. When we return to Iris, it is through a 1947 newspaper article announcing the discovery of a sailboat carrying the dead body of her husband, a distinguished industrialist.
What makes this novel Margaret Atwood's strongest and most profoundly entertaining is the way in which the three wonderfully rich stories weave together, gradually revealing through their interplay the secrets surrounding the entire Chase family — and most particularly the fascinating and tangled lives of the two sisters. *The Blind Assassin* is a brilliant and enthralling book by a writer at the top of her form.

'Absorbing....Expertly rendered....Virtuosic storytelling.'
The New York Times

$14.95

ISBN 0-385-72095-5

Cover illustration: Courtesy of the Advertising Archive, London
© The Curtis Publishing Co.
Cover design: Mario J. Pulice
Hand lettering: Anita Karl

READING GROUP GUIDE AVAILABLE AT
www.anchorbooks.com

READING AND SPEAKING
The Blind Assassin

1 Read the first part of *The Blind Assassin.* Which two words would you like your teacher to explain? Which statement do you agree with?

- The facts are presented coldly and clinically.
- The violence of the accident is described with great emotion.

2 Read the second part. Answer the questions.

1. Who are Laura, Richard, Mrs Griffen, and Alex? How are they related? (The narrator's name is Iris.)
2. What are the various suggested causes of the crash? How does Iris explain the crash to the policeman? Does she really believe this?
3. Why is she angry with her sister?

3 Read the final part. Answer the questions.

1. Why is Iris wondering what clothes to wear?
2. What impression do you have of her and her background?
3. Who is Reenie? What do we learn about the mother of Iris and Laura?
4. Who do you think the last line refers to?

4 When is Iris ...?

- calm   • nostalgic   • very angry
- clear thinking   • cold and factual

What evidence is there that Laura ...?

- didn't care about people's feelings   • had bad experiences in life
- felt guilty about something   • had suffered even as a child

Language work

1 The writer uses many dramatic words. Match a word from the extract with a more neutral description.

charred	turning and twisting
smithereens	things people do
plunged	knocking together (teeth)
swirling	making a loud cry (in pain)
suspended	very small pieces
chattering	lift quickly
deeds	badly burnt
scoop	fell suddenly downwards
howling	hung

What do you think?

1 The first chapter of this novel raises more questions than it answers. What has the author *not* told us? What do you want to know?

2 Which do you think is true?

- Laura's notebooks are ... her childhood diaries/a record of a secret relationship/a novel.
- Laura suffered because ... she was mentally ill/her mother died/she had an unhappy love life.
- Iris ... feels responsible for her sister's death/never loved her husband.

The BLIND ASSASSIN

CHAPTER I
The bridge

Ten days after the war ended, my sister Laura drove a car off a bridge. The bridge was being repaired: she went right through the Danger sign. The car fell a hundred feet into the ravine, smashing through the treetops feathery with new leaves, then burst into flames and rolled down into the shallow creek at the bottom. Chunks of the bridge fell on top of it. Nothing much was left of her but charred smithereens.

I was informed of the accident by a policeman: the car was mine, and they'd traced the licence. His tone was respectful: no doubt he recognized Richard's name. He said the tires may have caught on a streetcar track or the brakes may have failed, but he also felt bound to inform me that two witnesses – a retired lawyer and a bank teller, dependable people – had claimed to have seen the whole thing. They'd said Laura had turned the car sharply and deliberately, and had plunged off the bridge with no more fuss than stepping off a curb. They'd noticed her hands on the wheel because of the white gloves she'd been wearing.

It wasn't the brakes, I thought. She had her reasons. Not that they were ever the same as anybody else's reasons. She was completely ruthless in that way.

'I suppose you want someone to identify her,' I said. 'I'll come down as soon as I can.' I could hear the calmness of my own voice, as if from a distance. In reality I could barely get the words out; my mouth was numb, my entire face was rigid with pain. I felt as if I'd been to the dentist. I was furious with Laura for what she'd done, but also with the policeman for implying that she'd done it. A hot wind was blowing around my head, the strands of my hair lifting and swirling in it, like ink spilled in water.

'I'm afraid there will be an inquest, Mrs. Griffen,' he said.

'Naturally,' I said. 'But it was an accident. My sister was never a good driver.'

I could picture the smooth oval of Laura's face, her neatly pinned chignon, the dress she would have been wearing: a blue or steel grey or hospital-corridor green. Penitential colours – less like something she'd chosen to put on than like something she'd been locked up in. Her solemn half-smile; the amazed lift of her eyebrows, as if she were admiring the view.

The white gloves: a Pontius Pilate gesture. She was washing her hands of me. Of all of us.

What had she been thinking of as the car sailed off the bridge, then hung suspended in the afternoon sunlight, glinting like a dragonfly for that one instant of held breath before the plummet? Of Alex, of Richard, of bad faith, of our father and his wreckage: of God, perhaps, and her fatal triangular bargain. Or of the stack of cheap school exercise books that she must have hidden that very morning, in the bureau drawer where I kept my stockings, knowing I would be the one to find them.

When the policeman had gone I went upstairs to change. To visit the morgue I would need gloves, and a hat with a veil. Something to cover the eyes. There might be reporters. I would have to call a taxi. Also I ought to warn Richard, at his office: he would wish to have a statement of grief prepared. I went into my dressing room: I would need black, and a handkerchief.

I opened the drawer, I saw the notebooks. I undid the criss-cross of kitchen string that tied them together. I noticed that my teeth were chattering, and that I was cold all over. I must be in shock, I decided.

What I remembered then was Reenie, from when we were little. It was Reenie who'd done the bandaging, of scrapes and cuts and minor injuries: Mother might be resting, or doing good deeds elsewhere, but Reenie was always there. She'd scoop us up and sit us on the white enamel kitchen table, alongside the pie dough she was rolling out or the chicken she was cutting up or the fish she was gutting, and give us a lump of brown sugar to get us to close our mouths. *Tell me where it hurts*, she'd say. *Stop howling. Just calm down and show me where.*

But some people can't tell where it hurts. They can't calm down. They can't ever stop howling.

LISTENING AND SPEAKING
The money jigsaw

Our £2,000 jigsaw

1 Look at the headlines and photographs. With a partner, use the prompts to invent the story.

> walking to school / ripped up bank notes / flying all over / a bin / a plastic bag / jammed full / torn up notes / had to go to school

> after school playing / police / told them where / police took away / Bank of England / long time / gave back / stick together

Stick-up job on torn bank notes leaves schoolgirls £1,200 richer

What do you think?

Why do you think someone tore up the money? Rachel and her friend have two theories.

- Maybe an old lady decided she wasn't going to leave it to anyone.
- It could have been a divorce – one person didn't want the other to have it.

Do you agree? Do you have any better explanations?

2 **T 3.6** Listen to one of the girls, Rachel Aumann, being interviewed. Compare your story with hers. (*Sainsbury's* is the name of a supermarket.)

3 Answer the questions.
  1. Where did the girls find the money?
  2. How big are the pieces?
  3. Are they being allowed to keep it?
  4. Is it easy to stick the notes together?
  5. How do they do it?
  6. How long have they been doing it?
  7. How much money is there?

> **SPOKEN ENGLISH** *like*
>
> Rachel uses the word *like* a lot.
>
> > Yeah, it was … erm … like really out of the ordinary. … we traced it to like a bin.
>
> This use of *like* suggests that the speaker (often a younger person) is not making an effort to be precise when describing or reporting a situation.
>
> Look at the tapescript on p127. Find more examples of *like*. Which example shows the correct use of *like* as a preposition?

EVERYDAY ENGLISH
Showing interest and surprise

1 **T 3.7** Listen to the dialogue. Write in **B**'s answers. How does she show interest and surprise?

A Jade's got a new boyfriend.
B _____? Good for her!
A Apparently, he lives in a castle.
B _____? How amazing!
A Yes. She met him in Slovenia.
B _____? That's interesting.
A Unfortunately, he can't speak much English.
B _____? I thought everyone could these days!

2 **B** uses *echo questions* and *reply questions*. Which are which? Practise the conversation with your partner. Pay particular attention to the stress and intonation.

Music of English 🎵

To show interest, the intonation on echo and reply questions should start high, go down, and then go up high at the end.

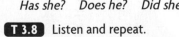

Has she? *Does he?* *Did she?* *Are you?*

T 3.8 Listen and repeat.

If you use these short questions without any intonation, you will sound bored and uninterested!

3 Complete the conversations with either an echo or a reply question.

1 **A** Sam wants to apologize.
  B _____?
  A Yes. He's broken your mother's Chinese vase.
  B _____? Oh, no!

2 **A** We had a terrible holiday.
  B _____?
  A Yes. It rained all the time.
  B _____?
  A Yes. And the food was disgusting!
  B _____? What a drag!

3 **A** I'm broke.
  B _____? How come?
  A Because I just had a phone bill for £500.
  B _____? Why so much?
  A Because I have a girlfriend in Korea.
  B _____? How interesting!

4 **A** It took me three hours to get here.
  B _____?
  A Yes. There was a traffic jam ten miles long.
  B _____? That's awful!
  A Now I've got a headache!
  B _____? Poor darling. I'll get you something for it.

5 **A** I'm on a mountain, watching the sun set.
  B _____?
  A Yes. And I've got something very important to ask you.
  B _____? What is it? I can't wait!
  A You'd better sit down. I'd like to marry you.
  B _____? Wow!

T 3.9 Listen and compare. Practise them with a partner.

4 Your teacher will read out some sentences about himself/herself. Respond, using a reply question or an echo.

4 Nothing but the truth

Questions and negatives · Prefixes and antonyms · Being polite

TEST YOUR GRAMMAR

1 Make the sentences negative. Sometimes there is more than one possibility.

> **I disagree/don't agree with you.**

1 I agree with you.
2 I think you're right.
3 I told her to go home.
4 'Is John coming?' 'I hope so.'
5 I knew everybody at the party.
6 I've already done my homework.
7 You must get a visa.
8 My sister likes hip-hop, too.

2 Write in the missing word in each question.

1 'What of music do you like?' 'Jazz.'
2 'How do you wash your hair?' 'Every other day.'
3 'Who do you look?' 'My mother.'
4 'How does it take you to get to school?' 'Nearly an hour.'
5 'What were you talking to the teacher?' 'Oh, this and that.'
6 'Do you know what the time?' 'Just after three.'

Ask and answer the questions with a partner.

TELLING LIES
Questions and negatives

1 Think of some lies that these people might tell.

> a teenage girl to her parents   a car salesman
> a student to the teacher   a politician
> a husband to his wife

2 All the people in the cartoons are lying. Who to? Why?

3 **T 4.1** Listen to what the people are really thinking. What *is* the truth? Why *did* they lie? Do you think any of the people have good reasons to lie?

4 Which question was each person asked before they lied? Put *a–f* in the boxes.

1 ☐ What did you make that face for? Doesn't it look good?
2 ☐ Can I speak to Sue Jones, please? It's urgent.
3 ☐ How come you're ill today? You looked just fine yesterday!
4 ☐ Who gave you that black eye? Haven't I told you not to get into fights?
5 ☐ Where are you going? How long will you be? I hope you won't be late.
6 ☐ I want to know if you'll marry me. I don't think you will.

LANGUAGE FOCUS

1 In exercise 4, find and read aloud …

Questions

… questions with auxiliary verbs.

… questions without auxiliary verbs.

… two ways of asking *Why?*

… a question with a preposition at the end.

… a question word + an adverb.

… an indirect question.

Negatives

… negative questions.

… a future negative.

… negatives with *think* and *hope*.

2 Indirect questions

Make these direct questions indirect using the expressions.

Where does he work? I don't know …

What's the answer? Have you any idea … ?

Did she buy the blue one? I wonder …

▶▶ **Grammar Reference p144**

PRACTICE

Quiztime!

1 Work in two groups. You are going to write some questions for a general knowledge quiz.

Group A Look at the information on p155.
Group B Look at the information on p156.

Write the questions for your quiz in your group. Ask and answer questions between groups.

2 Make comments about the answers in the quiz. Some of your sentences might be indirect questions.

We weren't sure …

We didn't have a clue …

We had no idea …

None of us knew …

We guessed …

Did you all know … ?

… how many legs a butterfly has.

… which theory Charles Darwin developed.

Asking for more information

3 We can respond to a statement with a short question to ask for more information.

Write short questions with a preposition to answer these statements.

1 She gave away all her money.
2 Can I have a word with you, please?
3 I danced all night.
4 I need £5,000 urgently.
5 I got a lovely present today.
6 I bought a birthday card today.
7 Sh! I'm thinking!
8 Do you think you could give me a lift?

4 Make the short questions into longer ones.

Who did you go out for a meal with?   *Where did she send it from?*

T 4.2 Listen and check your answers. Notice that all the questions end with the preposition.

Negative questions

5 **T 4.3** Listen and compare the use of negative questions in 1 and 2.

> 1 a Don't you like pizza? How unusual!
>   b Can't you swim? I thought everybody learned to at school these days!
>   c Hasn't the postman been yet? It's nearly midday!

> 2 a Haven't we met somewhere before? Wasn't it in Paris?
>   b Wasn't it your birthday last week? Sorry I forgot.
>   c Isn't that Hugh Grant over there? You know, the actor! I'm sure it is!

In which group …?

… does the speaker ask for confirmation of what he thinks is true and expect the answer *Yes*?

… does the speaker express surprise and expect the answer *No*?

T 4.3 Practise the negative questions. Pay attention to stress and intonation.

6 Give answers to the negative questions in exercise 5.

1 a **No, I've never liked pizza. Can't stand it, I'm afraid.**
2 a **Yes, that's right. It was at the sales conference in La Défense.**

7 Ask and answer about these things using negative questions.

> **Expressing surprise**
> like   ice-cream/learning English/your neighbours?
> have   ever been abroad/got a TV at home?

> **Asking for confirmation**
> is   it Tuesday today/this your pen?
> go   to the States last year/to the races next weekend?

T 4.4 Listen and compare.

Making negatives

8 Make a negative sentence about these people. Use your dictionary.

Vegans don't eat any animal products.

> vegans   atheists   teetotallers   insomniacs
> dyslexics   pacifists   animal rights campaigners
> naturists   anti-globalization protesters

9 **T 4.5** Listen to the first part of a description of a man called Norman. Which words in exercise 8 describe him? Make some negative sentences about him.

He can't sleep.   **He doesn't have a big place to live.**

> **SPOKEN ENGLISH** *How come?*
>
> *How come?* can be used instead of *Why?* in informal spoken English. However, they are not the same. Look at these sentences. Which question expresses surprise?
>
> > *Why are you learning English?*
> > *How come you're going to work today? It's Sunday.*
>
> Note that *How come?* is not followed by the usual inverted word order of question forms.

10 **T 4.5** Listen to the second part of the description of Norman. There are lots of contradictions. Complete the sentences about Norman below with a question using *How come?*

My mate Norman

He lives in a tiny one-roomed flat so **how come he came downstairs to the living room?**
He's an insomniac, so **how come he slept so well?**
He's single, so …
He hasn't got any pets, so …
He's an atheist, so …
He's dyslexic, so …
He's unemployed, so …
He's teetotal, so …
He's vegetarian, so …
He's anti-social, so …

Who is it?

11 Write a description of yourself using *only* negative sentences. Your teacher will distribute them amongst the students in the class. Read them aloud and guess who it is.

I can't cook.   **I never arrive on time.**
I didn't pass the test last week.

LISTENING AND SPEAKING
My most memorable lie!

Work in small groups.

1 Did you ever tell lies as a child? Can you remember any? Talk about them in your groups. Decide which is the most interesting lie in your group and tell the class.

2 **T 4.6** Listen to six people talking about their most memorable lie. Correct the statements.

 1 **Andrew** was playing in the swimming pool when his father came home.

 2 **Paul** only lied once as a child because he swore and stole biscuits.

 3 **Carolyn** went to America for her girlfriend's wedding.

 4 **Kiki** finally told her grandmother the truth.

 5 **Sean** learnt Judo at school.

 6 **Kate** was not punished for lying.

3 Listen again and answer the questions.

 1 Andrew says, *I completely denied all knowledge.* Of what? How had he tried to hide the evidence?

 2 Paul says, *bizarrely what you end up doing is lying ... so that you've got something to say.* Lying to who? When? Why is it bizarre?

 3 Carolyn says, *I had to tell a white lie.* What was it? Why was it a white lie? What *did nothing* for whose figure?

 4 Kiki says, *I know where I lost it.* What did she lose? Where did she lose it? What was her lie?

 5 Sean says, *somebody's mother rang my mother to get details.* To get details of what? Why did he lie in the first place?

 6 Kate says, *I put him in the box ... and I shut the lid.* Who did she put in the box? Which box? How does she excuse her behaviour?

4 Which words go with which lie? What do they refer to?

confession	frumpy	dressing up box	gold-filtered
a robbery	spanked	stubs necklace	the playground
a princess	a grate	a soldier sins	

What do you think?

- Which of the six lies do you think are 'good' reasons to lie? Which are 'bad'? Which are 'white lies'?

- Work alone. List other occasions when you think it might be good to lie and occasions when it is definitely not.

- Discuss your ideas with your group. Do you all agree about what are 'good' and 'bad' lies?

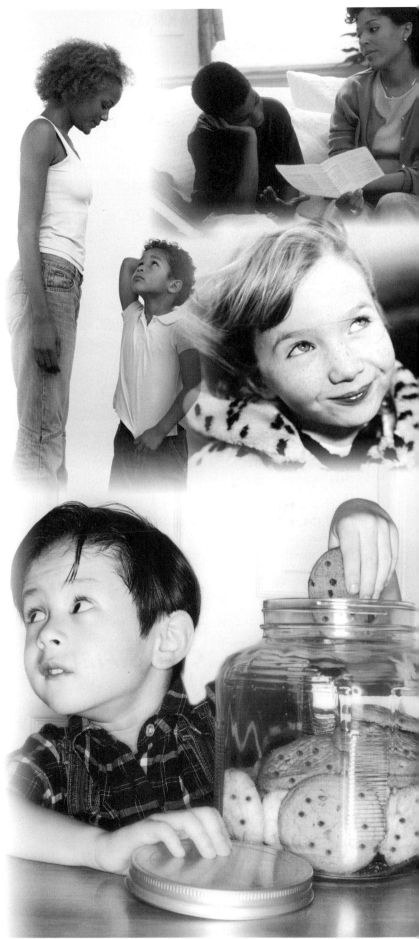

READING AND SPEAKING
Diana and Elvis shot JFK!

1 What do you know about the following events? Discuss in groups and share information.
- The deaths of President John F. Kennedy, John Lennon, Elvis Presley, Princess Diana.
- The Apollo moon landings.

2 There are many conspiracy theories about these events. What are conspiracy theories? How are they usually circulated nowadays? Do you know any about the events in exercise 1?

3 Read the introduction to three of the world's most popular conspiracy theories. Which events are mentioned? Why do people like these theories? What is a 'juicy' theory?

CLASSIFIED

EVERYBODY loves a good conspiracy theory. Whether it is the CIA shooting President Kennedy, or Elvis being alive and well and living on the Moon, there are few things that appeal to the imagination more than a mixture of mystery and a hint of evil-doing in high places. When horrifying, historic events shake our world we seek to make sense of them by creating bizarre theories. These theories, however unlikely, are preferable to the cold fact that sometimes accidents happen. Many of the juiciest theories circulate on the Internet.

4 Work in groups of three.

Student A Read the article on p39.
Student B Read the article on p40.
Student C Read the article on p41.

Answer the questions.

1 When and what was the event?
2 How many theories are mentioned? Write a list of the different ones in note form.
3 What proof is given to support them?
4 What reasons are suggested for hiding the true facts?
5 Which people, individual or groups, are mentioned in relation to the event?

Compare your answers with the others in your group.

Vocabulary work

Find words in your text to replace those in *italics*. Explain them to the others in your group.

Diana
1 The huge number of websites is *absolutely amazing*.
2 The florists *devised* a *clever but wicked* plot to murder Diana.
3 The car crash was a *carefully planned trick*.
4 I don't *believe* any of these theories.
5 Someone in the royal family *devised* a plot to *interfere* with the brakes.

Moon landing
1 Rumours have been *going round* for many years.
2 The US flag is seen *blowing* and there is no *wind* on the moon.
3 A *fantastic exhibition* of stars.
4 Scientists have *all* agreed that the theorists don't have *any argument at all*.
5 NASA has been desperately *trying to hide* evidence of life.

JFK Junior
1 There are many *strange* theories – one of the *craziest* claims he was murdered by Clinton supporters.
2 Explosives were *stuck* to the tail of the plane.
3 The plane *hit violent air movements*.
4 The crash happened *strangely and coincidentally* on the 30th anniversary.
5 Some explanations are *clearly stupid*. Others are *quite believable*.

What do you think?

- Which theories are the most believable/unbelievable?
- What is it about the Internet that breeds such theories?
- Think of a recent major news event and work in your groups to devise conspiracy theories about it. Describe the event and your theories to the class.

▶▶ **WRITING** Linking ideas – Conjunctions *p114*

CONSPIRACY THEORY 1

THE DEATH OF DIANA

The first Diana conspiracy site appeared on the Internet in Australia only hours after her death on August 31st, 1997. Since then an estimated 36,000 Diana conspiracy websites have been set up – breathtaking by anyone's standards. Hypotheses range from pure James Bond ('it was all an MI6 plot to protect the monarchy') to farce ('it was a fiendish murder plot thought up by the world's florists to sell lots of flowers'). And most popular of all, Diana, Princess of Wales, isn't dead after all – that terrible car crash in Paris was an elaborate hoax to enable the Princess and her boyfriend, Dodi Fayed, to fake their own deaths so that they could live in blissful isolation for the rest of their lives. Subscribers to this theory say that Diana was fed up with the intrusions into her private life and used the wealth and resources of the Fayed family to fake her death, and now she and Dodi are living on a small tropical island, communicating with her sons by satellite video conferencing. Think about it, they say, we never actually saw her body, did we?

'We never actually saw her body, did we?'

You don't buy into any of these theories? Don't worry. There are plenty more to choose from. For example, Paul Burrell, Diana's former butler, claims that the Princess predicted her own death in a car crash. Apparently, she was so frightened that ten months before her death she wrote to Burrell saying that a plot was being hatched by a member of the royal family and that her car's brakes would be tampered with and she would suffer serious head injuries. And all of this so that the Prince of Wales could marry again.

These theories multiply because it is so hard for us to believe that a princess, with all her wealth and bodyguards, could be killed by something as arbitrary and mundane as a traffic accident. Psychologically, we need conspiracy theories to make the tragedies of life more bearable. And the Internet helps feed the global paranoia.

CONSPIRACY THEORY 2 — THE APOLLO MOON LANDING

For over 30 years rumours have been circulating that the Apollo Moon landings were faked. They say astronaut Neil Armstrong made no 'giant leap for mankind', they assert that the 1969 Moon mission was a hoax to prove America won the space race, that the astronauts were 'astro-nots'! The high point in the Great Moon Landing Conspiracy came on 15 February 2001, the date that the Fox television network broadcast a programme entitled Did We Land on the Moon? This alleged that the whole Moon landing had been staged inside a film studio on a US military base somewhere in the Mojave desert.

The programme claimed:

1 The US flag planted on the Moon's surface is seen fluttering, and there is no breeze of any kind on the Moon.
2 The photographs taken by the astronauts do not include any of the Moon's night sky, where there would have been a stunning array of stars on view.
3 The shadows in the pictures are clearly coming from more than one angle – an impossibility on the Moon, where the only light source is the Sun, but more than plausible inside a film studio.
4 One of the famed Moon rocks brought back by the Apollo astronauts is marked with a telltale letter 'C', suggesting the markings not of some alien life force but of a film prop.

'Was the whole moon landing staged inside a film studio?'

After the programme the Internet went crazy with theories and counter-theories. However, scientists have unanimously agreed that the conspiracy theorists don't have even the beginnings of a case. Too many things about the Apollo missions were impossible to fake, from the radio signals picked up at listening stations around the world, to the Moon rocks, which have been subjected to repeated geological analysis and clearly date back several millennia.

Finally there are the UFO 'nuts'. They actually do believe that astronauts went to the Moon, and found not only a load of rocks, but also widespread evidence of an ancient alien civilization — a discovery so terrifying that NASA has been desperately seeking to conceal it from the public ever since.

Moon rock

CONSPIRACY THEORY 3

THE DEATH OF JOHN F KENNEDY JR.

John Kennedy Junior, son of assassinated US president JFK, was killed on July 17th 1999 when his tiny Piper Saratoga aircraft crashed over Martha's Vineyard, near Boston. He was piloting the plane on the way to a family wedding with his wife Carolyn. To millions of Americans, JFK Junior was the closest thing to royalty the United States has ever had, and, as with his father, with every anniversary of his death they come up with ever more bizarre conspiracy theories to explain the tragedy.

One of the wildest theories claims that Kennedy Junior, known as 'John John', was murdered by Clinton supporters because he planned to stand against Hillary Clinton in the New York senate race.

Another theory asserts that an explosion, heard over Martha's Vineyard at the time of the crash, suggests that terrorists placed a bomb on the tiny plane. It is claimed that leaked FBI documents record the discovery of explosives glued within its tail.

'Some of the explanations for the plane crash are patently ridiculous.'

A third theory blames Kennedy's beautiful blonde wife, Carolyn. It is suggested that she caused the crash by chatting on her mobile phone just as the plane ran into turbulence over Martha's Vineyard, thus interfering with the controls while her husband was desperately trying to make an emergency landing. However, the most popular theory of all blames the crash on the legendary Irish curse said to have taken the lives of so many of the Kennedy clan. This curse, reputed to have followed the Kennedy dynasty over from Ireland, is said to strike when Kennedy members are around water. John John's uncle Joseph Kennedy Jr. died in a flight over water during World War II, while another uncle, Teddy Kennedy, drove off a bridge into water at Chappaquiddick – spookily, the plane crash happened on the 30th anniversary of the Chappaquiddick incident.

'Some of the explanations for the plane crash are patently ridiculous,' says a Kennedy watcher. 'Others like the cell phone theory are based on recorded information and are pretty plausible.'

VOCABULARY
Saying the opposite

1 What part of speech are these words? Write antonyms for them using prefixes if possible.

Word	Antonym(s)
fake **adj**	genuine, real, authentic
like **vb**	dislike, hate, can't stand
tiny	
happiness	
guilty	
safe	
admit	
sincere	
success	
mature	
encourage	
kind/generous	
appear	

○ UP
○ UNDECIDED
○ DOWN

2 Complete the conversations with antonyms from the box. Put the words in the correct form.

> improve   safety   success   criticize   generosity
> fail   mean   encourage   get worse   danger

1 **A** Gary's a really _____ businessman.
  B Yeah, but he's a complete _____ as a family man. He never sees his children.

2 **A** My grandad's so _____, he gives me £20 every time I see him.
  B Lucky you. My grandad's famous for his _____. A fiver every birthday, if he remembers.

3 **A** Well, Henry, I'm pleased there's been some _____ in your behaviour this term, but sadly your work has _____.
  B Didn't I do OK in the test then?

4 **A** You're not going bungee jumping! It sounds really _____.
  B No, honestly, it's _____ enough as long as you're careful.

5 **A** Our teacher is always _____ us. I feel useless.
  B I know – it's not fair, he should give us more _____ if he wants us to work hard.

T 4.7 Listen and check.

3 What is the effect of using antonyms in these conversations?

A What **lousy** weather!
B Yes, it's not exactly **tropical**, is it?

A Jenny's **thick**, isn't she?
B Well, she isn't the **brightest of people**, it's true.

Write similar conversations with a partner about these topics. How could you describe the following both honestly and tactfully?

• a boring party   • an awful holiday   • a mean friend   • a difficult exam

T 4.8 Listen and compare.

4 What's the opposite of ... ?

1 a tough question
  tough meat

2 a clear sky
  a clear conscience

3 fair hair
  a fair decision

4 a hard mattress
  a hard exam

5 a live animal
  live music

6 a light colour
  a light sleeper

5 Match the words and their meanings.

1	**ab**used	not ever used
2	**dis**used	not used any more
3	**un**used	used cruelly or badly
4	**mis**used	used too much
5	**over**used	not used enough
6	**under**used	used in the wrong way

▶▶▶ **SONG** *I never loved you anyway* **Teacher's Book** *p145*

EVERYDAY ENGLISH
Being polite

1 What 'white lies' might you tell in these situations? Roleplay them with a partner.

> 1 You're having a meal with your host family. You've just forced yourself to eat something you don't like, when your host says, 'You must have some more!' What do you say?
>
> 2 A friend has just had a baby who you think looks like any other newborn baby. 'Isn't he gorgeous?' she coos. What do you say?
>
> 3 Your aunt invites you to go on holiday with her for two weeks. You love her, but know it would be a disaster and it would be no holiday for you. What do you say?

2 **T 4.9** Listen to the pairs of lines and conversations. After each one say which is more polite. In what ways? Look at the tapescript on p129 and practise the polite conversations with a partner.

3 Make these requests and offers more polite. Use the expressions below.

> 1 Give me a lift.
> 2 Help me find my glasses!
> 3 Come for a meal tomorrow evening!
> 4 Lend me your dictionary.
> 5 Look after my dog while I'm on holiday.
> 6 Where's the toilet?
> 7 Can I help you with this exercise?
> 8 Stop whistling!

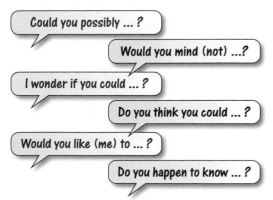

- Could you possibly ... ?
- Would you mind (not) ...?
- I wonder if you could ... ?
- Do you think you could ... ?
- Would you like (me) to ... ?
- Do you happen to know ... ?

Music of English

To sound polite, start quite high and go even higher on the main stressed word. Your voice should then fall and rise at the end of the sentence.

Could you possibly close the window, please?

T 4.10 Listen and repeat. If you use flat intonation, it sounds very aggressive in English!

---

4 Work with a partner. Take turns to make the requests and offers in exercise 3 and refuse them politely, using one of these expressions.

I'd love to, but ...	That's really kind of you, but ...
I'm terribly sorry ...	Believe me, I would if I could, but ...
I'm afraid I ...	

T 4.11 Listen and compare your answers.

Roleplay

5 Anna and Ben have invited their friends Kim and Henry to their house for dinner. Look at the conversation on p156. Work in groups of four to complete the conversation and then practise it, using the main stress shading to help you.

B   Kim! Hello! Great to see you. Come on in. Let me take your coat.

Kim Thanks very much. Oh, these are for you.

T 4.12 Listen and compare.

5 An eye to the future

Future forms · Hot verbs – *take, put* · Telephoning

1 Which future form expresses ...?

| an intention   a prediction   a future fact based on a timetable   an arrangement between people   a spontaneous decision   a suggestion |

1 Tomorrow's weather will be warm and sunny.
2 The train to Dover leaves at ten past ten.
3 I'm going to be a racing driver when I grow up.
4 We're seeing Sue for lunch on Thursday.
5 Shall we have a break now?
6 I'll make some coffee.

2 Name the different future forms.

HOW DO YOU SEE YOUR FUTURE?
Future forms

1 **T 5.1** Look at the pictures and listen to these people talking about the future. Who says what? Put a number 1–6 next to the names.

Elsie

Tony

Mickey

Katrina

Janine

Gavin

2 Answer the questions.

1 What is Katrina going to study?
   How long does her course last?
2 What is Mickey doing tomorrow?
   What time does the match start?
3 Why are Tony and Marie excited?
4 What's Elsie doing tomorrow?
   What will they do together?
5 Why is Janine packing?
   How's she getting to the airport?
6 What are Gavin's ambitions?

T 5.2 Listen and check.

3 Here are the answers to some questions.
Write the questions.

1 Bristol University. (*Which ...?*)
2 His son and some friends.
   Oxford United and Bristol Rovers.
3 Jamie or Hatty.
4 A sponge cake with jam in it.
5 It leaves at 10.30.
6 Twice what he's earning now.

T 5.3 Listen and check.

LANGUAGE FOCUS

1 Do these sentences refer to the present
or the future?

Marie's having a baby soon ...
At the moment I'm packing ...

I work in the City.
The plane leaves at 10.30.

2 What's the difference between these
sentences?

*What **do** you **do** in the evenings?*
*What **are** you **doing** this evening?*

*Get in the car. I**'ll give** you a lift.*
*I**'m going to give** Dave a lift to the
   airport tomorrow.*

*We**'ll have** supper at 8.00.*
*We**'ll be having** supper at 8.00.*

*I**'ll write** the report tonight.*
*I**'ll have** written the report by tonight.*

▶▶ **Grammar Reference pp144–146**

PRACTICE

Discussing grammar

1 Choose the correct form in the pairs of sentences.

1 `'ll see / 'm going to see`

I'm very excited. I _____ all my family this weekend.

I don't know if I have time to come this evening. I _____ .

2 `are you going to do / will you do`

So you're off to the States for a year! What _____ there?

I'm sure you will pass your exams, but what _____ if you don't?

3 `'ll come / 'm coming`

I _____ with you if you like.

I _____ with you whether you like it or not.

4 `are you doing / are you going to do`

Your school report is terrible. What _____ about it?

What _____ this evening?

5 `'m giving / 'm going to give`

I've had enough of her lazy attitude. I _____ her a good talking to.

I _____ a presentation at 3.00 this afternoon. I'm scared stiff.

6 `leaves / is leaving`

John! Peter _____ now. Come and say goodbye.

The coach _____ at 8.00, so don't be late.

7 `'ll see / 'll be seeing`

I _____ you outside the cinema at 8.00.

I _____ Peter this afternoon, so I'll tell him your news.

8 `'ll see / 'll have seen`

You _____ enough of me by the end of this holiday.

I'm going to make a success of my life. You _____ .

T 5.4 Listen and check.

2 Put the verb in brackets in the correct tense. Use Present Simple, Present Perfect, *will* or the Future Continuous.

'This is your captain speaking...'

Good morning, ladies and gentlemen. Welcome on board this British Airways flight to Rome. In a very short time we (1)_____ (take) off. When we (2)_____ (reach) our cruising speed of 550 miles per hour, we (3)_____ (fly) at 35,000 feet. Our flight time today is two and a half hours, so we (4)_____ (be) in Rome in time for lunch!

The cabin crew (5)_____ (serve) refreshments during the flight. If you (6)_____ (need) any assistance, just press the button and a flight attendant (7)_____ (come) to help you.

[Near the end of the flight]
In a few moments' time, the crew (8)_____ (come) round with duty-free goods. We (9)_____ also _____ (give out) landing cards. When you (10)_____ (fill) them in, place them in your passport. They (11)_____ (collect) as you (12)_____ (go) through passport control.

In twenty minutes' time we (13)_____ (land) at Leonardo da Vinci airport. Please put your seats in the upright position. You are requested to remain seated until the plane (14)_____ (come) to a complete standstill.

We hope you (15)_____ (fly) again soon with British Airways.

T 5.5 Listen and check.

3 Complete the sentences with the correct form of the verb. Use *will*, the Future Continuous, or the Future Perfect.

go

1 I can book the tickets. I _____ past the theatre on my way home.
2 I'll say goodbye now. You _____ by the time I get back.
3 He _____ mad when I tell him I've crashed his car.

make

4 'Tea?' 'It's OK. I _____ it.'
5 Dave is so ambitious. I bet he _____ a fortune by the time he's thirty.
6 You'll know where the party is. We _____ so much noise!

read

7 I'll lend you this book next time I see you. I _____ it by then.
8 We're studying Shakespeare next term so I _____ his plays over the summer.
9 I've just got an email from Megan. I _____ it to you.

Talking about you

4 Complete the questions with the most natural future form. Sometimes there are several possibilities.

1 Where _____ (you go) on holiday this year?
2 How _____ (you get) there?
3 How long _____ (you be) away for?
4 Which hotel _____ (you stay) in?
5 What time _____ (your flight arrive)?
6 What _____ (you do) while you're on holiday?

In pairs, ask and answer the questions about your next holiday. If you haven't got a holiday planned, make one up!

I hope so/I don't think so

5 **T 5.6** Listen to the conversations and complete them.

1 'Do you think you'll ever be rich?'
  'I _____ so.'
  'I _____ one day.'
  'It's possible, but I _____ it.'
  'I'm sure I _____.'
  'I'm sure I _____.'

2 'Are you going out tonight?'
  'Yes, I am.'
  'I think _____, but I'm not sure.'
  'I _____ be.'

3 'Do you think the world's climate will change dramatically in the next fifty years?'
  'I _____ so.'
  'I hope _____.'
  'Who _____? Maybe.'

6 Ask and answer similar yes/no questions about future possibilities in your life.

1 be famous
  go to Florida
  marry a millionaire
  speak perfect English
  have grandchildren

2 go to the cinema soon
  meet friends this weekend
  eat out in the next few days

3 we discover life on another planet
  people live for 150 years
  find a cure for cancer

COTE D'AZUR
TOUTE L'ANNÉE

TRAIN DE NOËL POUR
CHAMONIX
3 JOURS AUX SPORTS D'HIVER

INDIA

IMPERIAL

47

READING AND SPEAKING
Nobody listens to us

1 How do people of different ages see each other?

In your country, what do …

- old people think of young people?
- young people think of old people?
- parents think of teenagers?
- teenagers think of their parents?
- people think of students?

2 A group of 18–24 year-olds were canvassed for their opinions. Here is a list of ten social issues they said they cared about. What do you think their order of importance was?

- ☐ Improving public transport
- ☐ Raising standards in schools
- ☐ Reducing crime levels
- ☐ Improving the National Health Service
- ☐ Increasing the amount of aid we give to developing countries
- ☐ Ending the arms trade
- ☐ Ending globalization
- ☐ Addressing the causes of global warming
- ☐ Redistributing wealth from the richest to the poorest
- ☐ Ensuring equal rights for everyone, regardless of gender, sexual orientation, colour, or religion

Look at the correct order on p157. Look at the correct order on p157. Would your personal order be different?

3 Look at the heading and sub-heading of the newspaper article. What are the contrasting ideas in the sub-heading? What is the complaint of these young people?

4 Read the article. What are some of the surprise findings of the poll? What are some of the frustrations of these young adults? How do they spend their leisure time?

'WE WORK, WE VOTE, WE CARE'…

Selfish, work-shy, and uninterested in how their country and the world are governed – that is the popular view of our young adults. In fact, a new survey shows they are conscientious, idealistic, and care deeply about important issues, but feel they have no voice. Damian Whitworth and Carol Midgley report.

THIS is a story about people who believe that no one is listening.

They are concerned citizens, keenly aware that it is their civic duty to vote in the next general election, despite their disillusionment with politics and political leaders.

They worry about the future of the National Health Service, crime and schools, not trendy 'youth' issues such as legalizing soft drugs. They like to save their money, but are shouldering heavy debts. They have clear career plans.

This is the surprising picture of today's 18 to 24-year-olds. It is confirmed in numerous interviews, and in a huge number of emails from readers in response to our request to tell us how the world looks from early adulthood.

Perhaps the most intriguing findings relate to politics, where the message is that young people are alienated from politicians, but not from the issues. Nine out of ten say 'We all have a responsibility to vote'.

Two thirds say 'the main parties are so much alike that it doesn't make much difference who is in power'. 71 per cent say that 'politics matters, but political parties have nothing to say on the really important issues'.

> **❝ Nine out of ten say 'We all have a responsibility to vote'. ❞**

Almost half think that their parents' generation has no idea what it is like to be a young adult today. Two thirds think their grandparents are unaware of what it is to be young in the 21st century.

How do these people spend their time? Buying clothes is top, followed by purchasing and listening to CDs, both of which are well ahead of going to clubs, bars, and pubs. Next is eating out, and then drinking alcohol. Travel, going to the cinema or theatre, and reading books all came above sporting events and gigs and concerts, which came bottom of the list.

BUT NOBODY LISTENS TO US

www.stopwar.org.uk

5 Read the case studies on p50. Which person might have said ...?

1 I'm going to work and work.
2 I'm thinking of being self-employed.
3 This time next year I'll be living abroad.
4 I hope I'll have paid off my debts by the time I'm 31.
5 I certainly won't be working here forever.
6 I'll never be able to buy my own place.
7 I'm seeing my bank manager this afternoon to talk about getting a mortgage.

6 What is Amber's worry? Ellie's? Peter's?
What is Bob's intention? Kylie's? Joe's? Alex's?

What do you think?

- Are the frustrations and aspirations mentioned in the text similar to those of young people in your country?
- What are your aspirations for the future?

Language work

Complete the chart of adjectives and nouns. Mark the stress. The missing words are all in the article on p48.

Adjective	Noun
'popular	popu'larity
	awareness
disillusioned	
political	(x2)
criminal	
	intrigue
	alienation
responsible	
different	
powerful	

SPOKEN ENGLISH *thing*

Look at the examples of the word *thing* in the text.

> The thing is, a lot of social problems never seem to get dealt with properly.
> Politics just isn't my kind of thing.

The word *thing* is used a lot in English! In pairs, ask and answer the questions about you.

- How are things with you at the moment?
- What's the thing you like most about your best friend?
- Generally speaking, do you try to do the right thing?
- Do you like doing your own thing?
- Is horse racing your kind of thing?
- Do you ever say the wrong thing in company?
- Do you have a thing about people wearing fur?
- If your friend keeps you waiting, do you make a big thing of it?

Listen to us!

We carried out our own survey of the views of young people:

AMBER HONESS, 21
Student at Bristol University

This is my final year at university. I've been doing business studies for three years. Some of my friends will be going into finance companies; others don't really know what they'll be doing this time next year. But I know what I want to do – open a clothes shop with a friend of mine. We've got some great ideas.

My parents helped me a lot with money, but I still have debts of about £10,000. Terrifying, isn't it? It'll probably take me ten years to pay it off.

ELLIE GREEN, 24
Corporate lawyer

Young people are interested in politics, but it's very frustrating because you don't feel you can really make a difference.

The thing is, a lot of social problems never seem to get dealt with properly. We still have homeless people, the NHS doesn't seem to work no matter how much money is thrown at it, and more and more old people don't have adequate pensions.

I'm buying a house with my boyfriend soon, because I want to get on the property ladder before it's too late. I only hope I manage to keep my job. If that goes, I've had it. So I'm not very optimistic about the future.

PETER JAMIESON, 24
Trainee manager from Belfast

When my parents were young, they didn't have to worry about finding a secure job with prospects of promotion. They seemed to be a lot more relaxed about the future. These days we're put under pressure to get ahead in the rat race. No wonder so many young people take drugs.

One thing that really worries me is the cost of housing. I share a house with four other blokes, and I'll probably be living here for ever. There's no way I'll ever be able to afford a house of my own.

> **"I don't think any of them know what it's like to be our age nowadays."**

BOB WEST, 25
Plumber, London

I've never yet voted for the winning side in an election. Whoever I vote for, loses. So I guess I'm doing something wrong, somewhere. I still think it's important to vote, though. Let's face it, people would soon kick up a fuss if they weren't allowed to.

I'm saving money, and as soon as my application has been processed, I'm going to leave the country and live in Canada. Now there's a country that encourages young people and enterprise!

KYLIE WILLIAMSON, 24
Loans department in a bank

Politics just isn't my kind of thing. Dry, dull people, who bleat on about the same old things. I don't think any of them know what it's like to be our age nowadays.

A decent income is what matters to me, and as soon as I can, I'm going to start my own business.

JOE CASWELL, 20
Engineering student at Edinburgh

I know that if I don't graduate, I'll end up working in a dead-end job, just like my dad. So I know what I'm going to do – work my backside off to prove to my mum and dad that I can make it.

ALEX WILLIAMS, 24
Marketing account manager

There's no such thing as a job for life these days. Employers can make you redundant as soon as there's a downturn, so people don't feel the same loyalty. A lot of my friends are changing jobs to boost their career prospects. I expect I'll have several jobs before I'm 30, and I hope that in my working life I'll have several careers. I don't want to do the same thing for ever. I'm going for an interview next week. More money, more responsibility. 'Don't put off till tomorrow what you can do today' is my motto.

VOCABULARY
Hot verbs – *take, put*

1 There are many expressions with *take* and *put*. Look at these examples from the text on p50.

> It'll probably **take me ten years** to pay (the debt) off.
> These days we're **put under pressure** to get ahead in the rat race.
> No wonder so many young people **take drugs**.
> Don't **put off** till tomorrow what you can do today.

2 Put the words in the right box.

| offence   a stop to sth   place   your arm round sb   (no) notice   part |
| sb in charge of sth   sb/sth for granted   my advice   a plan into practice |
| a risk   your work first   responsibility for sth   pressure on sb   ages |

TAKE	PUT

3 Complete the sentences with expressions from exercise 2 in the correct form.

1 The wedding _____ _____ in an old country church. It was lovely, but it was miles away. It _____ _____ to get there.
2 My son's buying cigarettes, but I'll soon _____ _____ _____ to that. I won't give him any more pocket money.
3 Please don't _____ _____ but I don't think your work has been up to your usual standard recently.
4 I told you that boy was no good for you. You should have _____ _____ _____ and had nothing to do with him.
5 The older you get, the more you have to learn to _____ _____ for your own life.
6 My boss is _____ _____ on me to resign, but I won't go.
7 I tried to get the teacher's attention but she _____ _____ _____ of me at all.
8 Children never say 'Thank you' or 'How are you?' to their parents. They just _____ them _____ _____.

T 5.7 Listen and check.

4 Match a line in **A** with a line in **B**. Underline the expressions with *take* or *put*.

A	B
1 Take your time.	Put it in your diary.
2 The party's on the 21st.	What would you do?
3 Their relationship will never last.	Calm down. There's no need to panic.
4 'I told her a joke about the French, and it turned out she *was* French.'	There's no need to hurry.
5 Take it easy.	No one's out to get you.
6 Put yourself in my shoes.	Take my word for it. I know these things.
7 You always take things too personally.	'Whoops! You really put your foot in it, didn't you?'

Phrasal verbs

5 Use a dictionary. Complete the sentences with a phrasal verb with *take*.

> take sth back   take sth in
> take off   take sb on

1 The shop _____ _____ a lot of extra staff every Christmas.
2 The lecture was too complicated, and the students couldn't _____ it all _____.
3 My business really _____ _____ after I picked up six new clients.
4 You called me a liar, but I'm not. _____ that _____ and say sorry!

T 5.8 Listen and check.

6 Complete the sentences with these phrasal verbs with *put*.

> put sth out   put sb off
> put sth away   put sth on

1 _____ some music _____! Whatever you want.
2 That article about factory farming has really _____ me _____ eating chicken.
3 Could you _____ _____ your clothes, please. Your room's a total mess.
4 _____ your cigarette _____! You can't smoke in here.

T 5.9 Listen and check.

'Well, I wouldn't eat it, but don't let that put you off.'

LISTENING AND SPEAKING
The reunion

1 Three friends, Alan, Sarah, and James, were all at university together in Durham, a town in the north of England. Now, ten years later, they are planning a reunion. Divide into two groups.

Group A

`T 5.10` Listen to Alan phoning Sarah.

Group B

`T 5.11` Listen to Sarah phoning James.

Listen and complete as much as possible of the chart. The following names are mentioned.

> Claypath   the Lotus Garden   the Midlands
> The County   The Three Tuns   Leeds
> the Kwai Lam   Saddler Street   Sunderland

2 Check your answers with people in your group.

	Alan	Sarah	James
Travelling from?			
How?			
Leaving at what time?			
Arriving in Durham at?			
Staying where?			
Going to which restaurant?			
Where is it?			
Where are they going to meet?			
What time?			

3 Find a partner from the other group. Swap information to complete the chart.

4 What might go wrong with their arrangements? Or will everything work out all right? Who's meeting who where?

▶▶ **WRITING** Emailing friends *p115*

Alan   Sarah   James

EVERYDAY ENGLISH

Beginning a telephone conversation

1 **T 5.12** Listen to the beginning of three phone calls. What's the difference between them?
- When and why do we make small talk? Who with? What about?
- Why do organizations have recorded menus?
- Why do people find them frustrating?

2 Here is the beginning of a telephone conversation between two people who *don't* know each other. Put it in the right order.

[!] Hello. TVS Computers. Samantha speaking. How can I help you?

☐ (*pause*) OK. It's ringing for you now.

☐ Yes, please.

☐ (*ring ring*) Hello. Customer services.

☐ Good morning. Could I speak to your customer services department, please?

☐ (*pause*) I'm afraid the line's busy at the moment. Will you hold?

☐ Certainly. Who's calling?

☐ Thank you.

☐ This is Keith Jones.

[10] Hello, I was wondering if you could help me ...

T 5.13 Listen and check your answers.

Ending a telephone conversation

3 Here is the end of a telephone conversation between two work colleagues, Andy and Barry. Put it in the right order.

[1] **A** So, Barry. It was good to talk to you. Thanks very much for phoning.

☐ **A** I certainly will. And you'll send me a copy of the report?

☐ **A** That's great, Barry. Have a good weekend!

☐ **B** My pleasure. By the way, how's your golf these days? Still playing?

☐ **B** Same to you, too! Bye, Andy.

☐ **B** OK. Don't want to keep you. So, you'll give me a ring when you're back, right?

☐ **A** No, not much. I just don't seem to find the time these days. Anyway, Barry ...

☐ **B** It'll be in the post tonight.

☐ **A** It's true. Right, Barry. I must fly. I'm late for a meeting.

☐ **B** What a shame! You used to enjoy it so much.

[11] **A** Bye, Barry.

T 5.14 Listen and check your answers.

4 Discuss the questions.
- Who's trying to end the conversation?
- Who wants to chat?
- How does Andy try to signal that he wants to end the conversation?
- How do they confirm their arrangements?

5 Your teacher will give you a list of expressions and a role card for a phone conversation. Work in pairs. Decide if you think small talk is necessary, and if so, what you can talk about. Sit back to back and have the conversation.

6 Making it big

Expressions of quantity · 'export and ex'port · Business expressions and numbers

TEST YOUR GRAMMAR

1 <u>Underline</u> the words that can complete the expressions of quantity.

a few ... cars/traffic/hold-ups/pollution
not many ... crimes/criminals/violence/accidents
several ... times/letters/paper/rooms

very little ... time/room/hope/spaces
not much ... jobs/unemployment/work/experience
a bit of ... luck/opportunity/fun/help

a lot of ... enthusiasm/energy/people/ingredients
enough ... chairs/food/herbs/cutlery
plenty of ... fresh air/fluids/sleep/walks
hardly any ... money/experience/clothes/friends

2 What do you notice about the three groups of quantifiers?

THE NAKED CHEF
Expressions of quantity

1 Jamie Oliver is a famous British chef. Read the article. Why do you think he is called *the Naked Chef*?

2 Answer the questions.

1 How many TV series has he made?
2 How many books has he written?
3 How many live shows does he do a year?
4 How much did he earn cooking at his parents' pub?
5 How long did he spend in catering college?
6 How much time did he spend in France?
7 How many chefs did he work under in London?
8 How much experience did he have when he was first on TV?
9 How many fresh ingredients and herbs did he use?
10 How much interest in food programmes did his audience have previously?

Jamie Oliver

At only 28, JAMIE OLIVER is now an extremely successful and well-known chef, with his own acclaimed restaurant in the centre of London. He has made five TV series, written several books, and still does around twenty live shows a year. He doesn't have much free time any more. How did he make it big?

Well, his rise to fame and fortune came early and swiftly. By the age of eight he had already started cooking at his parents' pub. It was an easy way to earn a bit of pocket money! After two years in catering college, and some time spent in France, he started working in restaurants. He worked under three famous chefs in London before he was spotted by a TV producer at 21, and his life changed.

Even though he had very little experience, he had a great deal of enthusiasm for cooking, and was very natural in front of the camera. His first TV programme featured him zipping around London on his scooter buying ingredients and cooking for his friends, all to a rock and roll soundtrack. The recipes were bare and simple – they didn't involve complicated cooking techniques and used plenty of fresh ingredients and herbs. It attracted a completely new audience that previously had no interest in food programmes. Jamie Oliver became an overnight success.

So what's his recipe for success? 'A little bit of luck, a little bit of passion, and a little bit of knowledge!' he says.

3 **T 6.1** Listen to a similar text about Jamie Oliver. Write down the differences you hear.

4 Close your books. What can you remember about Jamie Oliver?

PRACTICE

Countable or uncountable?

1 With a partner, ask and answer questions.

How much ...?   *How many ...?*

1 money/in your pocket
2 cups of coffee/day
3 times/been on a plane
4 time/spend watching TV
5 sugar/in your coffee
6 pairs of jeans
7 books/read in one year
8 homework/a night
9 English teachers/had
10 films/a month

T 6.2 Listen and compare your answers.

2 Some nouns can be both countable (**C**) or uncountable (**U**).

Chocolate is fattening. **U**
Have a chocolate. **C**

I do a lot of business in Russia. **U**
We opened a business together. **C**

Complete the sentences with *a* or nothing.

1 I'd like ___ single room for the night.
Is there ___ room for me to sit down?

2 You mustn't let children play with ___ fire.
Can we light ___ fire? It's getting cold.

3 Scotland is a land of ___ great beauty.
You should see my new car. It's ___ beauty.

4 There was ___ youth standing in front of me.
___ youth is wasted on the young.

3 Find word pairs linked according to meaning. Which are normally count nouns, and which uncount? Write them in the correct column.

dollar lorry suitcase job furniture advice apple trouble fact money suggestion fruit journey chair problem work traffic information luggage travel

Count nouns	Uncount nouns
dollar	money

With a partner, choose a pair of words. Write two sentences to illustrate their use. Use the count nouns in the plural.

We need some new furniture.   *We need four more chairs.*

Expressing quantity

4 Rephrase the sentences. Use the prompts.

She earns five euros an hour.

much / very little / hardly any

She doesn't earn much money.
She earns very little money.
She earns hardly any money.

1 She's got two friends.

   many / very few / hardly any

2 There are six eggs in the fridge.

   some / a few / enough

3 There are two eggs in the fridge.

   many / only a couple of

4 There aren't any tomatoes.

   no / not a single / none

5 Did you spend many weeks in France?

   much / a lot of

6 I have five days' holiday a year.

   much / hardly any

7 I have put on 20 kilos!

   a huge amount of / far too much / loads of

8 Ninety per cent of my friends have a car.

   almost all / most / the majority

9 Ten percent of them smoke.

   very few / hardly any / not many

10 There isn't one of my friends who's married.

   none / not one

11 Ken works 100 per cent of the time.

   all / the whole

12 Yesterday I ate hardly anything at all.

   not much / very little / almost nothing

5 Choose the correct alternative.

1 I have *a few / few* cousins, but not many.

2 We have *very little / a little* money, I'm afraid.

3 I earn *less / fewer* money than I did in my old job!

4 *Less / fewer* people go to church these days.

5 *All people / Everyone* came to my party.

6 I was burgled last month. *All / Everything* was stolen.

7 *Everyone / All the people* was watching the Cup Final.

8 Last week the *all / whole* school had flu.

SPOKEN ENGLISH Expressing quantity

There are many ways of expressing quantity in spoken English.

*She's got **loads of** clothes.*

T 6.3 Listen and fill the gaps with the expression of quantity you hear.

| _____ of time | _____ of food | _____ of things |
| _____ of money | _____ of washing | _____ of people |

What have your friends got a lot of?

Tania's got millions of boyfriends.

A lifestyle survey

Conduct a survey of the habits of your class using the activities listed. When you are ready, give your feedback using expressions from the box.

- like shopping
- spend a lot of money on trainers
- watch *Friends*
- buy designer clothes
- like *The Simpsons*
- go to coffee shops
- go clubbing regularly
- do a lot of exercise

all of us
most of us
a few of us
hardly anybody
quite a lot of us
nobody
(nearly) everybody
none of us

Most of us like shopping.

▶▶ **WRITING** Report writing – A consumer survey **p116**

LISTENING AND SPEAKING
Advertisements

1 What's your favourite advertisement at the moment? What's it for? Does it have a story?

2 Talk about an advertisement from a newspaper or magazine. What's it for? Why do you like it?

3 **T 6.4** Listen to six radio advertisements and answer the questions. Write a number 1–6.

Which advert ...

... is advertising a football match?	☐
... is selling a chocolate bar?	☐
... is selling soap powder?	☐
... is for a new car with free insurance?	☐
... is for car insurance for women?	☐
... is advertising a shop's opening hours?	☐

4 Complete the chart.

	Name of the product	Characters involved	Setting/place
1			
2			
3			
4			
5			
6			

5 What is the selling point for each advert?

6 Answer the questions about each advert.

 1 Describe Sarah's play shirt.
 What's special about this washing powder?

 2 What do the men think of the woman driver?
 Why and how do they change their minds?

 3 What has the daughter done that she's so proud of?
 Why is her father so horrible to her?

 4 How can the daughter afford a new car?
 In what ways does she make fun of her father?

 5 What does the man want to invite Sue to do?
 In what ways does he say the wrong thing?

 6 How does the vicar try to hurry up the wedding?
 Why is he in a hurry?

Writing an advert

Devise a radio or television advert. Choose a product or service of your own, or one of the following.

a BMW sports car   Bonzo dog food
        Dazzle washing-up liquid
Blue Mountain coffee   a bank for students
        a restaurant in town
                a computer

STARBUCKS COFFEE

1 What do you know about these brands? What is their reputation? Are they popular among your friends and family? Who are their rivals?

2 Work in two groups.

Group A Read about Starbucks on this page.
Group B Read about Apple Macintosh on p59.

Read your article and answer the questions.

1 When and where did the company begin?
2 Who founded it?
3 Where did the name of the company come from?
4 Why did the product become a success?
5 Has the company's progress always been easy?
6 What makes the brand special?
7 What features of the product or company do people see as negative?
8 What are some examples of the company's products?

3 Find a partner from the other group. Compare and swap information.

4 Here are eight answers. Decide which four are about your article. Then write the questions.

- In Silicon Valley.
- Three or four.
- $5 billion.
- In 1997. (*When ... launched?*)
- Ten years. (*How long ... take ... ?*)
- Because he argued with his partner. (*Why ... resign?*)
- Because they can't compete. (*Why ... out of business?*)
- By selling some of their possessions. (*How ... ?*)

ANYONE FOR COFFEE? What about a Skinny Latte, or perhaps an Almond Truffle Mocha, or even a Raspberry Mocha Chip Frappuccino? These are just a few of the many speciality coffees on offer at Starbucks, the world's leading coffee roaster and retailer.

Starbucks serves over 25 million customers a week in 7,500 stores around the world. And this figure is increasing rapidly, with three or four new stores being opened every single day! So how did a company currently worth $5 billion get started?

Starbucks Coffee, Tea and Spice, as it was originally known, roasted its first coffee beans in 1971. This tiny coffee house in Seattle, named after a character in the novel *Moby Dick*, was the vision of three men – Baldwin, Siegel, and Bowker – who cared passionately about fine coffee and tea. Their determination to provide the best quality coffee helped their business to succeed, and a decade later, their fourth store in Seattle opened.

Meanwhile, in New York, Howard Schultz, a businessman specializing in kitchen equipment, noticed that a small company in Seattle was ordering a large number of a special type of coffeemaker. Out of curiosity, he made the cross-country trip to Seattle to find out more. Immediately he saw the Starbucks store, he knew that he wanted to be part of it. The three founder members weren't initially very keen, but a persistent Schultz was eventually hired to be head of Starbucks marketing in 1982. He modelled the Starbucks stores on Italian espresso bars, and made them comfortable places to relax. Within the next ten years, Schultz had already opened 150 new stores and had bought the company! There are now stores all over Europe, Asia, and the Middle East. Today Starbucks is one of the world's most recognized brands.

"3 or 4 new stores open every day."

But global success comes at a price. Although Starbucks has a company policy of fair trade and employee welfare, it has been the recent target of anti-globalization protests. Many people feel that big corporations, even responsible ones, are never a good thing, as small, independent companies can't compete and go out of business. However, Starbucks' continued success in the face of opposition shows that its blend of commercialism and comfy sofas is still proving an irresistible recipe for world domination.

Apple Macintosh

ARE YOU A MAC USER? For many, home computers have become synonymous with Windows and Bill Gates, but there has always been a loyal band of Apple Macintosh users, whose devotion to the Apple brand and its co-founder Steven Jobs is almost religious.

Steven Jobs and Steven Wozniak dropped out of college and got jobs in Silicon Valley, where they founded the Apple Computer company in 1976, the name based on Jobs' favourite fruit. They designed the Apple I computer in Jobs' bedroom, having raised the capital by selling their most valued possessions – an old Volkswagen bus and a scientific calculator. The later model, the Apple Macintosh, introduced the public to point and click graphics. It was the first home computer to be truly user-friendly, or as the first advertising campaign put it, 'the computer for the rest of us'.

When IBM released its first PC in 1981, Jobs realized that Apple would have to become a more grown-up company in order to compete effectively. He brought in John Sculley, the president of Pepsi-Cola, to do the job, asking him 'Do you want to just sell sugared water for the rest of your life, or do you want to change the world?' Sculley and Jobs began to argue bitterly, however, and after a power struggle, Jobs was reluctantly forced to resign.

"The computer for the rest of us."

By 1996 Apple was in trouble, due to the dominance of Windows software and the increasing number of PC clones which could use it. Jobs, having had great success with his animation studio Pixar, was brought back to the ailing firm for an annual salary of $1, and the company gradually returned to profitability.

Apple's computers cost more than most PCs, and have a more limited range of software available for them, but their great appeal has been the attention to design, making Apple the cool computer company. The launch of the stunning multi-coloured iMac in 1997, followed by the sleek new iMac in 2002, marked the end of the computer as an ugly, utilitarian machine, and brought the home computer out of the study and into the lounge. As Steve Jobs put it, 'Other companies don't care about design. We think it's vitally important.'

Apple's fortunes were transformed again with the development of the iPod in 2003, which soon became a must-have gadget and brought about a boom in Internet music sales. And of course, it was beautifully stylish.

Vocabulary work

Find adverbs ending in *-ly* in the texts that have these meanings.

Starbucks

a	at great speed
b	at the present time
c	in the beginning, before a change
d	with strong feeling and enthusiasm
e	at the beginning
f	after a long time, especially after a delay

Apple Macintosh

a	really/genuinely
b	in a way that produces a successful result
c	in a way that shows feelings of sadness or anger
d	in a way that shows hesitation because you don't want to do sth
e	slowly over a long period of time
f	in a very important way

What do you think?

1 What arguments do the anti-globalization protesters make against Starbucks and other multinational corporations? Do you agree?

2 Do you have a computer? What sort? What are your favourite websites?

VOCABULARY AND PRONUNCIATION
export: /'ekspɔːt/ or /ɪk'spɔːt/?

1 **T 6.5** Listen and repeat these words, first as nouns and then as verbs. How does the word stress change?

a export	c decrease	e progress	g refund	i permit	k insult
b import	d increase	f record	h produce	j transport	l protest

2 With a partner practise the words. Give instructions like this.

> c as a noun!
> 'decrease

> g as a verb!
> re'fund

3 Complete the sentences with one of the words in its correct form. Read the sentences aloud.

1 Scotland _____ a lot of its food from other countries. Its _____ include oil, beef, and whisky.
2 I'm very pleased with my English. I'm making a lot of _____ .
3 Ministers are worried. There has been an _____ in the number of unemployed.
4 But the number of crimes has _____ , so that's good news.
5 How dare you call me a liar and a cheat! What an _____ !
6 There was a demonstration yesterday. People were _____ about blood sports.
7 He ran 100m in 9.75 seconds and broke the world _____ .
8 Don't touch the DVD player! I'm _____ a film.
9 Britain _____ about 50% of its own oil.

T 6.6 Listen and check.

refuse: /'refjuːz/ or /rɪ'fjuːz/?

1 **T 6.7** These words have different meanings according to the stress. Check the meaning, part of speech, and the pronunciation in your dictionary. Listen and repeat.

a refuse	c minute	e content	g invalid
b present	d desert	f object	h contract

2 Practise saying the words in exercise 1 with a partner.

> g as an adjective!
> in'valid

3 Answer the questions using the words in exercise 1.

1 What's another name for a dustman?
2 What's a UFO?
3 What's the Sahara?
4 What do you get lots of on your birthday?
5 What are pages 2 to 5 of this book?
6 What's another way of saying ...?
   - happy
   - a written agreement
   - incorrect (PIN number)
   - very small
   - to say you won't do something

T 6.8 Listen and check.

SPEAKING
A business maze

Work in small groups.

> You have reached one of life's crossroads! You've been made redundant, and some big decisions about your future have to be made.

Discuss the problem on the card until you all agree on what to do next.

1

You were working as a chef in a large restaurant. You have been made redundant, as the restaurant is being converted into a cinema. You have received £15,000 redundancy money. You have a family to support, and cannot survive for long without an income. You want to start a restaurant in your local town, as you believe there is a need for one. It is going to require more than your £15,000, so what are you going to do?

Approach the bank for the extra funding to get your plans underway?
GO TO 8

Go into business with a partner. A friend of yours was also made redundant and received the same amount of money. Why not do it together?
GO TO 22

Your teacher will give you your next card with more information and more decisions. Keep discussing until you get out of the maze. You might succeed, or you might fail!

What do you think?

- Appoint a spokesperson from each group.

  Tell the rest of the class about the decisions that your group took.

  In retrospect, did you make any wrong decisions?

- Why are activities such as these used for management training exercises?

EVERYDAY ENGLISH
Business expressions and numbers

1 This exercise practises fixed expressions in a work context. Match a line in **A** with a reply in **B**.

> We need to get together sometime. When would suit you best?

> Monday and Tuesday are out for me, but Wednesday would be fine. Let's say 9.30.

A	B
1 Mike! Long time no see! How are things?	a Sorry, I didn't quite get that last bit. What was it again?
2 I'm afraid something's come up, and I can't make our meeting on the 6th.	b Sure. I'll email them to you as an attachment.
3 What are your travel arrangements?	c Hey! Mind your own business! You wouldn't tell anyone yours!
4 Could you confirm the details in writing?	d There's no point. I'm not qualified for it. I wouldn't stand a chance.
5 They want a deposit of 2½ percent, which is £7,500, and we … the two … thousand … ge… t…	e I'm getting flight BA 2762, at 18.45.
6 I'll give you £5,250 for your car. That's my final offer.	f Good, thanks, Jeff. Business is booming. What about yourself?
7 I don't know their number offhand. Bear with me while I look it up.	g Great! It's a deal. It's yours.
8 OK. Here's their number. Are you ready? It's 0800 205080.	h Never mind. Let's go for the following week. Is Wednesday the 13th good for you?
9 So what's your salary, Dave? 35K? 40K?	i No worries. I'll hold.
10 Have you applied for that job?	j I'll read that back to you. Oh eight double oh, two oh five, oh eight oh.

T 6.9 Listen and check.

2 Work with a partner. Cover the lines in **B**. Try to remember the conversations. Then cover the lines in **A** and do the same.

Music of English ♪♩

Use the stress shading to help you get the rhythm of each sentence right.

'No. Thursday's out. How about never – is never good for you?'

3 Practise the numbers in the conversations. How is the phone number said in two different ways?

4 Practise saying these numbers.

375   1,250   13,962   23,806   150,000   5,378,212
½ ¾ ⅓ ¼ ⅔

4.3   7.08   10.5   3.142   0.05

17 Sept   Feb 3   22 Nov   Aug 14

19th century   21st century   1960s

2007   1980   1786   1902

12.00 p.m.   12.00 a.m.   14.05   22.30

07775 360722   0800 664733   0990 21 22 23

(football) 2 – 0   (tennis) 30 – 0

T 6.10 Listen and check.

5 Write down some numbers. Dictate them to your partner. Ask your partner to read them back to you.

7 Getting on together

Modals and related verbs 1 • Hot verb *get* • Exaggeration and understatement

TEST YOUR GRAMMAR

1 Read the sentences 1–10 and <u>underline</u> the modal verbs. Rewrite them with a correct expression a–j.

  1 You shouldn't wear red, it doesn't suit you.

  2 May I make a suggestion?

  3 You can smoke in the designated area only.

  4 I can take you to the airport after all.

  5 You must obtain a visa to work in Australia.

  6 You should always make an appointment.

  7 You'll pass. Don't worry.

  8 You mustn't walk on the grass.

  9 I couldn't get through, the line was engaged.

  10 I won't discuss the matter any further.

> a I'll be able to …
> b I didn't manage to …
> c You're bound to …
> d You are required to …
> e Is it OK if …?
> f You're allowed to …
> g If I were you …
> h I refuse to …
> i It's always a good idea to …
> j You aren't permitted to …

2 **T 7.1** Listen and check.

3 Complete the lines a–j with your own ideas and compare with a partner.

I'll be able to come on Saturday after all.

WE CAN WORK IT OUT
Modals and related verbs

1 **T 7.2** Read and listen to the two conversations. Who are the speakers? What are they talking about? Find all the examples of modal verbs.

1 **A** What the … where d'you think you're going?
  B What d'you mean?
  A Well, you can't turn right here.
  B Who says I can't?
  A That sign does mate. 'No Entry'. Can't you read?
  B I couldn't see it, could I?
  A You should get your eyes tested, you should. You're not fit to be on the roads.

2 **T 7.3** Listen to two similar conversations. What expressions are used instead of modal verbs?

3 Choose one of the conversations. Learn it by heart and act it out to the class with your partner.

LANGUAGE FOCUS

1 Modal verbs have many meanings. Match a sentence in **A** with a meaning in **B**.

A	B
1 He can ski. 2 Can I go to the party? 3 You must stop at the crossroads. 4 You must see the film. 5 He must be rich. 6 I'll help you. 7 I won't help you. 8 You should stop smoking. 9 It will be a good party. 10 It might rain.	ability advice obligation permission probability (un)willingness

2 Which meanings in **B** do these related verbs express?

be able to   manage to   be allowed to   be bound to be supposed to   promise to   refuse to   have (got) to be required to   be likely to   had better   Why don't you ...?

3 What is the **question**, **negative**, and **third person singular** of these five sentences?

*I can speak Japanese.   I'm able to speak three languages.
I must go.   I have to go.   I've got to go.*

Put the sentences into the past and future.

▶▶ **Grammar Reference pp147–149**

2 A You won't tell anyone, will you?
  B Of course I won't.
  A You really mustn't tell a soul.
  B Trust me. I won't say a word.
  A But I know you. I'm sure you'll tell someone.
  B Look. I really can keep a secret, you know. Oh, but can I tell David?
  A That's fine. He's invited too, of course. It's just that Ben and I want a really quiet affair. It being second time around for both of us.

PRACTICE

Negotiating

1 Read the conversation. What is it about?

  A *If I were you*, I'd swallow *my* pride and forgive and forget.
  B Never! I *refuse to*.
  A You'll *have no choice* in the end. You *won't be able to* ignore each other forever.
  B *Maybe I'll* forgive him but *I'll never be able to* forget.
  A *Surely it's* possible to talk it over and work something out. You *have to* for the sake of the children.
  B Oh dear! I just don't know what to do for the best.

2 **T 7.4** Replace the words in italics with suitable modal verbs, then listen and compare.

3 **T 7.5** Do the same with this conversation.

  A I don't know if I'*ll be able to* come this evening.
  B But you *have to*. You *promised to*.
  A Yeah, but *I'm not supposed to* go out on weekday evenings. My parents won't let me.
  B *Why don't you* tell them that you're coming over to my house to do homework?
  A *Not possible*. Somebody's *bound to* see me and tell them.
  B We *have no choice but to* cancel the match then. Lots of kids *aren't able to* come to practice in term time.

4 Practise the conversations with a partner.

Discussing grammar

5 Work with a partner. Which of the verbs or phrases can fill the gap correctly? Cross out those which cannot.

1 I _____ be able to help you.

    a won't   b can't   c might   d may

2 Did you _____ keep it secret?

    a could   b manage to   c able to   d have to

3 You _____ be exhausted after such a long journey.

    a must   b can   c had better   d are bound to

4 The book is optional. Our teacher said that we _____ read it if we don't want to.

    a mustn't   b don't have to   c don't need to
    d aren't supposed to

5 I absolutely _____ work late again tonight.

    a will not   b should not   c might not   d refuse to

6 _____ hold your breath for more than a minute?

    a Are you able to   b Can you   c May you   d Could you

7 _____ tell me where the station is?

    a May you   b Could you   c Are you able to   d Can you

8 _____ I have some more dessert?

    a Could   b May   c Will   d Would

9 Will you _____ come on holiday with us?

    a can   b be able to   c be allowed to   d may

10 You _____ go to England to learn English.

    a should   b don't have to   c mustn't   d could

11 You _____ worry so much. You'll make yourself ill.

    a mustn't   b shouldn't   c don't have to   d can't

12 I _____ call home.

    a 'd better   b ought to   c am likely to   d had to

6 Rewrite the sentences using the words in brackets.

1 I just know it'll rain at the weekend. (*bound*)

2 He gave up smoking after three attempts. (*manage*), (*succeed*)

3 Can you tell which twin is which? (*able*)

4 My parents say I can't have a puppy. (*allow*), (*let*)

5 You should take it back and complain. (*If*), (*better*)

6 I should wear a suit for work, but I often don't. (*supposed*)

7 You mustn't tell anyone about it. (*better*), (*promise*)

8 He said he wouldn't put out his cigarette. (*refuse*)

Exciting news

7 Read one side of a telephone conversation between Miranda and Rick.

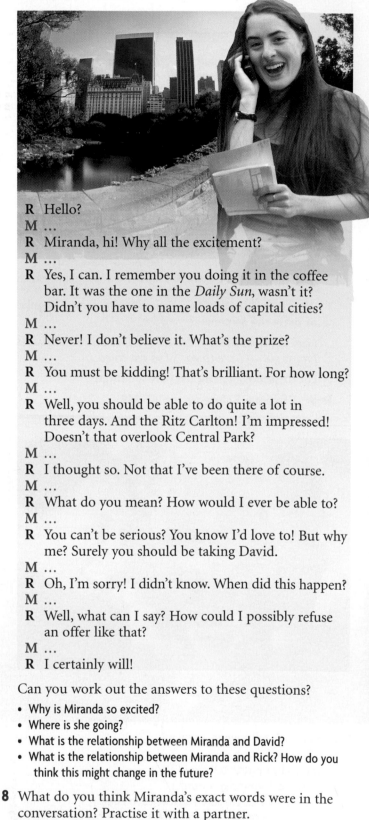

R Hello?
M …
R Miranda, hi! Why all the excitement?
M …
R Yes, I can. I remember you doing it in the coffee bar. It was the one in the *Daily Sun*, wasn't it? Didn't you have to name loads of capital cities?
M …
R Never! I don't believe it. What's the prize?
M …
R You must be kidding! That's brilliant. For how long?
M …
R Well, you should be able to do quite a lot in three days. And the Ritz Carlton! I'm impressed! Doesn't that overlook Central Park?
M …
R I thought so. Not that I've been there of course.
M …
R What do you mean? How would I ever be able to?
M …
R You can't be serious? You know I'd love to! But why me? Surely you should be taking David.
M …
R Oh, I'm sorry! I didn't know. When did this happen?
M …
R Well, what can I say? How could I possibly refuse an offer like that?
M …
R I certainly will!

Can you work out the answers to these questions?

• Why is Miranda so excited?
• Where is she going?
• What is the relationship between Miranda and David?
• What is the relationship between Miranda and Rick? How do you think this might change in the future?

8 What do you think Miranda's exact words were in the conversation? Practise it with a partner.

9 **T 7.6** Listen to the actual conversation between Miranda and Rick. Compare your ideas.

LISTENING AND SPEAKING
Getting married

1 Look at the photos of three weddings and describe them.

2 What do you think are good reasons to get married? What do you think are bad reasons? Discuss ideas with the class.

3 This is Pratima Kejriwal, an Indian lady who had an arranged marriage. What would you like to know about her marriage? Write questions with a partner.

Who arranged the marriage?

How old was she when she married?

4 **T 7.7** Listen to Pratima. Answer the questions.

1 Which of the questions you wrote are answered? What are the answers?
2 How did Pratima's father find the two men?
3 What did he want to know about them?
4 What were the similarities and differences between the two men?
5 Why did her father choose Shyam and not the first man?
6 Why did Shyam dress badly?
7 What happened between the time of the interview and the wedding?
8 How do you know that Pratima believes in arranged marriages?

SPOKEN ENGLISH Other question forms

1 What is unusual about these questions from the interview?

> And your father arranged your marriage?
> And this one your father chose?
> He had to?

These are *declarative questions*, and are used when the speaker thinks he/she has understood something, but wants to make sure or express surprise. Find more examples in the tapescript on p132.

2 Look at this question from the interview.

> For my sister, my elder sister, he saw over one hundred men before ...
> **He saw how many?**

What emotion does this question form express? Make similar questions in reply to these statements.

1 My friends went to Alaska on holiday. **They went ...?**
2 I got home at 5.00 this morning.
3 I paid €300 for a pair of jeans.
4 I met the president while I was out shopping.
5 He invited me to the palace for a drink.

T 7.8 Listen and check.

What do you think?

- Do you think arranged marriages are a good or bad thing? Work in groups and make a list of all the advantages and disadvantages that you can think of.
- What other ways do people meet marriage partners? Do you believe some ways are better than others? If so, which?

Discuss your ideas with the class.

▶▶ **WRITING** Arguing your case – For and against *p118*

READING AND SPEAKING
Meet the *Kippers*

1 When do young people usually leave home in your country? Why do they leave? Work in two groups. List reasons for and against leaving home when you grow up.

Group A Make a list from the children's point of view.
Group B Make a list from the parents' point of view.

Share ideas with the class.

2 Read the introduction to the article and answer the questions.
1 Who are the *Kippers*? What do they refuse to do?
2 What do the letters stand for?
3 What exactly does 'eroding retirement savings' mean?
4 What does 'fly the nest' mean?

3 Read about two *Kipper* children and answer the questions in your groups.
Group A Read about **Vicki**.   **Group B** Read about **Martin**.

1 Who does she/he live with? How do they get on together?
2 Why does she/he still live at home?
3 Has she/he ever lived away from home?
4 What advantages and disadvantages are mentioned?
5 What do her/his friends say?

Work with someone from the other group and compare the two children. Who do you think is the most spoilt?

4 Read about two parents of *Kippers*, Bill and Sandra. Compare their views.
1 Who is happy with the arrangement? Why? Who is not? Why not?
2 Who is at their 'wits' end'?
3 What do they say about foreign travel?
4 What do they say about money?

Vocabulary work

Complete the sentences with words to do with money from the text. Who does each sentence refer to?

1 She isn't able to **r**_____ a flat.
2 He couldn't **a**_____ to pay **o**_____ his **d**_____.
3 Her friends are always **s**_____ for **c**_____ because they have to pay **h**_____ rents.
4 She **c**_____ to the phone **b**_____.
5 She doesn't **c**_____ him **r**_____ because he wouldn't pay it.
6 He **a**_____ debts of £4,000.
7 He sponges **o**_____ his mother in many ways.
8 He can **s**_____ all his **s**_____ on enjoying himself.
9 He believes that **m**_____ isn't **e**_____.

What do you think?

- Check your list of reasons from exercise 1. Which were mentioned?
- What's your opinion of Vicki and Martin?
- Do you sympathize more with Bill's views or Sandra's? Why?
- Is it possible to 'grow up' while still living at home?
- Do you know any *Kippers*?

MEET

Who are they?
They're the children who just WON'T leave home.

Kippers is an acronym for 'Kids In Parents' Pockets Eroding Retirement Savings'. Or, to put it another way, it refers to all those grown up children who stay at home into their 20s and 30s, unwilling or unable to fly the nest.

THE CHILDREN

VICKI SARGENT, 30, lives with her father, Norbert, 65.

IF I WASN'T living at home, I wouldn't be able to afford to live in such a beautiful house. I would only be able to rent a room in a flat. This way I have my father for company and money for a social life. It's just too comfortable to move out.

My dad and I get on so well. We usually have dinner together and if I'm not out, I'll spend the evening with him watching TV. He spoils me a lot and treats me at least once a week to a meal at a nearby restaurant.

My friends don't get it. They say I'm living in a bubble away from the real world, and I suppose they're right, but they also admit they're jealous – they are always so strapped for cash because of their high rents. I don't pay my father any rent but I buy the food and contribute to the phone bill.

Apart from three months when I went travelling in my early 20s, I have never lived away from home.

THE K.I.P.PE.R.S

MARTIN GIBBS, 28, lives with his parents Kathy, 52, and Robert, 54.

I HAVE TO admit that I'm spoiled at home, so it's hard to imagine moving out. My mum always has my tea on the table when I return from work. We all get on really well together – although my parents can get on my nerves when they tell me what to do. I'm sure I get on their nerves as well sometimes.

At 23, I moved out for two years. I lived with a friend for a short time, then went travelling in Australia. It was a brilliant experience but I got into debt, about £2,000, and I had to come back and live at home again so that I could afford to pay it off. My parents don't charge me rent, so I can spend all of my salary on enjoying myself. Sometimes girls call me a 'mummy's boy', but I think they like it. It's a lovely, cosy place to bring girls back to because there is always an open fire and something cooking in the oven.

THE PARENTS

BILL KENNEDY tells why his children, Anna, Simon, and Andrew can stay as long as they like!

NO ONE TOLD ME, but it seems I was the father of Kippers for years, without knowing it. My three children all lived at home well into their late 20s. I know there'll be some parents at their wits' ends with their 'lazy kids sponging off them'. Actually, we don't want an empty nest. What puzzles me is why parents should ever want their children to leave home at 18. My wife, Judy, and I made it very easy for them to stay with us. It allowed them to postpone growing up. And it helped us postpone getting old. Honestly, I would happily forfeit any number of retirement perks – golfing, snorkelling holidays in Portugal, Paris, Peru or wherever – for just a few more years with our children at home. And why? Because money isn't everything. Family is.

SANDRA LANE, 49, says it's domestic hell with her son, Alan, 27.

THE FRIDGE IS the main issue, he's always helping himself to some titbit that I've been saving for dinner and he puts empty milk cartons back. The phone is another cause for complaint – he's always getting in touch with his mates, but when I get angry he just says I should get a mobile phone. And he borrows the car without asking and so I suddenly find myself unable to go out. He's been living at home since he graduated from university five years ago. By the time he finished his studies he had accumulated £4,000 in debt. I can't charge him rent, there's no point. He couldn't and wouldn't pay it. But he's always got money for clothes and nights out. I'm at my wits' end with it all. I had been planning to go on a dream cruise as soon as Alan left home. Now that's all it can be – a dream.

VOCABULARY AND SPEAKING
Hot verb *get*

1 The verb *get* is very common in English. It has many different uses. Here are some examples from the texts on pp66–67.

1 My dad and I **get on so well**.
2 My friends don't **get it**.
3 ... my parents can **get on my nerves** ...
4 ... it helped us postpone **getting** old.
5 ... when I **get** angry ...
6 He's always **getting in touch with** his mates.
7 He said I should **get** a mobile phone.
8 He's always **got** money for clothes.

Replace the words in **bold** with one of the expressions from the box.

> annoy/irritate me   buy
> become   contacting   growing
> have a good relationship
> has   understand

Talking about you

2 Ask and answer these questions with a partner.

1 How do you get on with your parents?
2 What have you got to do when you get home tonight?
3 How do you get to school?
4 What time do you usually get to school?
5 When did you last get angry? Why?
6 Have you got a pet/a PC?
7 If you have a problem with your computer, who do you get to help you?
8 How often do you get your hair cut?
9 In what ways is your English getting better?
10 What are two things that always get on your nerves?

Work together to rewrite the questions without using *get*. Is *get* generally more formal or informal?

Phrasal verbs with *get*

3 *Get* can combine with many particles to make phrasal verbs. Complete each group of sentences with the same particle from the box below. (Careful, only six of the particles are used.)

> at   away   into   off   on   out   over   round   through   up

1	You always get How did our secret get I got a great book	_____	of doing the washing up. It's not fair. ? Everyone knows now! of the library. You can borrow it after me.
2	You're always getting What are you getting I can't get	_____	me! Leave me alone! ? Just say what you mean! the sugar. It's at the back of the cupboard.
3	It took me ages to get He couldn't get his point I can't get	_____	the operation. to me at first. He had to explain it again. how much your children have grown!
4	That boy is always getting We got I had to get	_____	to something naughty! to page 56 in the last lesson. at 5 a.m. to catch the plane.
5	I couldn't get We got I failed, but Sue got	_____	to Joe. I don't think his phone's working. loads of money whilst we were in Paris. the exam with flying colours.
6	She can always get I'm sorry. I just haven't got I can't see how we can get	_____	her father and get exactly what she wants. to replying to your invitation yet. this problem. It's a difficult one.

'How is the cat getting on with your new pet snake?'

'It's the only way I can get the kids to take notice.'

▶▶ **SONG** *Fast car* Teacher's Book **p159**

EVERYDAY ENGLISH
Exaggeration and understatement

1 Which nationalities have a reputation for being passionate, spontaneous, and temperamental? Which nationalities are more controlled and reserved?

2 Which of these declarations of love are exaggerated? Which are understated?

I adore you and I can't live without you.

I'm really rather fond of you.

I'm absolutely crazy about you.

We get on pretty well, don't you think?

I worship the ground you walk on.

3 Match a line in **A** with a line in **B**. Use your dictionary to look up new words.

A	B
1 ☐ I'm absolutely dying for a drink!	a Yes, it was a nice **little** break, but all good things must come to an end.
2 ☐ His family are pretty well off, aren't they?	b You're not kidding. **He's as** thick as two short planks.
3 ☐ You must have hit the roof when she told you she'd crashed your car.	c Yes, my throat's a bit **dry**, I must say.
4 ☐ I think Tony was a bit rude last night.	d Too right! He was **totally** out of order!
5 ☐ I can't stand the sight of him!	e I suppose it is a bit **chilly**.
6 ☐ He isn't very bright, is he?	f Yeah, they do seem **to get** on quite well.
7 ☐ I'm fed up with this weather! It's freezing.	g OK. I feel a bit out **of breath**, too.
8 ☐ Well, that was a fantastic holiday!	h Well, yes, I was a bit **upset**.
9 ☐ I'm knackered. Can we stop for a rest?	i You can say that **again**! They're absolutely loaded!
10 ☐ They're obviously madly in love.	j I must admit, I'm **not too** keen on him either.

4 **T 7.9** Listen and check your answers. Which words are examples of exaggeration? Which are understatements? Practise the conversations with a partner.

Music *of* English 🎵🎶

With exaggerations, the *absolutely* and the adjective both have strong stress.

I'm absolutely exhausted. Aren't you?

With understatements, the main stress is on the qualifier.

Well, I am a bit tired.

T 7.10 Listen and repeat.

5 Work with a **partner**. Take turns to read aloud these understated **remarks** and give an exaggerated reply.

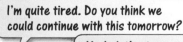

I'm quite tired. Do you think we could continue with this tomorrow?

Yeah, let's stop now. I'm absolutely exhausted.

1 Is that a **new** watch? I bet that cost a bit.
2 It's a bit **chilly** in here, don't you think?
3 These shoes are rather nice, aren't they?
4 Can we stop at the next service station? I could do with something to eat.
5 I think those two like each other, don't you?
6 I bet you **were** a bit upset when your team lost.

T 7.11 Listen and compare.

8 Going to extremes

Relative clauses · **Participles** · **Adverb collocations** · **The world around**

TEST YOUR GRAMMAR

1 Complete the sentences with one of the relative pronouns.

who	which	where	what	when	whose

1 The man _____ you met was my brother.
2 My other brother, _____ lives in London, is a teacher.
3 He suddenly decided to give up teaching, _____ came as a bit of a shock.
4 He says that _____ he wants to do is move to Australia.
5 His girlfriend, _____ parents live in Melbourne, is delighted.
6 They don't know exactly _____ or _____ they are going.
7 Their flat, _____ they bought only last year, is up for sale.
8 The flat _____ I want to buy is in Acacia Avenue.

2 In which sentences can the relative pronoun be replaced by *that*?

3 Underline the present and past participles in these sentences. Rewrite them with relative pronouns.

1 The woman standing next to him is his wife.
2 Most houses built in the sixteenth century are listed buildings.

PILOT SUPERSTAR
Relative clauses and participles

1 What do you know about John Travolta? Look at the photos and read the text quickly. What do you learn about his lifestyle? What is his passion?

2 Read the text again and complete it with the clauses a–j.

a which is built
b who lives
c who isn't full of his own importance
d where the super-rich can commute
e including a Gulfstream executive jet
f whose $3.5 million mansion
g Walking out of his door
h which means
i previously owned by Frank Sinatra
j most of whom share

T 8.1 Listen and check your answers.

JUMBOLAIR
HOME OF JET PILOT JOHN TRAVOLTA

3 Answer the questions.

1 What kind of people live in Jumbolair?
2 Does John Travolta own three planes or more than three?
3 Who owned the Boeing 707 before Travolta?
4 What is Travolta's home like?
5 Why is it called 'the ultimate boys' fantasy house'?
6 What is 'apt' about the name of his son?
7 Why don't the neighbours complain about the noise?
8 Does Travolta behave like a typical film star?

Welcome to JUMBOLAIR, Florida – the world's only housing estate (1)_____ to work by jet plane from their own front doors.

Jumbolair's most famous resident is Hollywood film star John Travolta, (2)_____ is big enough to park a row of aeroplanes, (3)_____ , a two-seater jet fighter, and a four-engined Boeing 707, (4)_____ .

Travolta holds a commercial pilot's licence, (5)_____ he's qualified to fly passenger jets. He can land his planes and taxi them up to his front gates. His sumptuous Florida home, (6)_____ in the style of an airport terminal building, is the ultimate boys' fantasy house made real. As well as the parking lots for the jets, there is a heliport, swimming pool and gym, stables for 75 horses, and of course a 1.4-mile runway. Family man Travolta, (7)_____ with wife Kelly, daughter Ella Bleu, and aptly named son Jett, flies daily from his home when filming. (8)_____ and into the cockpit, he is airborne in minutes. His neighbours, (9)_____ his love of aviation, don't seem to mind the roar of his jets. They say that it's nice to meet a superstar (10)_____ . 'He's just a regular guy, very friendly', says one neighbour.

LANGUAGE FOCUS

Relative clauses

Relative clauses are like adjectives. They give more information about nouns.

*We have a German neighbour **who comes from Munich**.*

1 Read these sentences aloud paying attention to the punctuation. <u>Underline</u> the relative clauses.

I met a man who's a pilot.
My friend Adam, who lives in London, is a pilot.

The house which you walked past is my aunt's.
My aunt's house, which I don't like, is very modern.

2 In each pair of sentences which relative clause …

… tells us exactly *who* or *what* is being talked about? (A **defining** relative clause)

… gives us an extra piece of information? (A **non-defining** relative clause)

Explain the use of commas. How do they affect the pronunciation?

3 In which sentence in 1 can the relative pronoun be omitted? Why?

Present and past participles

<u>Underline</u> the participles in these sentences. Which are adjectives? Which are present and which past?

Who is that boring man standing at the bar?
The curtains and carpets included in the sale were old and worn.
They own four houses, including a ruined castle in Scotland.
Having lost all his money, he was a broken man.

▶▶ **Grammar Reference pp149–150**

PRACTICE

Pronunciation and punctuation

1 Work with a partner. Read the sentences aloud, then write in the correct punctuation where necessary.

1 The area of London I like best is Soho.
2 My father who's a doctor plays the drums.
3 The book that I'm reading at the moment is fascinating.
4 Paul passed his driving test first time which surprised everybody.
5 People who smoke risk getting all sorts of illnesses.
6 I met a man whose main aim in life was to visit every capital city in the world.
7 The Channel Tunnel which opened in 1995 is a great way to get from England to France.
8 What I like best about work is the holidays.
9 A short bald man seen running away from the scene of the crime is being sought by the police.

T 8.2 Listen and compare your pronunciation. Repeat the sentences.

Discussing grammar

2 Read these sentences and decide which need *more* information to make sense.

1 The apple tree in our garden _____ needs to be cut down.
2 People _____ live longer.
3 She married a man _____.
4 The Great Barrier Reef _____ is the largest coral reef in the world.
5 Did I show you the photographs _____?
6 Let me introduce you to Petra James _____.
7 I'm looking for a book _____.
8 I was speaking to someone _____.

3 Put these sentences in the correct sentences in exercise 2, rewriting them as relative clauses. Leave out the pronoun if possible.

a She works in our Paris office.
b You know this person.
c We took them in Barbados.
d She met him on holiday in Turkey.
e It practises German grammar.
f They do regular exercise.
g My grandfather planted it sixty years ago.
h It is situated off the north-east coast of Australia.

Depress -ed or *depress -ing*?

4 Which adjectives in **B** do you think go with the topics in **A**?

A	B
1 exam results	challenging/challenged
2 a holiday	shocking/shocked
3 gossip	disappointing/disappointed
4 a journey	boring/bored
5 a job	relaxing/relaxed
6 a hard luck story	exhausting/exhausted
7 a TV documentary	amusing/amused
8 a social situation	embarrassing/embarrassed

T 8.3 Listen to conversations about the topics. For each, say how the woman feels and why. Use the adjectives in **B**.

'It's raining again!'
'Oh, no! Another miserable day when we're stuck indoors.'

She's depressed.   The weather is depressing.

5 Complete each pair of sentences with the correct form of the same verb, once as a present participle (*-ing*) and once as a past participle.

1 I hurt my leg _____ football.
  Bridge is a card game _____ by four people.
2 It says _____ *in Korea* on my camera.
  I have a job in a café _____ sandwiches.
3 I've spent the whole morning _____ an essay.
  On the wall was some graffiti _____ in big letters.
4 Goods _____ in the sales cannot be refunded.
  I've spent all my money _____ Christmas presents.
5 The police caught the burglar _____ into a house.
  Careful! There's a lot of _____ glass on the floor.

Making descriptions longer

6 Add *all* the words and phrases from the box to this short sentence to make one long sentence.

A woman was sitting in her garden.

| lost in her thoughts   lazily going from rose to rose   beautiful |
| country   watching a bee   gathering honey   young |

T 8.4 Listen and check.

7 Work with a partner. Choose two sentences and make them longer. Read them aloud to the class. Who has the longest sentence?

1 *A man walked along the road.*
2 *Peter has a house in the countryside.*
3 *Ann Croft, the actress, was seen having lunch in a restaurant.*
4 *The holiday was a disaster.*
5 *A boy found a wallet in the street.*

T 8.5 Listen and compare your ideas.

8 Find a picture in a magazine, or use the one your teacher gives you. Describe it to a partner, without showing it. Can your partner draw it?

LISTENING AND SPEAKING
Extreme experiences

1 What's the coldest, hottest, or wettest you've ever been? Where were you? What were you doing? Work in groups, and then tell the class.

2 You are going to listen to Simone and Anna recalling their extreme experiences of heat and cold. Look at the words and discuss what you think happened.

Simone	Anna
a night club	a tram
the pyramids	scarves
sunrise	frozen nostrils
a taxi	an anonymous landscape
a motorbike	huge blocks of flats
heat exhaustion	an old lady
rehydration salts	bonfires

3 **T 8.6** Listen to Simone and answer the questions.

1 Where was she?
2 What was the temperature?
3 What did she do that was stupid or silly?
4 What kind(s) of transport did she use?
5 Where was she going to? Why?
6 What did she see when she arrived?
7 Who did she meet? Was this person helpful?
8 How did the temperature affect her?
9 What happened in the end?

4 Guess the answers to the same questions about Anna's story. Use the words in exercise 2 to help.

5 **T 8.7** Listen and answer the questions in exercise 3 about Anna. Compare your ideas.

Language work

6 Complete the sentences with the adverbs used by Simone and Anna.

> completely   dramatically   exactly   extremely
> profusely   properly   really   seriously   stupidly

1 It was _____ hot and _____ we decided to go dancing.
2 We were sweating _____.
3 The temperature rises _____.
4 My brain wasn't working _____.
5 It was _____ anonymous, this landscape.
6 They all looked _____ the same.
7 I was beginning to _____, _____ panic.

SPOKEN ENGLISH Adding a comment

In conversation we can add a comment with *which* as an afterthought. This often expresses our reaction to what we have said.
   He gave me a lift home, which was nice.

1 Add a suitable comment from **B** to Simone's and Anna's comments in **A**. Sometimes more than one is correct.

A	B
1 We went dancing in temperatures of over 40°C,	which is hard to believe.
2 My friends were worried I'd get lost,	which was just amazing.
3 We visited the pyramids at sunrise,	which was rather a stupid thing to do.
4 My nostrils actually froze,	which was no joke.
5 This motorbike broke down in the desert,	which was no laughing matter.
6 The old lady didn't understand a word I said,	which was understandable.
	which is hardly surprising because my Russian's lousy.

T 8.8 Listen and check. Practise saying the comments with a partner.

2 Write sentences ending with a comment from **B**. Tell the class.
   I missed the last bus home, which was no laughing matter.

READING AND SPEAKING
Chukotka, the coldest place on earth

1 Look at the photos. What do you think links Roman Abramovich with the two places?

2 Read these facts about Chukotka, the coldest place on earth. Which facts do you find surprising? Which not surprising? Why? Discuss with a partner.

> The people don't use fridges or freezers.
> There's no crime.
> It is a remote territory of Russia.
> Its capital, Anadyr, is a boom town.
> It's too cold to play football.
> One of the world's richest men lives there.
> The only flowers are the plastic ones.

3 Read the article quickly. Answer these questions and share information with the class.

1 There are five headings. What does each refer to?

2 For each fact in exercise 2 find some related information.

> *The people don't use fridges or freezers. They hang their meat outside in plastic bags.*

4 Read the article again and answer the questions.

1 Where exactly is Chukotka?
2 What is the climate like? In what ways does it have 'weird weather'?
3 How does the climate affect the daily lives of the people? Give examples.
4 What is the connection between Chukotka and Chelsea Football Club?
5 How has the lifestyle of the inhabitants changed since Roman Abramovich became governor?
6 What do the people find difficult to understand?
7 What does Abramovich own which shows his extreme wealth?
8 Why does he say he is interested in Chukotka? What do some people suspect?

What do you think?

Discuss in groups.

- Why do you think people live in a place like Chukotka? What would you find most difficult there?
- What do you think the lives of the people were like *before* Abramovich became Governor?
- Imagine a year in the life of Roman Abramovich. What do you think is a typical year for him?
- Most people take holidays in warm countries. Are there any cold places in the world you have visited or would like to visit? Where and why?

THE COLDEST

Welcome to CHUKOTKA, where it's currently -30°C and so windy that in the capital, Anadyr, ropes are tied along the streets to stop its inhabitants from blowing away.

It's so cold here that people don't use freezers. They hang their meat in plastic bags on nails above their windows. Spring and summer, when they arrive in June, last a mere eight weeks. The Bering sea, one of four seas that wash against Chukotkan shores, freezes hard enough to support weights of up to 35 tons. There's no crime because it's just 'too damn cold'!

Where yesterday collides with today

Chukotka is, in fact, a remote territory of Russia. It covers 284,000 square miles of frozen landscape, bordering the Bering Strait and straddling the Arctic Circle. Nine time zones ahead of Moscow, it lies right behind the International Dateline, where yesterday collides with today. There is nowhere else on earth earlier than here. Conditions are cruel, and there may seem little to be passionate about other than reindeer, vodka, and the weird weather, but Chukotka has captured the interest of one of the world's richest men, the oil billionaire Roman Abramovich.

From hospitals and cinemas to supermarkets

Roman Abramovich

Roman Abramovich, whose fortune is in excess of $14 billion, is the world's 22nd-richest person, and four years ago he was voted governor of Chukotka. Since then, he has been pouring money into this frozen province. Despite not having been born or raised in Chukotka, he has spent an estimated $300 million of his personal fortune on the region. In Anadyr alone he has rebuilt the hospital, dental clinic, and primary school, modernized the airport, opened its first supermarket and cinema, and sent 8,500 local children on holiday. He even owns the local radio station, the aptly named Blizzard FM. Abramovich not only owns a radio station, he also owns a football club, but not in Chukotka, where it's too cold to play football. The club he owns is over 5,000 miles away in London, England, where, in 2003, he bought Chelsea Football Club.

– 42°C and falling

The inhabitants of Chelsea, England, could not imagine the life of the inhabitants of Chukotka. Locals like to boast that last winter the wind chill took the recorded temperature of −42°C down to −100°C. Schools were closed for a month. It's generally too cold for outdoor sports or any kind of café society, but there are some restaurants and a bar in the supermarket. Snow covers the ground from September to May, which means there are no gardens or woodland: the only flowers are the plastic ones which adorn restaurant tables. But for all this, Abramovich has made Anadyr into a boom town. People find it difficult to understand what he has done and why he has done it.

From reindeer meat to French camembert

Roman Badanov, news editor of Chukotka TV says: 'Anything Abramovich does is news here because so little happens. Why did he choose us? No one knows – it's a secret he keeps to himself.' But he did choose them and they are grateful. In the supermarket you can buy everything from carved walrus tusks to French camembert, Greek olive oil and Scottish whisky. A few years ago there was only frozen reindeer meat, often eaten for breakfast, lunch, and dinner. And Abramovich takes his duties as a governor seriously – he flies in most months on board his private Boeing 767. He has built a Canadian-style wooden house, thereby earning himself the unique distinction of owning homes in St Tropez, Knightsbridge (London), Moscow, and Anadyr. Far from being resentful that he visits only monthly, the local people are astonished that he comes at all. Such is his popularity that the locals refer to BA and AA: Before Abramovich and After Abramovich.

'Why doesn't anyone believe I find this place interesting?'

Abramovich himself asks: 'Why doesn't anyone believe I find this place interesting? I think I can change things here – after all, I have achieved success in business.' But some suspect that he's hoping for vast returns on Chukotka's natural resources, which include 1.2 billion tons of oil and gas and the second-largest gold reserves in Russia. But his motives don't trouble most of the 73,000 population. Just one person, Nathalia, who runs the local Internet service, sounded a note of caution: 'The people are fools because one day Abramovich will go. This is our moment, but it is only a moment.'

VOCABULARY AND PRONUNCIATION
Adverb collocations

Extreme adjectives

Work with a partner.

1 Look at the adjectives in the box.
Find some with similar meanings.

> good bad marvellous huge nice
> wet clever enormous fabulous
> excited surprised valuable small silly
> funny interesting thrilled delighted
> priceless amazed tiny hilarious
> wonderful fantastic ridiculous awful
> brilliant pleased fascinating gorgeous
> big soaking excellent beautiful

Which adjectives go with which of
these adverbs? Why?

very   **absolutely**

2 Complete the conversations with suitable
adverbs and adjectives. Practise them with
your partner.

1 **A** Did you get very wet in that shower?
  B Shower! It was a downpour. We're ... !

2 **A** I bet you were quite excited when your
       team won.
  B Excited! We were ... !

3 **A** I thought she looked rather silly in that
       flowery hat, didn't you?
  B Silly! She looked ....!

4 **A** Come on, nobody'll notice that tiny
       spot on your nose.
  B They will, I just know they will! It's ... !

5 **A** I thought the last episode of *Friends*
       was absolutely hilarious.
  B Mmm. I wouldn't say that. It was ... but
       not hilarious.

6 **A** Len left early. He wasn't feeling well.
  B I'm not surprised. When I saw him this
       morning he looked ... !

3 **T 8.9** Listen and check. Practise again.
Make similar conversations with your
partner. You could talk about films,
people you know, the weather ...

Quite

4 **T 8.10** The adverb *quite* has different meanings. Listen and repeat
these sentences. Which in each pair is more positive?

> 1 **a** She's quite clever.   2 **a** He's quite nice.
>   **b** She's quite clever.   **b** He's quite nice.

5 Read these sentences aloud according to the meaning.
1 The film was quite interesting; you should go and see it.
2 The film was quite interesting, but I wouldn't really recommend it.
3 I'm quite tired after that last game. Shall we call it a day?
4 I'm quite tired, but I'm up for another game if you are.

T 8.11 Listen, check, and repeat.

A night at the Oscars

6 Read the speech. Who is speaking? Why? Rewrite the speech and make
it sound more extreme by changing and adding adjectives and adverbs.

> " I am very surprised and pleased to receive this award. I am grateful
> to all those nice people who voted for me. 'Red Hot in the Snow' was a
> good movie to act in, not only because of all the clever people involved
> in the making of it, but also because of the beautiful, exciting and
> often quite dangerous locations in Alaska. None of us could have
> predicted that it would be such a big success. My special thanks go to
> Marius Aherne, my director; Lulu Lovelace, my co-star; Roger Sims, for
> writing a script that was both interesting and funny, and last but not
> least to my wife, Glynis, for her valuable support. I love you all. "

7 **T 8.12** Listen and compare your choices.

EVERYDAY ENGLISH
The world around

1 Look at the signs. Where could you … ?

- … borrow money to buy a flat?
- … buy a hammer, a screwdriver, and some glue?
- … go to get fit?
- … get rid of your newspapers and bottles?
- … get an inexpensive bed for the night?
- … get help with legal problems?
- … have your body decorated?
- … replace some of the parts on your car?

2 **T 8.13** Listen to five conversations. Where are they taking place?

3 In pairs, write similar conversations that take place in two or three of the other places. Read them out to the rest of the class. Where are they taking place?

▶▶ **WRITING** Describing places – My favourite part of town *p119*

9 Forever friends

Expressing habit • *used to do/doing* • Homonyms/Homophones • Making your point

TEST YOUR GRAMMAR

1 Match a line in **A** with a line in **B**.
Underline the words that express habit.
Which are past and which are present?

2 Choose the correct ending for these
sentences.

| He used to work hard | because he's a builder. |
| He's used to hard work | but now he's retired. |

	A		B
1	A reliable friend		my Dad would read me a story at bedtime.
2	In the 1960s, hippies		are always talking about themselves.
3	I think my sister's in love.		will never let you down.
4	When I was a kid		She'll spend hours staring into space.
5	My first girlfriend was Alice.		used to wear flowers in their hair.
6	Big-headed people		We used to go to the cinema on a Friday, and then we'd go for a pizza afterwards.

FRIENDS REUNITED
Expressing habit – *used to do/doing*

1 One of the most popular websites in Britain
is *Friendsreunited.co.uk*. What sort of website
do you think it is? Is there a similar website
in your country?

2 Read the email from Alison to an old
school-friend. Complete it with the lines a–l.

a used to sit	g went
b 'd get	h was
c got	i used to call
d 's always talking	j used to calling
e used to go	k were always giggling
f 'd go	l 'll always end up

T 9.1 Listen and check.

3 Which actions in the email happened again
and again? Which only happened once?

Friends Reunited .co.uk

From: Alison Makepeace <AliMakepeace72@glosmail.uk.com>
Date: Mon 17 September, 18.36
To: sallydavies@talksmail.co.uk
Subject: Allendales School

Dear Sally

I'm sending this through Friends Reunited. Do you remember me?
We 1_____ to Allendales School together. You were the first person
I 2_____ to know when I started there.

We 3_____ next to each other in class, but then the teachers made
us sit apart because we 4_____ so much.

I remember we 5_____ back to your house after school every day
and listen to music for hours on end. We 6_____ all the Beatles
records as soon as they came out. Once we ate all the food in your fridge
and your mother 7_____ furious.

Do you remember that time we nearly blew up the science lab? The
teacher 8_____ crazy, but it wasn't our fault. We 9_____ him
'Mickey Mouse' because he had sticky-out ears.

I still see Penny, and she's still as mad as ever. We meet up every now
and again, and we 10_____ chatting about old times together. She
11_____ about a school reunion. So if you're interested, drop me a line.

Looking forward to hearing from you.
Your old schoolmate

Alison Makepeace

PS I'm not 12_____ you Sally Davies! To me, you're still Sally Wilkinson!

4 Look at these two sentences.

> We used to go to school together ...
> We'd go back to your house ...

Which sentence is more factual?
Which is more nostalgic?

5 Match a line in **A** with a line in **B**. Practise saying them. Pay attention to contracted forms and weak forms.

A	B
we used to go	him 'Mickey Mouse'
we used to sit	to school together
we were always giggling	you Sally Davies
we'd go back	so much
we used to call	to your house
I'm not used to calling	next to each other

T 9.2 Listen and check.

PRACTICE

What's she like?

1 Choose an adjective from the box to describe the people in the sentences.

> easy-going   clumsy   mean   absent-minded
> argumentative   sensitive   sensible   stubborn

1 He's always losing things, or forgetting where he's put things.
2 She'll always cry at the end of a sad film.
3 Nothing ever upsets her, or annoys her, or worries her.
4 I'm always dropping things, or bumping into things.
5 She's ruled by her head, not her heart. She'll always think things through before she acts.
6 He just won't listen to anyone else's suggestions.
7 I remember that bloke Dave. He'd never buy you a drink.
8 And he'd pick a fight with anyone about anything.

2 Add similar sentences to support these statements.

1 My flatmate is the untidiest person in the whole world.
2 My boyfriend is insanely jealous.
3 Marc is just the coolest guy I know.
4 My mother really gets on my nerves.
5 But my grandma was so sweet.
6 My dog Bruno was my best friend.
7 Your problem is you're self-obsessed.
8 My sister's so nosy.

Discussing grammar

3 In pairs, decide which line in **B** best continues the line in **A**.

A	B
1 My friend Joe buys and sells cars. 2 He's always buying new things for himself – a DVD, a palm top. 3 He'll buy a shirt and only wear it once.	He's a real techno-geek. Don't you think that's wasteful of him? He earns loads of money.
4 When I was young, we used to have holidays by the seaside. 5 My dad and I would build sandcastles and go swimming together. 6 One year we went to East Africa.	What an adventure that was! We'd go to the same place year after year. I remember those days with such fondness!
7 John usually does the cooking 8 He used to do the cooking 9 He's used to doing the cooking 10 He's getting used to doing the cooking	because he's been doing it for years. but he still burns things. Maybe one day he'll get it. but then he stopped. but he isn't tonight. I am.

Parents

4 **T 9.3** Listen to four people talking about their relationship with their parents. Is/Was it a good relationship?

5 **T 9.3** Listen again. These lines are similar to what they say. What are their actual words?

1 ... she talked to me very openly ...
... we used to go out shopping ...

2 My wife always asks me questions ...
... we didn't talk very much ...
... every week he took me to the hairdresser.

3 ... she always tells me to pick things up ...
She goes on for hours ...

4 We did a lot together as a family.
... he brought us each a treat ...

6 Write a few sentences about the relationship between you and your parents. Tell your partner about it.

Answering questions

7 Answer the questions with a form of *used to do, be /get used to doing/sb/sth*.

1 **A** You don't like your new teacher, do you?
   B Not a lot, but _we're getting used to her_.

2 **A** How can you get up at five o'clock in the morning?
   B No problem. I _____.

3 **A** How come you know Madrid so well?
   B I _____ live there.

4 **A** How are you finding your new job?
   B Difficult, but I _____ it bit by bit.

5 **A** Do you read comics?
   B I _____ when I was young, but not any more.

6 **A** You two argue so much. How can you live together?
   B After twenty years' marriage we _____ each other.

T 9.4 Listen and check.

LISTENING AND SPEAKING
A teacher I'll never forget

1 Look at the pictures. What are the teachers doing? What are the students doing? How have teaching styles changed over the years?

'*That's an interesting question Timmy, I suggest you ask your search engine.*'

2 **T 9.5** Listen to four people talking about a teacher they'll never forget. What characteristics of a good and a bad teacher do they mention?

3 Discuss the questions.

1 Why did Alan like his teacher? What are some of the things he'd do?

2 Why didn't John like his teacher? What are some of the things he used to do?

3 What does Liz say about her teacher? What will she never forget?

4 Why does Kate have two opposing views of Mr Brown?

5 What comments do they all make about their teacher's name?

What do you think?

Who is a teacher you'll never forget? Why? What was/is she/he like?

SPOKEN ENGLISH Adjective intensifiers

Look at these lines from the tapescript.

> All the kids were **scared stiff** of him.
> ... she made it seem **dead easy**.

These are compounds that intensify the meaning of the adjective.

Complete the sentences with a word from the box.

> brand   stiff   freezing   tiny   wide   great   boiling   fast

1 They live in this _____ big house in the centre of London.

2 I made one _____ little mistake in my driving test, but I still failed.

3 Careful with the soup – it's _____ hot. Don't scald yourself.

4 It's _____ cold in here. Can't we put on the heating?

5 Do you like my car? It's _____ new.

6 Don't worry. You won't wake the children. They're _____ asleep.

7 I have a cold shower every morning. After that I feel _____ awake.

8 'I'm fed up with this lesson.' 'Me, too. I'm bored _____.'

READING AND SPEAKING
Friends past

1 Discuss the questions.

1 What kind of TV programmes are these?

soap opera	sitcom	quiz show
documentary	reality TV	current affairs

Think of examples of each in your country. What are your favourites?

2 What American programmes are on TV in your country? Do you watch any of them?

2 **T 9.6** Listen to the theme tune of *Friends*, one of the most successful American sitcoms ever. Can you remember any of the lines?

3 What do you know about *Friends*? Why do you think it was so successful?

4 Read the first half of the article and answer the questions.

1 What line in paragraph 1 summarizes the stories in *Friends*?
2 How long did the series last?
3 Why, according to Steve Beverly, was the show so popular?
4 What is so enviable about the *Friends'* lifestyle?
5 *Zeitgeist* is a German word meaning *the spirit or feeling of a period in history*. How did *Friends* capture the zeitgeist? Give two examples of how it defined it.
6 Why did *Friends* become more popular after 9/11?
7 How did the series change our language, hair, and drinking habits?

5 Read the second half of the article.

1 Who is related to who? Who is in love with who? What is the mixed emotion described at the end of the article?
2 What is each character like? Find some examples of their behaviour that illustrate the kind of person they are.

6 **T 9.7** Listen to people describing a character in *Friends*, but without saying who it is. Which character is being described?

Language work

Match a word from the first part of the text in **A** with a similar word in **B**.

A	B
the small screen	looked for
trials	met
trendy	feeling deep sadness
encountered	difficulties
grieving	television
sought	fashionable

What do you think?

• Who is your favourite TV character? Why?
• Describe one of your closest friends.

IT WAS THE AMERICAN SITCOM THAT DEFINED A GENERATION – and introduced one of the world's most famous haircuts. The six stars of *Friends*, among the longest-running, most successful series ever to hit the small screen, went their separate ways after 237 episodes and a decade together as flatmates, sharing the trials of their lives, loves, and careers in a trendy New York apartment. The last episode was seen by an estimated world audience of over 100 million viewers.

'*Friends* had a huge influence on American TV history,' said Steve Beverly, professor of communication arts. 'This group of six reflected a microcosm of what people their age encountered in their daily lives. Viewers related to them. We *all* wanted a life like theirs – the cool New York flat with table football and easy chairs, and the social circle of beautiful, supportive friends.'

We also wanted to drink endless cappuccinos. Interestingly enough, the first New York Starbucks store opened in the same year that *Friends* started. The dual rise of coffee culture and *Friends* was one example of how the show captured the *zeitgeist*. At other times it defined it. The 'Rachel' haircut was copied by millions of women.

The series has even been credited with influencing how many of us speak. Researchers analysed every episode to explore whether popular culture influenced how we speak. Prior to the series, the commonest way to intensify an adjective was by using *very* or *really*. On *Friends*, the most common intensifier was *so*. 'This guy is like so cool,' they said, and now we all say it.

The show enjoyed a huge surge in ratings after the 11 September terrorist attacks, as grieving New Yorkers struggled to make sense of the real horrors that had unfolded around them. In the familiar comforts of the show, they sought the return of a feel-good factor, according to Robert Thompson, professor of television and popular culture. '*Friends* is set not in the real New York, but in the New York of some Utopian fantasy where the rooms in the apartments are huge, everybody leaves their doors unlocked and people don't fly planes into buildings,' he said.

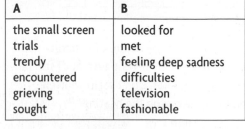

F·R·I·E·N·D·S PAST

It was much more than a brilliant comedy, says **Claire Rooney** – it changed our language, our hair, and even our drinking habits

So who are these characters?

Ross has been in love with Rachel, the best friend of his sister Monica, since childhood, and throughout the whole series they have an on-off romance. In the final episode they actually do get back together again. Ross is a bit of a bore and a geek. He's always whining.

Chandler, a computer programmer, used to share an apartment with Joey. He's constantly telling jokes and making everybody laugh. He had a few relationships throughout the series, mostly disastrous because he would always find flaws in the women he dated, but then married Monica.

Joey is a New York Italian. He's an actor who manages to spend most of the series unemployed. Nevertheless he has total belief in his talents. He's rather dense, but lovable and charming. He'll cheer himself up with food or women. Either will do, but both at the same time is best.

Rachel is a spoilt little rich girl who gets a job in the local coffee house, and later becomes a fashion consultant. She is terrible in a crisis, and will throw her arms up in despair. Rachel and Ross get together so many times, but things keep going wrong, until they finally make it permanent in the last episode.

Phoebe is the group hippy. She is wild and very eccentric, and she's always smiling. She is a spiritual masseuse, who is always communicating with the dead and chanting about auras. She is best known for her unique guitar playing – her most famous song is *Smelly Cat*.

Monica, hard as it is to believe, used to be fat. She is a deeply insecure character and is always tidying up. She's also bossy, and has to have her own way. Her desire is to find her dream man, get married, and have babies. Eventually she settles down with Chandler.

More like a way of life

Friends is more than just a sitcom, it's a way of life. Our attitudes to the *Friends'* lives is a mixture of envy – 'How do they get to sit on sofas all day sipping coffee and being witty?' – and disdain: 'Don't they have anything better to do with their time, like earn a living to pay for that Manhattan apartment?'

They were supposed to be in their mid-twenties, with lives untroubled by work and responsibility. With the cast approaching forty, the show had to come to an end. But of course, *Friends* will last forever.

VOCABULARY AND PRONUNCIATION
Homonyms and homophones

1 Work on your own. What do these words mean?

> fine   match   park   book   cross   mean

2 **T 9.8** Write down the words you hear.

3 Work with a partner. Compare your answers to exercises 1 and 2. Do you have any differences? What are they?

Homonyms

4 Homonyms are words with the same spelling and more than one meaning.

> a **bank** in the High Street
> the **bank** of a river
> I've supported you up till now, but don't **bank** on it forever.

Complete the pairs of sentences with the same word used twice.

1   You'll like Paul. He's a really _____ guy. Easy-going, and very good looking.

   There was a lovely _____ breeze coming off the sea.

2   'What's today's _____?' 'The third.'

   I've got a _____ tonight. I'm going out with Carol.

3   *Friends* is _____ in New York.

   My wife bought me a chess _____ for my birthday.

4   He goes to the gym every day. He's very _____ .

   The trousers are too small. They don't _____ you.

5   I can't _____ people who never stop talking about themselves.

   My four-year-old son won't go anywhere without his teddy _____ .

5 Think of two meanings for these words.

> wave   suit   fan   miss   type
> point   train   right   mind   fair

Homophones

6 Homophones are words with the same pronunciation, but different spellings and different meanings.

> /rəʊd/   the **road** to the town centre
> She **rode** a horse.
> I **rowed** across the river.

Write the word in phonetics in the correct spelling.

1   /həʊl/   the _____ world
   a _____ in the ground

2   /piːs/   a _____ of cake
   war and _____

3   /flaʊə/   a rose is a _____
   _____ to make bread

4   /seɪlz/   a yacht has _____
   buy clothes in the _____

5   /sel/   salespeople _____ things
   a prisoner lives in a _____

7 Think of a homophone for these words.

> bored   caught   war   hire   pair   plain   waist   seas   sure   aloud

8 **T 9.9** A lot of children's jokes are made with homonyms and homophones. Here are two! Which word makes the joke?

A How do you keep cool at a football match?

B I don't know.

A Sit next to a fan.

A Why did the teacher wear sunglasses?

B I don't know.

A Because her students were so bright.

T 9.10 Listen to some more jokes. Which word makes the joke? Practise telling them to each other.

EVERYDAY ENGLISH
Making your point

1 **T 9.11** Listen to Vicky, Al, and Beth-Anne talking about whether people should pay more tax on fast food. Who is for it, who is against it, and who is undecided?

2 Match a line in **A** with a line in **B** as they appear in the tapescript on p135.

A	B
If you	is that ...
Another thing	the point.
That's not	I understand it ...
The point	you the truth ...
To tell	my opinion ...
I suppose	worries me is that ...
As far as	I'm trying to make is that ...
Anyway, as I	point is that ...
If you want	the problem is that ...
As	was saying ...
But the main	I'm concerned ...
What really	ask me ...

T 9.12 Check your answers. Listen carefully and practise the lines.

> **Music of English** 🎵
>
> Notice the stress patterns in the expressions for making your point. It's important that you get the stress pattern right if you want to make your point forcefully.

3 Write the adverbs that end in -*ly* in tapescript 9.11.

firstly　*secondly*　*personally*

4 Match a line in **A** with a line in **B**.

A	B
1 First of all,	there are problems with the cost.
2 As well as this,	I'd like to give my conclusion.
3 Finally,	I'd like to look at the general problem.
4 In my opinion,	how do you educate people to have a better diet?
5 Generally speaking,	fast food should be totally banned.
6 The problem is,	as a nation we don't do enough exercise.
7 As far as I know,	I don't know the answer to this problem.
8 To be exact,	there are five others like this.
9 To be honest,	this problem is quite common.

5 Have a class debate. Choose a topic you feel strongly about, something local to your situation perhaps, or one from this list.

- Being vegetarian
- Diets
- Smoking in public places
- Experiments on animals

Divide into groups to prepare your ideas. When you're ready, conduct the debate.

▶▶ **WRITING** Writing for talking – *What I want to talk about is ... **p120***

10 Risking life and limb

Modal auxiliary verbs 2 · Synonyms · Metaphors and idioms – the body

TEST YOUR GRAMMAR

1 All modal verbs can be used to express degrees of probability. Which of these sentences do this? Put a (✓). Which don't? Put a (✗).

1 She must be very rich.
2 I must do my homework.
3 I can't sleep because of the noise.
4 They can't be in. There are no lights on.
5 I think that's Jane but I might be wrong.
6 You should see a doctor.
7 I could swim when I was five.
8 Cheer up! Things could be worse.
9 The train may be late due to bad weather.
10 May I make a suggestion?

2 Put sentences 1–6 in the past.

T 10.1 Listen and check.

ÖTZI THE ICEMAN
Modal auxiliary verbs in the past

1 The body of a 5,300-year-old man was discovered in the Italian Alps in 1991. It had been preserved in ice. He was named Ötzi after the Ötz Valley where he was found. Look at the pictures.

What do you think ...

... he was?
... he wore?
... he ate?

Where did he live?
How did he die?
How old was he when he died?

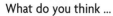

> He was probably a hunter.

> He could have been a warrior.

2 **T 10.2** Listen to two people, Alan and Bill, discussing the questions in exercise 1. Give one of their answers to each question.

3 Answer these questions about Ötzi using the words in *italics*.

1 What was he?

  a hunter/shepherd   *could*

2 What was he doing in the mountains?

  looking after his sheep/got lost   *might*

3 Where did he live? What did he wear?

  a cave   animal furs   *must*

4 How did he die?

  asleep/cold and starvation   *may*

5 Was it a good idea to go so high?

  so high on his own   *shouldn't*

  protective clothing   *should*

6 What did he eat?

  a lot of meat and berries   *must*

  crops like cereals to make bread   *might can't*

  meat   *'d have thought*

7 Did they travel much?

  (not) much at all   *wouldn't have thought*

  stayed in the same area   *must*

8 How old was he when he died?

  between forty and forty-five   *could*

  quite old in those days   *must*

4 **T 10.3** Listen and check. Practise the sentences, paying attention to contracted forms and weak forms.

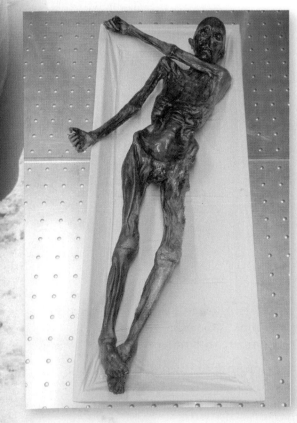

5 Here are some more things found on or near Ötzi's body. How can you explain them?

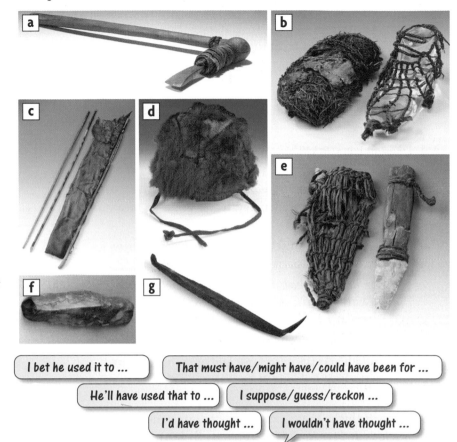

I bet he used it to ...

That must have/might have/could have been for ...

He'll have used that to ...

I suppose/guess/reckon ...

I'd have thought ...

I wouldn't have thought ...

6 Read the results of recent tests done on Ötzi on p157. Were Alan and Bill right or wrong in their assumptions? Were *you* right in *your* assumptions?

LANGUAGE FOCUS

1 Write *certain* or *possible* next to these modal auxiliary verbs according to the degree of probability they express.

They'll have They must have		
They might have They could have They may have	arrived.	
They can't have They won't have		

2 What concept do these modal verbs express? Choose a definition on the right.

You shouldn't have told a lie.
You needn't have cooked. No one's
* hungry.*
You idiot! You could have killed
* yourself!*
	You did this but it wasn't
	  necessary.
	This was possible but you
	  didn't do it.
	You did this but it was wrong.

▶▶ **Grammar Reference p151**

PRACTICE

Discussing grammar

1 <u>Underline</u> the correct answer.

1 Sorry I'm late. I *should have gone/had to go* to the post office.

2 I looked for Pearl but I *couldn't find/couldn't have found* her.

3 I don't know where Paul is. He *had to go/must have gone* home early.

4 I *had to work/must have worked* hard when I was at school.

5 You *needn't have said/shouldn't have said* anything to Pam about her birthday party. It was going to be a surprise.

6 You *needn't have bought/couldn't have bought* a new vacuum cleaner. I managed to fix the old one.

7 You *should have asked/must have asked* me earlier. I *might have given/would have given* you a lift.

8 You *can't have done/needn't have done* your homework already! You only started five minutes ago.

9 You *could have told/must have told* me the lesson had been cancelled! I *shouldn't have got/wouldn't have got* up so early.

10 You were lucky to get out of the car unharmed. You *would have been/could have been* badly hurt.

2 Complete the sentences with a modal verb in the past.

1 I *did* tell you about Joe's party. You _____ listening.

2 Thanks so much for all your help. I _____ managed without you.

3 Flowers, for me! Oh, that's so kind, but really you _____ .

4 Come on! We're only five minutes late. The film _____ started yet.

5 I don't believe that Kathy's going out with Mark. She _____ told me, I know she would.

6 We raced to get to the airport on time, but we _____ worried. The flight was delayed.

7 We've got a letter here that isn't for us. The postman _____ delivered it by mistake.

8 You _____ gone swimming in such rough sea. You _____ drowned!

T 10.4 Listen and check. Practise the sentences with a partner.

Making assumptions

3 **T 10.5** You will hear one half of a telephone conversation. Who are the people? What are they talking about? Make assumptions.

> They must be divorced.

> They might just be separated.

4 Work with a partner. Look at the tapescript on p136. Write what you think is the other half of the conversation. Compare with other students.

5 **T 10.6** Do the same with the second conversation.

SPOKEN ENGLISH Expressions with modals

There are many fixed expressions with modal auxiliary verbs often found in spoken English. Match a line in **A** with a line in **B**.

A	B
1 'That exam was totally impossible!' 2 'You might as well apply for the job, even though you're too young.' 3 I know I shouldn't have eaten a whole tub of ice-cream … 4 'I'm going to tell her exactly what I think of her.' 5 'You might have told me that Jackie and Dave had split up!'	a 'Sorry! I thought you knew.' b 'You can say that again!' c but I just couldn't help it. d 'Yes, why not! After all, I've got nothing to lose.' e 'I wouldn't do that if I were you.'
6 'I think you should forget all about her and move on.' 7 'You should have been here yesterday! You'd have died laughing!' 8 'Then I found out that Annie's been going out with … guess who? Dave!' 9 I'd known this guy for five minutes when he asked me to marry him! 10 'I could do with a break.'	f 'Me, too. I'm dying for a coffee.' g 'Believe me, I would if I could.' h 'Why? What was so funny?' i 'Huh! I could have told *you* that.' j I just couldn't believe it!

T 10.7 Listen and check. What extra lines do you hear? What are the contexts? Practise the conversations with a partner.

▶▶ **SONG** *One of these things first* Teacher's Book **p162**

It all went wrong!

6 Write some notes about an occasion in your life when everything went wrong. Tell the class. They can comment and ask questions.

> Couldn't you have …?
> Why didn't you …?
> You must have been terrified!
> I'd have thought you could have …
> Don't you think you should have …?
> You might well ask!
> You can say that again!
> I know I shouldn't have … , but I couldn't help it.
> I couldn't believe it!

SPEAKING
The murder game

> Four men are sitting in the library of a country house. Suddenly one of the men drops dead.
> # Who did it?

1 Your teacher will give each of you a card with information about the murder. You can't show your card to anyone else, but you can say what's on it.

2 Work as a class to solve the murder. The best way to do this is through organization and co-operation, knowing when to speak and when to listen.

If you work together well, you should solve the murder in about twenty minutes. If you don't work together, you'll never solve it!

3 When you have finished, discuss these questions.

- How did you organize yourselves?
- Was everybody involved, or did one person dominate?
- How could you have solved the murder more quickly?
- What should you have done?
- Games such as these are used on management training courses. Why, do you think?

▶▶ **WRITING** Formal and informal letters and emails – Do's and don'ts **p121**   Unit 10 · Risking life and limb   89

READING AND SPEAKING
How the West was won

1 Do you know any films about cowboys and Indians? What is a typical plot? Who are the 'good guys' and who are the 'bad guys'? Do you have a favourite western?

2 What do you understand by the title of the article? Look at the six sub-headings. Make guesses about the contents of the paragraphs.

3 Read the first two sections. Answer the questions.

1 Why did the white settlers want to head west? (There are several reasons.)

2 What were some of the natural dangers to overcome? What could go wrong? What accidents could have been avoided?

3 What do these numbers refer to?

1843	14,000	2,000	4½	15	25

4 Read about the Donner family. Complete the sentences using the verb in brackets and a modal verb.

1 They _____ (set out) so late in the year.
2 They _____ (follow) an established route.
3 They _____ (spend) the winter in the mountains.
4 They _____ (take) enough food.
5 They _____ (be) really starving to do what they did.

5 Read the rest of the article. Answer the questions.

1 Describe the early relationship between new and Native Americans. What was the main reason for this to change?

2 Describe the American Indians' culture. Over what issues were they bound to clash with the settlers?

3 How did the white people help the Native Americans? How did they exploit them?

4 How was the spirit of the Native Americans finally broken?

5 Find different ways in which the white people and the Indians are referred to.

What do you think?

• In which other countries have settlers taken the lands of native inhabitants? What has happened there?

• Do you think native inhabitants of today should receive financial compensation for the land that was taken from their ancestors?

• What are the arguments for and against developing remote parts of the world such as rainforests, deserts, and Antarctica?

HOW THE

'GO WEST, YOUNG MAN!'

The American West covers a vast area from the Mississippi River to the Pacific coast. It was largely unexplored by white settlers until the beginning of the nineteenth century. Land was scarce in the East, so many white people who wished to farm went West in search of a new life. The US government promised these pioneers land in the newly-acquired states of California and Oregon. Many Americans believed that there should be one large American republic stretching from the Atlantic to the Pacific. They thought that this was part of God's plan, and they had the right to claim the land from the primitive natives.

THE HAZARDOUS JOURNEY

Large-scale migration began in 1843. By 1848, over 14,000 settlers had followed. Much of the land they crossed consisted of mountains, deserts, and huge, treeless plains. To avoid the worst of the winter blizzards in the mountains, travellers normally began their journey in late April or early May. It was not possible to travel earlier in the year, as there was not enough grass on the Great Plains to feed the livestock. If everything went according to plan, the 2,000-mile journey took around four and a half months, covering about fifteen miles a day. Any delay meant that fierce snowstorms would be encountered in the Sierra Nevada mountains. Migrants suffered from disease, violent dust storms, wagons stuck in mud, and plagues of insects such as mosquitoes. One in 25 of the migrants failed to make their destination. Many deaths were self-inflicted. Not experienced in the use of guns, they frequently shot themselves or each other by mistake.

WEST WAS WON

The 2,000-mile journey took four and a half months.

THE TRAGEDY OF THE DONNER FAMILY

In 1846, a group from Illinois decided to emigrate to California. One of the families was called Donner. Their story was to become one of the best-known tragedies in the history of Western emigration. They made two vital mistakes. They started late, and followed an untested route and got lost. Morale became poor, tempers flared, and one of the men was stabbed to death. It was late October by the time they started to climb the Sierra Nevada mountains, and they were desperately short of food. It became clear that the snow had made the mountains impassable. They prepared to spend the winter in the mountain snow. Starving, they ate glue, fur, and dogs. Eventually, they ate their own dead. Out of 81 travellers, over half died.

FIRST CONTACTS WITH NATIVE AMERICANS

When the white people first explored the American West, they found Native Americans living in every part of the region, many of them on the Great Plains. White people saw the Plains Indians as savages, but in fact each tribe had its own complex culture and social structure. They didn't believe that land should be owned by individuals or families, but it should belong to all people. They believed that human beings were indivisible from all the other elements of the natural world: animals, birds, soil, air, mountains, water, and the sun. In the early days of migration, relations between the pioneers and Native Americans were generally friendly. Trade was common, and sometimes fur traders married and integrated into Indian society. The travellers gave Native Americans blankets, beads and mirrors in exchange for food. They also sold them guns and ammunition. In the 1840s attacks on wagons were rare and the Plains Indians generally regarded these first white travellers with amusement.

GOLD FEVER AND CONFLICT

Then in 1849 came an event which greatly changed the relationship between new and Native Americans – the Gold Rush. Thousands of men of many different nationalities flocked to California, and later to Colorado and Nevada, to search for gold. With the rush came the development of mining camps and the growth of industries, towns, shops, road systems, and railroads. All of this on sacred hunting grounds. Inevitably, conflict ensued. To the white people, the Great Plains were a wilderness waiting to be tamed, a resource to be exploited, and a potential source of profit. They were not concerned about damage to the environment. Native Americans did little farming and mining. They were hunters, and central to their way of life was the wild buffalo. There had been enormous herds of buffalo, estimated at 60 million, but by the mid-1880s they were virtually extinct, having been hunted by white Americans.

BROKEN AND DEFEATED

The whites took over more and more of the Indian homelands, until tensions finally exploded into war in the 1860s. Hostilities continued for over twenty years, and terrible atrocities were committed. In 1890, the Seventh Cavalry surrounded and disarmed a band of Sioux at Wounded Creek. Fighting broke out, and 146 Sioux men, women and children were slaughtered. This was the last great act of violence against the Plains Indians. The spirit of the Native Americans had finally been broken. They were persuaded to live in reservations, where government officials encouraged them to adopt an American way of life.

LISTENING AND VOCABULARY
Synonyms – the story of Jim and the lion

In 1907 Hilaire Belloc published *Cautionary Tales for Children*. They are humorous verses with a moral.

1 Look at the title of the poem and the pictures. Guess the answers to these questions.

  1 Where did his nurse* take him?

  2 Was Jim a well-behaved little boy who always did what he was told? Or was he naughty?

  3 How far did he get when he ran away?

  4 How did the lion go about eating him?

  5 Who tried to help Jim? Did this work?

  6 How did his parents react?

    *Nowadays we would say *childminder*, not *nurse*.

2 **T 10.8** Listen and check.

3 Complete the lines with a word on the right. Think of style, rhythm, and rhyme. It might help to say the poem out loud. Do the first verse.

4 **T 10.8** Listen and check your answers to the first verse. Then do the same for the rest of the poem.

5 What is the moral of this poem? What is the tone?

Jim's parents, we are told, were 'concerned' about their son. Why is this funny?

What do you think?

• What were your favourite stories as a child? Tell the class about one of them.

• Were they scary? Funny?

• Who were the main characters? Were the stories based on real life, or fantasy?

• Did they have a moral? A happy ending?

Jim, who ran away from his nurse, and was eaten by a lion

There was a boy whose name was Jim;
His _____ were very good to him.
They gave him tea, and cakes, and jam,
And slices of _____ ham,
And read him _____ through
   and through,
And even took him to the zoo –
But there it was the _____ fate
Befell him, I now _____.

buddies / friends

delicious / tasty
novels / stories

dreadful / appalling
describe / relate

You know – at least you ought to know,
For I have _____ told you so –
That children never are _____
To leave their nurses in a crowd;
Now this was Jim's especial foible,
He ran away when he was able,
And on this _____ day
He slipped his hand and _____ away!

frequently / often
allowed / permitted

unlucky / inauspicious
hurried / ran

He hadn't gone a yard when – bang!
With open jaws, a lion _____,
And hungrily began to eat
The boy: _____ at his feet.
Now just _____ how it feels
When _____ your toes and then
   your heels,
And then by gradual degrees,
Your shins and ankles, calves and knees,
Are _____ eaten, bit by bit.

sprang / leapt

beginning / commencing
imagine / guess
initially / first

gradually / slowly

No wonder Jim _____ it!
No wonder that he _____ 'Hi!'
The honest keeper heard his cry,
Though very _____, he almost ran
To help the little gentleman.
'Ponto!' he cried, with _____ frown
Let go sir! Down sir! Put it down!
....
The lion having reached his head,
The _____ boy was dead!

loathed / detested
shouted / screamed

fat / overweight

furious / angry

miserable / unfortunate

When nurse _____ his parents they
Were more _____ than I can say:-
His mother, as she dried her eyes,
Said, 'Well – it gives me no _____,
He would not do as he was told!'
His father, who was _____
Bade all the _____ round attend
To James' miserable _____,
And always keep a-hold of nurse
For fear of finding something worse.

told / informed
concerned / upset

shock / surprise

reserved / self-controlled
kids / children
fate / end

EVERYDAY ENGLISH
Metaphors and idioms – the body

1 Complete the sentences with a part of the body.

> Your _____ is associated with intelligence.
> Your _____ are associated with manual skills.
> Your _____ is associated with emotions.

2 In which one of these sentences is the word in *italics* used literally? Rephrase the words used metaphorically.

1 Can you give me a *hand* to move this sofa? It's so heavy.
2 She's so clever. She's *heading* for great things in life.
3 But she's not at all *big-headed*.
4 We shook *hands* and introduced ourselves.
5 My daughter has a very good *head* for business.
6 I'd offer to help, but I've got my *hands* full at the moment.
7 I know she shouts a lot, but really she's got a *heart* of gold.
8 We had a *heart-to-heart* talk, and things are much clearer now.
9 My parents wanted me to be a lawyer, but my *heart* wasn't in it. Now I'm a journalist.

3 Complete the sentences with one of these expressions.

> face the fact   putting a brave face   on its last legs   goes to their head
> pulling your leg   finding my feet   a sharp tongue

1 My car's done over 200,000 kilometres. It's _____ now. I'll have to buy a new one.
2 With so many celebrities, success _____ and they start to believe they're really special.
3 She's being very courageous and _____ on it, but I know she's in a lot of pain.
4 I'm in my first term at uni, and it's all a bit strange, but I'm slowly _____ .
5 I'm nearly seventy-five. I simply have to _____ that I'm not as young as I was.
6 'Oh no! I've forwarded your email complaining about work to the boss!' 'Are you serious?' 'No, I'm just _____ .'
7 'Sue says some really cruel things.' 'Yes, she's got _____ .'

4 **T 10.9** Listen to three conversations. Replace some of the phrases used with an expression on this page.

T 10.10 Listen and check.

5 Look up another part of the body in your dictionary. Find one or two useful idioms or metaphorical uses. Explain them to the rest of the class.

11 In your dreams

Hypothesizing · **Expressions with *if*** · **Word pairs** · **Moans and groans**

TEST YOUR GRAMMAR

1 Helen is feeling very sorry for herself. Read column **A**. What are her problems?

2 **T 11.1** Join a line in **A** with a wish in **B**. Listen and check.

3 Write down one thing you're not happy about. Tell the class what you wish.

A		B
1 It's raining again.		I was.
2 I'm not going out tonight.		I did.
3 There's nothing good on TV.		I didn't.
4 I don't like my job.	I wish	I could.
5 My boyfriend and I split up last week.		he would.
6 I know he won't call me.		there was.
7 I feel really depressed.		it wasn't.
8 I can't talk to anyone about it.		we hadn't.

IF ONLY...
Hypothesizing about the past and present

1 Look at the photos. Each one illustrates someone's regret or wish. What do you think the regret or wish is?

2 **T 11.2** Listen to the people talking. Who says what? Number the pictures in the order you hear.

c

a

b

3 **T 11.2** Listen again and complete the lines. Who is speaking?

1 I shouldn't have …
  If only I hadn't …
  I wouldn't worry …

2 If only we could …
  That would …
  I'd just …
  Sometimes I wish …

3 What would you give … ?!
  Which one would you choose if … ?
  … if I won the lottery I'd …
  I wouldn't – I'd …

4 Don't you wish you … ?
  But *you* could have …

5 I shouldn't have …
  Surely you could … ?
  Supposing you … ?

4 Work with a partner. Use the lines in exercise 3 to help you remember the conversations. Practise them.

5 What are the facts behind some of the wishes and regrets?

I shouldn't have gone out last night.
She did go out last night. She went to a party.

d

e

LANGUAGE FOCUS

Hypothesizing – past and present

1 All of these sentences are hypothetical. That is, they imagine changing certain facts. What are the facts?
  a *I wish I **knew** the answer.*   **I don't know the answer.**
  b *If only I **could come**.*
  c *If only I**'d told** the truth.*
  d *If I **didn't get** so nervous, I**'d get** better results.*
  e *If you**'d helped** us, we**'d have finished** by now.*
  f *I **should have listened** to your advice.*
  g *I wish I **spoke** French well.*
  h *I wish you **would speak** to him.*

2 Which of the sentences are about present time? Which are about past time?

3 Look at sentences *c*, *d*, and *e*. What are the full forms of the contractions *I'd*, *you'd*, and *we'd*?

4 Other expressions are also used to hypothesize. Complete the sentences with the facts.

  It's time you **knew** the truth. The fact is that you …
  I'd rather you **didn't smoke**. The fact is that you …
  I'd rather they **hadn't come**. The fact is that they …
  Supposing you**'d fallen** and **hurt** yourself? Fortunately you …

▶▶ **Grammar Reference** pp151–152

PRACTICE

1 Express a wish or regret about these facts. Use the words in brackets.

1 I don't speak English fluently. (*wish*)

2 You speak very fast. I don't understand. (*If*)

3 I'm an only child. (*wish*)

4 We don't have enough money for a holiday. (*If only*)

5 I get up at six o'clock every morning. I have to go to work. (*wouldn't/if*)

6 I didn't learn to ski until I was forty. I'm not very good. (*If*)

7 My thirteen-year-old sister wants to be older. (*She wishes*)

8 My best friend always borrows my things without asking. (*I'd rather*)

9 I don't know anything about computers. I can't help you. (*If*)

10 We want to have a break. (*It's time*)

Broken dreams

2 Read Sozos's sad story. Explain the title. Complete his final regret.

Politeness doesn't pay!

SOZOS PAPADOPADOS A RETIRED BOAT BUILDER

IN THE 1970s, Sozos was a newly arrived Greek immigrant in Australia. Each and every week he bought a lottery ticket. One week he was queuing to buy a ticket, when an old lady stepped into the shop also wanting to buy one. Sozos, being a polite young man and remembering his mother's words, 'always be kind to old people', offered the woman his place in the queue. The next week, to his shock and horror, he saw on TV that the winning ticket was the one the old lady bought. She had won $6 million.

Sozos says: 'I think about it to this day. How different my life would have been if only I ... !'

3 Use these words to form sentences about Sozos.

1 Sozos shouldn't/allow the old lady/jump the queue.

2 If he/not follow/mother's advice/his life/very different.

3 If he/contact the old lady/she might/give him/money.

4 What/happen if he/keep his place/the queue?

5 Supposing he/not give away his place/the queue?

Answer question 5. Use your imagination.

4 **T 11.3** Listen to **Marty** talking about a holiday he and his ex-wife **Carrie** had in Vanuatu in the South West Pacific a few years ago. Work with a partner and complete these sentences about them.

1 If they'd known that ...
2 They should have ...
3 They shouldn't have ...
4 If they hadn't ...
5 They wish they ...

Compare your answers with the class.

5 Form the question and answer it.

What/happen/if there/not be/earthquake?

Talking about you

6 What do you wish was different about your life? Make a wish list about some of these things and discuss it with other students.

My wish list

- home   • social life   • money
- family   • work   • relationships
- friends   • holidays

| If only
I wish | I
you
he
she
we
they | was/were ...
wasn't/weren't ...
did/didn't ...
had/hadn't ...
could ...
would/wouldn't ... |

SPOKEN ENGLISH Expressions with *if*

There are many fixed expressions with *if* often found in spoken English. Match a line in **A** with one in **B**.

A	B
1 Would it be OK if	if you've got a minute?
2 If all goes well,	I'd never forgive myself.
3 If you knew what I know,	If anything, he's a bit shy.
4 Could I have a word with you	I left a bit early today?
5 If anything went wrong,	we can always postpone it.
6 Win? What do you mean? If you ask me,	you'd never go out with him again.
7 It was a Thursday, not a Tuesday,	if any at all.
8 Well, if the worst comes to the worst,	they don't stand a chance.
9 You haven't made much progress,	we should be finished by Friday.
10 I don't think he's cold or arrogant.	if I remember rightly.

T 11.4 Listen to the conversations and check. What extra lines do you hear? What are the contexts? Practise with a partner.

VOCABULARY AND PRONUNCIATION
Word pairs

> There are many pairs of words joined by a conjunction.
> The order of the words is fixed.
>
> **1** Read these sentences aloud.
> **Each and every week** he bought a ticket.
> To his **shock and horror** he saw her on TV.
>
> **2** Complete these well-known ones.
> Life's full of **ups and** _____ .
> There are always **pros and** _____ in any argument.
> We'll find out the truth **sooner or** _____ .

1 Match a word pair with a definition.

A	B
ifs or buts	compromise/be flexible
wait and see	excuses or arguments
ins and outs	be patient and find out later
give and take	generally speaking
by and large	exact details
grin and bear it	accept it or refuse, I don't care.
odds and ends	tolerate it as best you can
take it or leave it	things

2 Complete the sentences with a word pair from above.

1 In any relationship you have to be prepared to _____ .
   You can't have your own way all the time.
2 I didn't buy much at the shops. Just a few _____ for the kids.
   Socks for Ben and hairbands for Jane.
3 I don't want to hear any _____ . Just finish the job as soon as you can.
4 It's difficult to explain the _____ of the rules of cricket. It's so
   complicated.
5 'What have you got me for my birthday?' 'You'll have to _____ .'
6 'Oh, no! The Burtons are coming for lunch! I hate their kids!'
   'I'm sorry, but you'll just have to _____ . It's only for an hour or so.'
7 OK, you can have it for £90. That's my final offer, _____ .
8 Britain has lots of faults, of course, but _____ , it's a pleasant place to live.

T 11.5 Listen and check.

3 Work with a partner. Match a word in **A** with a word in **B** and a word
in **C**. Look for synonyms and antonyms.

A	B	C
now sick more	and	tired quiet sound
touch peace safe	but	surely then go
slowly there	or	then less

Try to put each pair into a sentence. Read the sentences aloud to the class.

4 **T 11.6** Listen to a conversation between two friends. What are they
talking about? Note down all the word pairs you hear.

5 Look at the conversation on p157. Practise it with your partner,
paying particular attention to the stress and intonation.

READING AND SPEAKING
Have you ever wondered?

1 As you go through your day do you
ever wonder about things? Have you
ever puzzled over these questions?
Discuss them in groups. Which can
you answer? Make notes of your ideas.

1 **Why do we dream?**

2 What are falling stars?

3 **What would happen if the
gravity on Earth was
suddenly turned off?**

4 Why do aeroplanes take
longer to fly west than east?

5 **What would happen if there
was no dust?**

6 What is the origin of the @
symbol ?

2 Read the answers to the questions on
pp98 and 99. Check your ideas and
discuss them with your group.

Have you ever wondered?

Answers to some important questions in life

1 Why do we dream?

Two different schools of thought exist as to why we dream: the physiological school, and the psychological school. Both, however, agree that we dream during the REM, or rapid eye movement, phase of sleep. During this phase of sleep, our closed eyes dart rapidly about and our brain activity peaks.

The physiological theory centres upon how our brains function during the REM phase. Those who believe this theory say that we dream to exercise the brain cells. When awake, our brains constantly transmit and receive messages and keep our bodies in perpetual motion. Dreams replace this function.

Psychological theorists of dreams focus upon our thoughts and emotions, and say that dreams deal with immediate concerns in our lives, such as unfinished business from the day. Dreams can, in fact, (1)____. Connections between dreams and the human psyche have been made for thousands of years. The Greek philosopher Aristotle wrote in his *Parva Naturalia*, over 2,200 years ago, of a connection between dreams and emotional needs. Sweet dreams!

2 What are falling stars?

Contrary to popular belief, 'falling (or shooting) stars' are not stars at all, but meteors, solid bodies that travel through space. Meteors (2)____ to huge objects weighing many tons, which are visible to the naked eye at night. Most meteors, except the really huge ones, burn up when they enter the Earth's atmosphere. If they do land successfully, they are renamed meteorites.

Usually meteors travel together in swarms like bees. Nature's spectacular fireworks show, a 'meteor shower,' comes into view when these swarms hit the Earth's atmosphere and then fall towards the Earth in a brilliant display of light. One must be quite patient to witness the most spectacular meteor storms, as these cross the Earth's path only once every 33 years.

3 What would happen if the gravity on Earth was suddenly turned off?

Supposing we could magically turn off gravity. Would buildings and other structures float away? What happened would depend on how strongly the things were attached to the Earth. The Earth is rotating at quite a speed, (3)____. If you spin something around your head on a string it goes around in a circle until you let go of the string. Then it flies off in a straight line. 'Switching off' gravity would be like letting go of the string. Things not attached to the Earth would fly off in a straight line. People in buildings would suddenly shoot upwards at a great speed until they hit the ceiling. Most things outside would fly off into space. Some things, like trees and many buildings, which are rooted into the Earth, would not find it so easy to fly off.

4 Why do aeroplanes take longer to fly west than east?

It can take five hours to go west–east from New York to London but seven hours to travel east–west from London to New York. The reason for the difference is an atmospheric phenomenon (4)___ . The jet stream is a very high altitude wind which always blows from the west to the east across the Atlantic. The planes moving at a constant air speed thus go faster in the west–east direction when they are moving with the wind than in the opposite direction.

5 What would happen if there was no dust?

Most of us who have ever cleaned a house would be much happier if there was less dust. However, without dust there would be less rainfall and sunsets would be less beautiful. Rain is formed when water molecules in the air collect around particles of dust. When the collected water becomes heavy enough (5)___ . Thus water vapour would be much less likely to turn to rain without the dust particles.

The water vapour and dust particles also reflect the rays of the sun. At sunrise and sunset, when the sun is below the horizon, the dust and water vapour molecules reflect the longer, red rays of light in such a way that we can see them for more time. The more dust particles in the air, the more colourful the sunrise or sunset.

6 What is the origin of the @ symbol ?

History tells us that the little @ in email addresses, commonly referred to as the '*at* sign', stemmed from the tired hands of medieval monks. During the Middle Ages, before the invention of printing presses, every letter of a word had to be painstakingly transcribed by hand in Latin for each copy of a book. The monks that performed these tedious copying duties looked for ways to reduce the number of individual strokes for common words. Although the word *ad*, the Latin word for *at*, is quite short, it was so common that the monks thought it would be quicker and easier to shorten it even more. As a result, they looped the 'd' around the 'a' and eliminated two strokes of the pen.

With the introduction of email the popularity of the @ symbol grew. (6)___ , for instance, *joe @uselessknowledge.com*. There is no one universal name for the sign but countries have found different ways to describe it. Several languages use words that associate the shape with some type of animal. These include:

snabel	Danish for 'elephant's trunk'
klammeraffe	German for 'hanging monkey'
papaki	Greek for 'little duck'
kukac	Hungarian for 'worm'
dalphaengi	Korean for 'snail'
grisehale	Norwegian for 'pig's tail'
sobachka	Russian for 'little dog'

Reading

3 Read the texts again. These lines have been removed from them. Which text does each come from?

a moving at over a thousand miles per hour at the equator.

b It separates a person's online user name from their mail server address.

c range in size from that of a pinhead

d the water droplets fall to the earth as rain

e teach us things about ourselves that we are unaware of

f known as the jet stream

4 Answer the questions.

1 What does REM stand for?
2 What kind of things do dreams deal with?
3 What is the difference between a meteor and a meteorite?
4 What travel like swarms of bees?
5 What would happen to buildings and the people inside them if gravity was turned off?
6 How does the jet stream affect how fast planes fly?
7 What would happen to rain and sunsets if there was no dust?
8 Why did the monks invent the @ sign?
9 What is the @ sign called in different languages?

Vocabulary work

Find the highlighted words in the texts. Try to work out their meaning from the contexts.

What do you think?

- Which questions did you find most interesting?
- Which facts were new to you? Which did you already know? Use some of these phrases to express your reactions.

I already knew that . . .	Did you know that . . .?
What surprised me was . . .	Everyone knows that . . .
I don't believe that . . .	I had no idea that . . .

- What do *you* call the @ sign? Which language's animal word do you think best describes it?
- Small children often ask lots of 'Why' questions.

Why is the grass green?   Why doesn't our cat talk to me?

Think of some good 'why' questions about the world. In pairs, try to answer them as if you were talking to a child. (The child will often answer with another 'Why?' question!)

Why doesn't our cat talk to me?   Because cats can't talk.

Why can't cat's talk?   Because . . .

LISTENING AND SPEAKING
The interpretation of dreams

1 Everybody dreams but some people remember their dreams better than others. Discuss these questions in groups.

1 Did you dream last night? Can you remember anything about it?
2 What often happens when you wake up from a dream and try to describe it to someone?
3 What do you think are common themes in dreams?

2 Read these descriptions of dreams. Discuss what you think each dream might mean.

1
Fall guy
Many times, as I'm going to sleep, I dream that I am walking along the road and suddenly trip up and fall towards the pavement. I always wake up before I hit the ground. Why do I dream this?

J.H, PERTH, AUSTRALIA

2
Underneath it all
My dreams are often set in a small decaying cellar. I always wake up feeling bad about life when this happens. What does this dream mean?

D.J, WINNIPEG, CANADA

3
Hidden treasure
I am digging in the garden of my childhood home and uncover a box of treasure. My life has been pretty bad lately. Does my dream indicate a change for the better?

P.T, SWINDON UK

3 Read the interpretations of the dreams on p158. Which do you think goes with each dream? Why? Compare them with your ideas.

4 **T 11.7** Listen to Paul describing a dream. What is really strange about the dream? Are these statements true or false? Correct the false ones.

1 Paul describes himself as a sensible, rational person.
2 He was in his room at university when he had the dream.
3 He was asleep with his girlfriend.
4 The dream took place in his home town.
5 In the dream, he and his girlfriend had arranged to meet in front of the station.
6 His girlfriend had a similar dream.
7 His girlfriend had never visited his home town.
8 He believes their dreams were as a result of a TV programme they'd been watching.

Language work

Read the tapescript on p137.

1 Find four things in the story that Paul describes as *strange*.
2 Find other words which are similar in meaning to *strange*.

What do you think?

• Discuss Paul's dream in your groups and try to interpret it. Share your ideas with the class.

• Describe any memorable dreams that you have had.

• Do you ever have the same dream or dreams with common features?

▶▶ **WRITING** Narrative writing 2 – Linking words and expressions *p122*

EVERYDAY ENGLISH
Moans and groans

It's not fair!
What a pain!
I don't believe it!

1 Read the complaints in **A**. Match them with a response in **B**. Which of the items in the box do they refer to?

> a leather jacket   email   boots   ordering by phone
> a bookcase   a TV programme   a dishwasher   ~~an exam~~

A	B
1 [e] I could kick myself. As soon as I'd handed it in, I remembered what the answer was. *an exam*	a What a pain! Have you tried ringing the computer helpline?
2 ☐ I don't believe it! I've spent all morning trying to send this, and *all I get* is 'Ooops! Your message wasn't sent. Try again later'.	b Give me a break! I was in a hurry. Anyway, they're only a *bit* muddy.
3 ☐ These instructions don't make any sense to me at all. If you can follow them, you're a genius.	c I'm awfully sorry, sir. I'm afraid there's nothing I can do about it. It's out of my hands.
4 ☐ It's not fair. I'd been looking forward to watching it all day and then the phone goes and rings!	d I know, it drives me mad. But worse still is that you never get to speak to a real person anyway!
5 ☐ How many times do I have to tell you? Take them off *before* you come into the house!	e Oh, I hate it when that happens! But do you think you've still passed?
6 ☐ This has gone beyond a joke. You promised you'd deliver it by Tuesday at the latest. Now you're saying next month!	f It's such a shame. It would have gone so well with your white jeans.
7 ☐ I went away to think about it, and of course, when I went back it had been sold. I wish I'd just bought it there and then.	g Don't ask me! This flatpack stuff is a nightmare! I had exactly the same trouble trying to put up a bedside table.
8 ☐ What a waste of time! Ten minutes listening to music and 'All our lines are busy. Thank you for waiting'.	h Typical! And who was it? Anyone interesting?

2 [T 11.8] Listen and check your answers. Read them aloud with a partner and add another line.

> **A** I could kick myself. As soon as I'd handed it in, I remembered what the answer was.
> **B** Oh, I hate it when that happens! But do you think you've still passed?
> **A** Who knows? I'll just have to wait and see.

> ### Music *of* English ♫♪
> When people moan about something, there is an exaggeration on the rise and fall of the word with main stress.
>
> ⌢↘   ⌢↘
> *I don't believe it!*   *It's not fair!*
>
> [T 11.9] Listen and repeat.

3 What are some of the events in a typical day in your life? For each event think of something to moan about.

> *What a pain! I got up and had to wait ages before the shower was free. But worse still, the water was freezing cold!*

4 Do you have any moans and groans about anything that's happened recently in your country or in the world?

'Press 1 for classical, press 2 for easy listening, press 3 for jazz.'

12 It's never too late

Articles • Determiners • Hot words – *life, time* • Linking and commenting

TEST YOUR GRAMMAR

1 Tell the story of Mary's grandfather, matching a line from **A** with a line from **C**. Use the correct article from **B** to connect the lines. Tell the story to a partner.

2 **T 12.1** Listen and check. What extra information do you hear?

	A	B	C
1	My grandfather used to be		dinner with him.
2	He retired		captain of the ship.
3	He decided to go on		sea cruise.
4	He enjoyed	a/an	cruise very much.
5	He sailed all round	one	year before last.
6	He met	the	judge.
7	He invited her to have	*no article*	love at any age.
8	They got on really well with		another.
9	My grandfather says you can find		world.
10	They were married by		attractive widow.

THE PACE OF LIFE
Articles and determiners

1 Do the quiz about your pace of life. Circle *a*, *b*, *c*, or *d*. Discuss your answers with a partner. Turn to p158 and find out what kind of person you are. Do you agree?

2 Find these highlighted words in the quiz. Underline the nouns that follow. Which are followed by *of*?

enough	the whole	all	each	plenty
a great deal	hardly any	several	none	
no	(a) few	(a) little	most	every

3 These lines are similar to those in the quiz but not the same. Find them in the quiz. What are the differences?

1 I leave sufficient time for relaxation.
2 Non-stop all of the time.
3 More than enough things.
4 Lots of enthusiasm.
5 Very few, just a couple of minor things.
6 There aren't any uncompleted projects.
7 I see every one of my projects through.
8 I don't have any patience.
9 I have hardly any hobbies or leisure time.
10 In quite a few ways.
11 In all kinds of ways.
12 Nearly all of the time by email.

How well do you

1 How would you describe the pace of your life?
a Easy-going. I just take life as it comes.
b Quite fast, but I leave enough time for relaxation.
c At times frantic, at times relaxed.
d Non-stop the whole time but I like it that way.

2 How do you tackle all the things you have to do each day?
a I do those things I feel like doing.
b I prioritize. I do the important things and put off all the rest.
c There's either not enough time to do everything or too much time with nothing to do. I find this difficult.
d I have a daily 'to do' list that I tick off after each item is completed.

3 How many things have you begun and not finished in the last few years?
a Plenty of things. I begin with a great deal of enthusiasm but then get bored.
b Hardly any, just one or two minor things.
c Several things. Sometimes I get distracted and move from one thing to another.
d None. There are no uncompleted projects in my life. I see each of my projects through before I start the next.

4 When do you switch off your mobile phone?

a Do most people have mobile phones these days?
   I haven't got round to buying one yet.
b In some public places and when I need some
   peace and quiet.
c Not as often as I should.
d Only if I have to.

5 What is your attitude to punctuality?

a I don't waste time worrying about it.
b Being late is impolite and inefficient so I try to
   be punctual.
c I like to be on time in theory but in practice
   I'm often late.
d I'm always on time. I have no patience with people
   who are late.

use your   time?

6 How do you spend your leisure time?

a Doing a bit of this and that. I don't know where
   time goes.
b I recharge my batteries with a few hobbies and
   being with friends.
c I keep trying different things that people suggest,
   but nothing really grabs me.
d I have few hobbies and little leisure time. I try
   to put the whole of my life to good use.

7 How do you keep in touch with friends?

a I wait for them to get in touch with me.
b In several ways – emails, texting, but also
   I like to phone them for a proper chat.
c In any way I can – but it can be difficult.
   I think 'I must contact X' but time
   passes and I find I haven't.
d Most of the time by email. It's quick and efficient.

8 Which of these is closest to your philosophy on life?

a Whatever will be will be.
b Life is not a dress rehearsal.
c There is a season for everything.
d Grasp every moment.

4 What is the difference between these pairs of sentences?

| I have a few hobbies. | I have a little leisure time. |
| I have few hobbies. | I have little leisure time. |

5 Is there a difference in meaning between these sentences?

| I completed **each** project. | I completed **every** project. |

Which can mean you had only two projects? Which *can't* mean you had only two projects? Which can mean you had lots of projects?

LANGUAGE FOCUS

Determiners
Determiners help identify nouns and express quantity.

1   Look at the examples. Which determiners go with which nouns? Which group expresses quantity?

the other another many other his only such a what a	book books good book		both neither each/every little all the whole no	book books time

2   Determiners can join a noun using *of + the/my/our/ this/that*, etc. Which expressions can you make from these examples?

both neither each all some the whole none	of	the my those	book books time

▶▶ **Grammar Reference p152**

PRACTICE

Talking about you

1   Complete the sentences with determiners which make them true for you.

1   I have _____ time to relax.
2   _____ my friends think I work too hard.
3   _____ my teachers think I work hard.
4   I spent _____ weekend relaxing.
5   I have _____ interests and hobbies.
6   _____ my hobbies are sports.
7   _____ my parents look like me.
8   _____ my family have fair hair.
9   My aunt gives _____ us birthday presents.
10   My grandparents watch TV _____ time.

Discussing grammar

2 Work with a partner. What is the difference in meaning between these pairs of sentences?

1 I spoke to all the students in the class.
   I spoke to each student in the class.

2 None of them knew the answer.
   Neither of them knew the answer.

3 The doctor's here.
   A doctor's here.

4 There's a man at the door.
   There's some man at the door.

5 There's a pair of socks missing.
   There's a couple of socks missing.

6 Whole families were evacuated from their homes.
   All the families were evacuated from their homes.

3 Match a line in **A** with a line in **B**.

A	B
Would you like Do all birds lay Where did I put	eggs? the egg? an egg?

A	B
I have two cars. Borrow It was great to see I have five nieces. I gave £10 to	each one. everyone. either one.

A	B
Love A love The love	I have for you is forever. is everything. of animals is vital for a vet.

A	B
Both All Every	my friends like dancing. person in my class is friendly. my parents are Scottish.

4 **T 12.2** Listen and respond to the lines with a sentence from exercise 3.

I don't like cereal for breakfast.

Well, would you like an egg?
A boiled egg and some toast?

T 12.3 Listen and check. Pay particular attention to stress and intonation. Look at the tapescript on p138 and practise the conversations with a partner.

SPOKEN ENGLISH Using demonstratives and determiners

Demonstratives and determiners are often found in idiomatic language.

Look at these examples of the demonstratives *this*, *that*, *these*, and *those* from the quiz on p102.

> (I like) doing a bit of *this and that*.
> Most people have mobile phones *these days*.
> I do *those things* I feel like doing.

Find examples of the determiners *each*, *every*, and *all* in the quiz.

5 Demonstratives – *this/that/these/those*

Complete the sentences with the correct demonstrative.

1 What's _____ song you're singing?

2 Look at _____ ladybird on my hand!

3 Did you hear _____ storm in the middle of the night?

4 Mmm! _____ strawberries are delicious!

5 Take _____ dirty shoes off! I've just cleaned in here.

6 I can't stand _____ weather. It's really getting me down.

7 Who was _____ man you were talking to _____ morning?

8 Do you remember when we were young? _____ were the days!

9 Children have no respect for authority _____ days, do they?

T 12.4 Listen and check.

these that this those

6 Determiners – *each*, *every*, or *all*

T 12.5 Listen to some short conversations. What is each about? Complete the replies. They all contain expressions with *each*, *every* or *all*. Practise the conversations with a partner.

1 **A** What was the meal like?
  B . . .

2 **A** Did you apologize to all the guests?
  B . . .

3 **A** They didn't all pass, did they?
  B . . .

4 **A** Sorry, I only have 50p on me.
  B . . .

5 **A** When do you think you'll get there?
  B . . .

6 **A** Do you fancy a quick pint?
  B . . .

all each every

▶▶ **WRITING** Adding emphasis in writing – People of influence *p123*

LISTENING AND SPEAKING
Happy days

1 Work in small groups. What is the average life expectancy in your country? Suggest ages for these stages of life. What is typical behaviour for each stage? Give examples and discuss with the whole class.

0 – ☐	infancy
☐ – ☐	childhood
☐ – ☐	teenage years
☐ – ☐	adulthood
☐ – ☐	middle age
☐ – ☐	old age

2 You are going to listen to Bernie, Hayley, Tony, and Tommy talking about themselves. Here are some of the things they said (two for each person). Which stage of life do you think they are at?

1 I want to see the world, meet lots of people, get a good career before I settle down.
2 This time though, after the operation I knew immediately it would be OK.
3 We have buckets and spades.
4 Lizzie and I are quite content just to potter in the vegetable patch, or cut the grass, or weed the flower beds.
5 Most of us just get off on dancing.
6 I think the world has gone to pot.
7 It's got big, big wheels, hugest wheels ever.
8 These days the only thing that makes me unhappy is meeting people who don't realize what a gift life is.

3 **T 12.6** Listen to the four people. After each one discuss these questions.

1 At which stage of life is the person?
2 Which lines in exercise 2 did he or she say?
3 What does the person do or say that is typical or not typical for their age?
4 What makes the person happy or unhappy?

What do you think?

• Which stage of life do you think is best? Which worst? Why?
• Are there advantages and disadvantages for each stage? Discuss.
• Do you know people who you think are typical or not typical for their age? Are you?

READING AND SPEAKING
You're never too old

1 What age do you consider to be old? Think of some 'old' people you know.

> How old are they?
>
> What are they like?
>
> What do they do every day?
>
> Which of these activities are typical for old people?
> - finding it difficult to sleep
> - liking routine
> - going to university
> - studying foreign languages
> - going to church
> - talking about the past
> - losing your memory
> - using the Internet
> - living in the centre of a city
> - watching TV

2 Read the text quickly. Which of the activities in exercise 1 are part of Mary Hobson's life? Explain the title: 'A life in the day'.

3 Read the text again. Find the highlighted lines and answer the questions about them.

1 l.04 What is 'it'? Why does 'it' do this?

2 l.10 What is 'it'? How did Marcus Aurelius help Mary?

3 l.22 What does she work at for nothing? What does this imply about Mary's lifestyle?

4 l.24 Who is 'he'? Who is 'some old bat'?

5 l.30 What was hell for who? What did Mary do about it?

6 l.35 What was the session? What did Mary do in it?

7 l.47 Is 'the time of your life' a good or bad time? What was the time of Mary's life?

8 l.55 Why do they think this?

9 l.65 What is 'it'? What does Mary mean by this?

10 l.67 What is 'it'? Why does she sleep so badly?

A life in the day

Mary Hobson, 77, gained a degree in Russian in her sixties and a PhD at 74. A mother of four, she lives in south London.

'I've started to learn ancient Greek. It doesn't urge you to communicate, only to learn, and I find the early hours of the morning the perfect time for that. I love ritual and routine. I wait until 6am to have tea; at 7am I phone my youngest daughter and we start the day with a chat. At 7.30 I make breakfast – All-Bran, wholemeal toast, and a pot of black coffee – and I take it back to bed along with the Roman emperor Marcus Aurelius.

I am a dedicated atheist. I regard religion as complete lunacy. You've got only one opportunity to be alive: for goodness' sake don't waste it waiting for an afterlife. I read Marcus Aurelius every day; it was his philosophy that got me through my son Matthew's death, four years ago in a motorcycle accident. Aurelius said: 'What we cannot bear removes us from life.' Matthew's death was such a waste. At first I would rather have been dead too, but then I thought: 'No. I mustn't do less. I must do more!'

After a bath I spend the morning translating. A special committee was convened to organize the translation of the works of Pushkin for his centenary. Unpaid, of course. I'm an expert at working for nothing. Poor old Pushkin: some of his letters were scandalous. Really very rude indeed. How was he to know that, 200 years later, some old bat would be poring over every line?

I am what you might call a late developer. I was 40 before I wrote my first novel, 62 when I went to university. My husband, Neil, was a talented jazz musician, but at 25 he developed a cerebral abscess, losing his speech and the use of the right side of his body. It was hell for him and a nightmare for us. We were so broke, we lived on national assistance for ages. When things got really bad, I'd collect up old china and give it to the children to smash out their frustrations on the wall outside.

I wrote my first novel while Neil had his weekly music therapy. That 50-minute session was all I had. I used to sit in the ABC café in Earls Court and write and write while couples had life-and-death quarrels around me. Neil was terribly difficult. None of it was his fault, of course, but after 28 years I thought: 'It's not my fault either.' I was going down with him. I left and Matthew stayed with him to stop me going back – I was very grateful for that.

Having snatched a bit of life back, I had to do something with it. My daughter Emma gave me *War and Peace*, and I loved it so much. Then it hit me: I hadn't read it at all, I'd only read a translation, and I so longed to read the actual words. A marvellous elderly Russian lady taught me the basics and I enrolled on the Russian-

Mary Hobson

by Caroline Scott

WINNER OF THE PUSHKIN GOLD MEDAL FOR TRANSLATION

'I was 40 before I wrote my first novel, 62 when I went to university.'

language degree course at the University of London. People talk about 'the time of their lives'. Well, that was mine. Don't let anyone tell you your memory goes with age. It's there if you want it enough. Gradually I forced it into action – it was such an
50 exhilarating experience. Oh, the joy of learning!

I have such good friends. After a late lunch, I might go and play Scrabble with a Russian lady. I write poetry en route, on buses and trains. I love London. Give me the town over the country any day. I try to go to Moscow every year in the coldest weather.
55 My Russian friends think I'm mad; it hits minus 40 and they find it hellish. I adore lying in bed listening to snow being scraped from the pavements.

I have an overpowering feeling that I don't want to waste any time. There's so much out there. I won't be able to get about
60 forever, so when I can't stagger down my front steps, I'll perfect my Greek. I order my groceries on the Internet, so I have everything sent. As long as I have my books I'll be happy.

If I'm not going out, I make supper and get into bed, simply because my feet are awful. Then I phone everyone I can think of.
65 I can't bear TV – it makes me feel as if everyone else is living and I'm only watching. I don't have a newspaper; I get my news through Radio 4. I sleep rottenly, so I have it on all night. Dreams are horrendous. Mine are all about anxiety and loss. I much prefer the day – at least you know you're in charge.

Language work

There is *one* mistake in each of these sentences. Find it and discuss why it is wrong with a partner. Check your answers in the text.

1 I make breakfast and I take it back to the bed.
2 I am a dedicated atheist. My husband was talented jazz musician.
3 You've got only an opportunity to be alive.
4 I enrolled on the Russian-language degree course at University of London.
5 I try to go to Moscow every year in coldest weather.
6 Having snatched a bit of the life back, I had to do something with it.
7 Give me the town over a country.
8 I make supper and get into bed, simply because the feet are awful.

What do you think?

• It's easy to think of all the advantages of being young and the disadvantages of being old. But try it the other way round. Work in two groups.

Group A List all the disadvantages of being young.

Group B List all the advantages of being old.

• Find a partner from the other group and discuss your lists.

• Discuss as a class. What do you think is the best age to be in life?

VOCABULARY AND LISTENING
Hot words – *life* and *time*

1 Work with a partner. Complete the expressions below with either the word *life* or *time*. Use a dictionary to help.

Having the **time** of your **life**!	
not on your _____	you can bet your _____
take your _____	better luck next _____
get a _____	get a new lease of _____
kill _____	it's high _____
third _____ lucky	for the _____ being
no _____ to lose	stand the test of _____
that's _____	see _____
not before _____	in the nick of _____
any old _____	dead on _____
a cushy _____	anything for a quiet _____

2 Complete these lines with an expression from exercise 1.

1 No need to hurry. Take . . .
2 For goodness sake hurry up. There's no . . .
3 The operation was so successful that grandpa got a new . . .
4 Shakespeare's writing is still relevant today. It's really stood . . .
5 I got to the bank in the . . . It was just about to close.
6 You can give them back any . . . I'm not going skiing again until next year.
7 OK, OK stop crying. You can have another ice-cream. Anything . . .

3 **T 12.7** Listen to the conversations. What are the people talking about? Which of the expressions from exercise 1 do you hear? Turn to p139 and practise the conversations with your partner.

A song

4 **T 12.8** Close your books and listen to a song called *That's life*, recorded by Frank Sinatra and Robbie Williams. Then read the words on this page. There are many differences. Listen again and note them all.

5 **T 12.8** Listen again and sing along!

THAT'S LIFE

That's life, that's what they all say.
You're full of life in April,
Shot down in May.
But you bet I'm gonna play that tune,
When I've got a new lease of life in June.

That's life, strange as it seems.
Some people get their kicks,
Jumpin' on dreams;
But I don't allow it to get me down,
'Cause this ol' world continues turning around.

I've been a puppet, a pauper, a pilot,
A policeman, a pawn and a king.
I've been up and over and in and out
And I know a few things:
Every time I find myself down on my face,
I pull myself up and get back in the race.

That's life, I can't deny it,
I thought of giving up,
But my head just won't buy it.
If I didn't think it was worth a try,
I'd roll up in a corner and cry.

EVERYDAY ENGLISH
Linking and commenting

1 Look at these lines from the first tapescript in T12.6. The expressions in **bold** link or comment on what has been said or what is going to be said. They are mainly adverbs.

Personally, I'm just happy to be alive.
You see, I'd recently married …

Anyway, I had some tests …
In fact the transplant failed …

Find other examples from the tapescripts on p138.

2 Read these conversations. Choose the correct linking or commenting expression.

1 A Did you see the match last night?
   B No, but *apparently / obviously* it was a good game. We won, didn't we?
   A *Probably / Actually*, it was a draw, but it was really exciting.

2 A What do you think of Claire's new boyfriend?
   B *Personally / Certainly*, I can't stand him. I think he'll dump her like all the rest. *Ideally / However*, that's her problem, not mine.
   A Poor old Claire! She always picks the wrong ones, doesn't she? *Anyway / Honestly*, we'll see soon enough.

3 A I don't know how you can afford to buy all those fabulous clothes!
   B *Still / Hopefully*, I'm going to get a bonus this month. My boss has promised. *After all / Presumably*, I did earn the company over £100,000 last year. *Basically / Absolutely*, I deserve it.

4 A She said some terrible things to me. I hate her!
   B *Generally speaking / All the same*, I think you should apologize to her. *If you ask me / Apparently* you lose your temper too easily. You're being very childish. It's time you both grew up!
   A What?! I never thought I'd hear you speak to me like that.
   B *Still / Honestly*, I'm not taking sides. I just think you should make up.

5 A So, Billy. You say that this is the last record you're ever going to make?
   B *Surely / Definitely*.
   A But *surely / actually* you realize how upset your fans are going to be?
   B *Obviously / Hopefully*, I don't want to hurt anyone, but *certainly / basically*, I'm fed up with pop music. I'd like to do something else. *After all / Ideally*, I'd like to get into films.

T 12.9 Listen and check your answers. Practise some of the dialogues.

3 Complete these with a suitable line.
1 They had a dreadful holiday. **Apparently …**
2 It should have been a happy marriage. **After all, …**
3 I know you don't want to go to Harry's party. **All the same, …**
4 I had the interview yesterday. **Hopefully, …**
5 I'd rather you didn't let this go any further. **Obviously, …**
6 I couldn't believe it, he just walked out and left her. **Presumably, …**
7 I don't like flying very much. **As a matter of fact, …**
8 So that's that. All's well that ends well. **Anyway, …**

Writing

UNIT 1 APPLYING FOR A JOB – A CV and a covering letter

1 What is a CV? What is the aim of one? Have you ever written one? What information did/would you include?

2 What is the purpose of a covering letter?

3 Write the headings from **A** in the correct spaces in the CV in **B**.

A

Profile	Additional information
Education	~~Name~~
References	Work experience
Personal details	Interests

4 Answer the questions.

1 Where did Kate go to school?
2 What did she study at university?
3 Who is Prof Jane Curtis?
4 Does she have a lot of work experience?

5 How is a CV different in your country?

B

Name _____

Kate Henderson

DOB 17/04/83

Address   31 Rendlesham Way
           Watford
           Herts
           WD3 5GT

Phone   01923 984663
Mobile   07764 733689
Email   katehenderson@hotshot.com

_____

A highly-motivated, well-travelled, and enthusiastic graduate, with practical experience of working with children of all ages.

_____

Watford Grammar School
8 GCSEs
3 A-levels

Bristol University
BA (Hons) Psychology and Education

_____

June 2000
Life guard and supervisor at KLC Leisure Centre

July 2001
Athletics coach at training centre

June 2003
Teaching assistant at secondary school

_____

Dance, athletics, volleyball, travel, cinema

_____

One of my main interests is dance, which I have done since I was three, passing many exams, and performing in annual dance festivals. I have organized sports events and training sessions for dance, athletics, and trampoline. I have travelled widely throughout the world, in Europe, the Far East, and the USA.

_____

Prof Jane Curtis	**Mike Benson**
Dept of Education	Head Teacher
Bristol University	Bailey School
BS5 7LA	Watford, Herts
	WD3 8JG

6 This is the job that Kate is applying for. Is she well qualified for it?

ACTIVITY HOLIDAY ORGANIZER IN THE CANARY ISLANDS

Are you …
- aged between 18–30?
- energetic?
- good at organizing people?

Do you …
- like kids?
- like sport?

Then come and join us as a leader for an Easter holiday of fun, looking after groups of kids at sports camp!

Send your CV to Mark Sullivan at 106 Piccadilly, Bristol BS8 7TQ

7 Read Kate's covering letter. Which parts sound too informal? Replace them with words on the right.

31 Rendlesham Way
Watford
Herts
WD3 5GT

01923 984663

Mark Sullivan
106 Piccadilly
Bristol
BS8 7TQ

17 March 2004

Dear Mark

I am applying for the post of camp leader, which I saw advertised somewhere recently. Here's my CV.

I reckon I have just about everything needed for this job. I have worked loads with kids, doing all kinds of stuff. They generally do what I tell them, and we manage to have a great time together. Having studied psychology and education at university, I know quite a bit about the behaviour of kids.

I am really into sport, and have lots of experience of organizing training events. I am a very practical person, easy-going, and it's no problem for me to make friends. I've been all over the place, and enjoy meeting new people.

I can't wait to hear from you.

Best wishes

Kate Henderson

Kate Henderson

extensively with young adults
respect my leadership abilities
I find it easy
very interested in
have a certain understanding of
Please find enclosed
look forward to hearing
considerable
many of the relevant
qualifications
have travelled widely
Mr Sullivan
Yours sincerely
in the March edition of the magazine *Holiday Jobs for Graduates*
feel
organizing a variety of activities
establish a good working relationship

Is this how a formal letter is laid out in your country? What are the differences?

8 Write your CV and a covering letter for a job that you would really like to do and are well qualified for.

1 Teachers sometimes use these symbols when correcting written work.

Correct the mistakes in these sentences.

1 I born in 1971 in one small town in Mexico.

2 My father is diplomat, so my all life I live in differents countries.

3 After the school, I went for four years in a busyness college.

4 I'm married since five years. I knew my wife while I was a student.

5 My town isnt as exciting than London. Is very quite at the evening.

6 I learn English for five years. I start when I had eleven years.

7 My father wants that I work in a bank becaus is a good work.

8 I do a evening course in English. I enjoy very much to learn languages.

WW	Wrong word
Sp	Spelling
T	Tense
Gr	Grammar
⅄	Word missing
P	Punctuation
Prep	Preposition
WO	Word order
/	This word isn't necessary

2 Read the letter. Answer the questions.

1 Where was the letter written?
2 Who is the guest? Who is the host?
3 Which city is described? What is it like?
4 What season is it?

3 Work with a partner. Find the mistakes and put the symbols on the letter. Then correct the mistakes. The first line has been done to help you.

4 Write a letter (about 250 words).

Either …
You are going to stay with a family in an English-speaking country.

Or …
An English-speaking guest is coming to stay with you.

Give some information about yourself – your family, interests, school, your town.

Check your work carefully for mistakes!

Avenida Campinas 361 ap. 45
01238 São Paulo Brasil

23 December

Dear James

Thank you your letter. I receive it the last week. Sorry I no reply you before, but I've been very busy. It's Christmas soon, and everyone are very exciting!

In two weeks I am with you in England. I can no belief it! I looking forward meet you and your familly very much. I'm sure we will like us very well.

My city, São Paulo, is biggest and noisyest city in Brasil. Is not really for tourist. Is a centre commercial. Also it have very much pollution and traffic. But there is lot of things to do. I like very much listen music. There are bars who stay open all night!

My friend went in London last year, and he has seen a football match at Arsenal. He said me was wonderfull. I like to do that also.

My plane arrive to Heathrow at 6.30 am in 3 Janury. Is very kind you meet me so early morning.

I hope very much improve my english during I am with you!

See you soon and happy New Year!

Fernando

1 Have you ever been in a dangerous situation? Write some notes about when, where, who you were with, and what happened. Discuss your notes with a partner and compare the situations.

2 Put the adverbs or adverbial phrases in the correct place in these sentences. Sometimes more than one place is possible.

1 I used to go skiing.	*in winter, frequently*
2 I enjoyed going to Colorado.	*with my family, especially*
3 I had a bad accident.	*two years ago, then, really*
4 I skied into a tree.	*headfirst*
5 I broke my leg.	*in three places, unfortunately,*
6 I'd like to go skiing again.	*definitely, one day*
7 But I don't feel confident.	*yet, enough*
8 My family go skiing.	*however, still, every February*

Read the completed story aloud with your partner.

3 Read through the story of two British mountain climbers, Rachel Kelsey and Jeremy Colenso. Where were they? What went wrong? How were they saved? What does the text message mean?

4 Place the adverbs on the right of the story in the correct place in the same line (sometimes more than one place is possible). Add punctuation where necessary.

5 What background information are you given in the article? When does the actual story of what happened start?

6 Using the notes you made earlier, write the story of your dangerous experience (about 250 words).

- Begin with background information
- Describe the events in the order they happened.
- Make sure you use plenty of adverbs to describe people's feelings and actions.

Share your stories as a class, reading some of them aloud.

TEXTING TO THE RESCUE

On a mid-September day, British climbers Rachel Kelsey and Jeremy Colenso were climbing in the Swiss Alps.	several years ago high / with great confidence
They were both experienced climbers, and when they left their base, the weather was good. They reached the summit, but as they started the climb down, an electric storm struck the mountain. Snow began to fall, making it difficult to see where they could put their hands and feet on the rock. After several frightening minutes, they found a narrow ledge and climbed on to it, hoping the snow would stop and they could continue their descent.	relatively easily suddenly / heavily / extremely safely gratefully / desperately
The snow did not stop and the temperature dropped to −10°C. 'We had to stay awake,' said Rachel, 'because it was so cold that we would have died. So we told stories and rubbed our fingers and toes to keep them warm.'	however / dangerously afterwards / undoubtedly continuously
They decided that they had to get help. But what could they do? Rachel had brought her mobile phone with her, but the only number contacts she had were in London. She sent a text message at 1.30 a.m. to get help. She sent the same text to five friends in the UK. It read: 'Need heli rescue off north ridge of Piz Badile, Switz'. They were all asleep, so nothing happened. At 5.00 a.m., one friend, Avery Cunliffe, got the message. He jumped into action, called the rescue services in Switzerland, and called Rachel to tell her that help was coming.	eventually / possibly / fortunately unfortunately in fact urgently for hours / then immediately then
The weather was too bad for the helicopters to operate, but Avery kept sending text messages to the climbers. At about 10.00 p.m. they were lifted off the mountain. 'We owe our lives to Avery', they said when they were back at base.	for the next 24 hours finally / safely exhaustedly

1 Use the conjunctions *but*, *although*, and *however* to join these two sentences.

She's rich and famous.   She's unhappy.

2 Conjunctions can join sentences to express **contrast**, **reason** and **result**, **time**, and **condition**. In each group complete the sentences with suitable conjunctions.

| Contrast | however   although   despite   even though |

1 _____ I can't speak much Spanish, I can understand a lot.
2 I can't speak Spanish well. _____, I can understand most things.
3 He can't speak Spanish well, _____ he lives in Spain.
4 _____ living in Spain, he can't speak Spanish.

| Reason and Result | such ... that   so   as   since   because   so ... that |

1 I didn't sleep well last night, _____ I'm tired.
2 I'm tired _____ I didn't sleep well last night.
3 I wanted to go, but _____ it was late, I decided not to.
4 _____ John can't be here today, I've been asked to chair the meeting.
5 He always looks _____ innocent _____ he gets away with murder.
6 He's _____ a terrible liar _____ no one believes him.

| Time | when(ever)   while   as (soon as)   until   after   since |

1 I called you _____ I could.
2 He refused to talk to the police _____ his lawyer arrived.
3 I feel sad _____ I hear that song.
4 They were burgled _____ they were away on holiday.
5 I've known her _____ I was a small child.
6 I'll help you with this exercise _____ I've had dinner.

| Condition | if   as long as   unless   in case |

1 _____ I'm going to be late, I'll call you.
2 You won't pass _____ you work harder.
3 Take an umbrella _____ it rains.
4 You can borrow my car _____ you drive carefully.

3 Discuss what you know about the film star, Marilyn Monroe.

4 Read about Marilyn's death and the conspiracy theories that surround it. Choose the correct conjunctions to join the sentences.

5 Research and write about someone famous who interests you. Use the plan below to help you.

Paragraph 1: Introduction and your interest in this person
Paragraph 2: Early life
Paragraph 3: Career path
Paragraph 4: Period of fame
Paragraph 5: Later life (and death)

MARILYN MONROE
THE DEATH OF A STAR

It is over 40 years (1) *since/after* Marilyn Monroe died, (2) *however/but* theories concerning her death still fascinate the world. (3) *Whenever/While* her name is mentioned, people recall the mystery of her final hours and (4) *although/despite* the official verdict was suicide, many believe that she was murdered by the Mafia or the FBI.

Marilyn had a reputation as a dumb blonde who had (5) *so/such* a problem with drink, drugs, and depression that she could never remember her lines. (6) *However/But*, her beauty and fame brought her into contact with some of the biggest names of the day. She dated Frank Sinatra, (7) *even though/despite* he had connections with the Mafia, and she also had affairs with President John Kennedy and his brother Bobby.

(8) *When/Until* Marilyn was found dead in bed at her home in Los Angeles in the early hours of Sunday, August 5, 1962, police assumed it was suicide (9) *but/as* there was an empty bottle of sleeping pills on the table beside her. (10) *Despite/However*, witnesses, including her psychiatrist and some of her friends, insisted she was not suicidal at the time. Other witnesses said they saw Bobby Kennedy visit her house that night, (11) *as long as/even though* he claimed to be in San Francisco. There were other suspicious events. Marilyn's housekeeper disappeared immediately (12) *after/since* she was found, only to reappear a year later as an employee of the Kennedys. Why would they employ her (13) *unless/if* they wanted her to keep silent? Marilyn's diaries also disappeared. Were they (14) *so/such* revealing that they had to be destroyed?

Marilyn's ex-husband Joe DiMaggio was convinced the Kennedys had her killed. He never spoke about it (15) *while/during* he was alive (16) *in case/unless* he also met an untimely death, but he did in his memoirs, which were published (17) *as soon as/since* he died.

1 How does writing an email differ from writing letters? List some differences.

2 Emails to friends are usually very informal and grammar words are often left out. How could you express these typical email phrases more formally?

> Glad you're OK.
> Great news – got the job!
> Sorry, can't make next Sat.
> You still OK for Friday?
> Thanks loads.
> Sounds fantastic.
> Can't wait to see you.
> Speak soon.

3 Read the email and note any features that are typical to emails. What changes would you make if it were a letter? Go through and discuss with your partner.

4 Read the letter from Jane to a friend. What is the main reason for writing? What parts of the letter give extra information?

Work with a partner and discuss how to make it more like an email.

5 Write an email in reply to Jane (about 250 words).

- Begin by reacting to her news
- Reply positively to her invitation
- Suggest arrangements for meeting her
- End by giving some news about yourself.

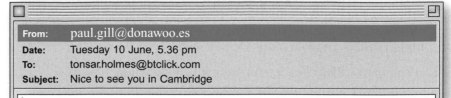

From:	paul.gill@donawoo.es
Date:	Tuesday 10 June, 5.36 pm
To:	tonsar.holmes@btclick.com
Subject:	Nice to see you in Cambridge

Hi Tony and Sarah

GREAT to see you in Cambridge last week and catch up on all your news. Wasn't the Old Church Hotel nice? (Hey, but what about the lousy breakfast service!). The party seemed to go OK. Wonder what the group photo will be like this year? Also, the bottle (or two!) of champagne in the bar after – MOST enjoyable!

Got back to Spain after a 2 day drive – stopped off at lovely 3 star hotel in village of Brioude on way to Montpellier. Kids loved the indoor pool and jacuzzi. Came as a welcome break from driving for us.

Hope all is well with you. Pam is off with kids to Aqualandia, swimming. Remember when we went up there with yours once – many moons ago?

Keep in touch. Would be great if you could get out here to visit us.

lots of love
Paul & Pam
& Hannah and Freddie

Wandsworth
London

July 8th

Dear Rob,

It was so good to see you and Jenny a few weeks ago. We really must get together more often, we always have so much to talk about.

On the subject of get-togethers, I just had a postcard from – guess who? Graham Pellowe. Do you remember 'gorgeous' Graham who was studying zoology? Well, he's in town. Apparently he's a real high-flier these days. He works for an international environmental agency, would you believe. Anyway, he's coming to London next Thursday and he really wants to meet up and discuss old times. He's staying with friends in Maida Vale, close to where I used to live. I know a great restaurant there called the Green Olive, or else there's the Red Pepper – both are excellent. Anyway, I am assuming and desperately hoping that you can come that evening – I don't fancy a whole evening with old Graham on my own. I finish work at about six and he can't make the restaurant until 8.30, which gives us some time to catch up. Let me know if any of this is possible.

Please call me or email when you can and I'll book the restaurant. It could be a fun evening.

Love
Jane

1 What do you understand by fast food? What fast food outlets are popular in your country? What do you understand by organic food? Do you ever buy it?

2 A company called the Organic Burger Company has commissioned a consumer survey to find out who their customers could be in the future. The results of the survey are presented to them as a report. Here are some headings from the report.

FAO (For the attention of ...)   ___
Title (of report)   ___
Background and objectives   ___ ___ ___
Research and findings   ___ ___ ___ ___
Summary and recommendations ___ ___
Action next   ___ ___

Match these expressions with the headings.

a   In conclusion,
b   The Managing Director
c   The purpose of this report
d   two main findings
e   The history of this issue
f   'Survey into Potential Demand for Organic Burgers.'
g   We recommend that
h   The results
i   We propose that
j   were asked to say what they thought
k   within the next six months
l   We were asked to investigate
m not enough evidence

3 Read the report based on the consumer survey conducted for the Organic Burger Company and complete it with the expressions from exercise 2.

The Organic Burger Company

FAO: (1)_____, Organic Burger Company
Title: (2)'_____'.
Date: 30th November

Background and objectives

(3)_____ is that there has recently been a drop in customers at traditional fast-food outlets such as McDonalds. The Organic Burger company wants to fill the growing gap in the market.

(4)_____ is to survey consumer attitudes by doing preliminary research with the young people of Nottingham, a medium-sized English town.

(5)_____ what the customers would want from the experience of buying and eating a high-quality organic burger.

Research and findings

We surveyed 120 people. The age range was:

16–19: 31%   **20–24:** 34%   **25–35:** 19%
36–50: 12%   **51+:** 4%

They (6)_____ about the following statements:

1 I prefer to eat organic meat in my burger.
                                                      SA A DK D SD

2 I prefer to have a restaurant interior that is tasteful and modern.   SA A DK D SD

3 I prefer my food to be grown with respect for the environment.   SA A DK D SD

4 I prefer all the other ingredients to be fresh and organic.   SA A DK D SD

5 I am prepared to pay more than I pay now.
                                                      SA A DK D SD

(SA = Strongly Agree, A = Agree,
DK = Don't Know, D = Disagree,
SD = Strongly Disagree)

(7)_____ are as follows:

1 46% agreed or strongly agreed
2 47% agreed or strongly agreed
3 77% agreed or strongly agreed
4 39% agreed or strongly agreed
5 22% agreed or strongly agreed

The (8)_____ are:

1. there is a growing preference for organic food.
2. there is (9)_____ that there is a large market yet.

Summary and recommendations

(10)_____ we believe that our survey showed that:

• the tastes of young people in a typical western town are changing

• demand exists for more stylish fast food and that this demand is growing.

(11)_____ the company loses no time in preparing for a push into all western markets.

Action next

(12)_____ further research is now carried out, on a larger scale and in other countries. This should be completed (13)_____.

WRITING A SURVEY AND A REPORT

4 You work for a firm of marketing consultants. Your client is a supermarket chain. Your brief is to find out if shoppers in your town would be prepared to buy more *Fairtrade* products in the local supermarket. *Fairtrade* products cost more, because they pay the producers in developing countries a better price for their products.

• Think of four or five statements like the ones used in the survey for the Organic Burger Company.

   I want to know where the things I buy come from.

   SA A DK D SD

• Ask at least 20 people, either in your class or outside your class.

• Take data about age. Possibly also male / female.

• Add up the statistics.

5 Write the report (about 250 words). Use expressions from exercises 2 and 3, and use the structure of the report as a model.

1 Do you send emails? If so who to and when? What emails have you received or sent recently? Discuss with a partner then with the class.

2 Is email a good or a bad thing? Brainstorm ideas as a class. Divide the blackboard into two. Appoint two students to take notes, one for each column.

PROS (+)	CONS (–)

Discuss your results. On balance, which side wins? What's your opinion?

3 Read through the article quickly. How many of the points you made are mentioned? How many other points did you make?

4 Study the article more carefully.
1 How is the topic introduced?
2 What personal examples does the writer include throughout the article?
3 For each point on the plus side underline the words and expressions used to connect the ideas.
First of all email is easy.
4 Compare the words and expressions used to connect the ideas on the minus side. Which are similar?
5 How is the article concluded? How does the writer express his opinion?

5 Brainstorm the arguments for and against one of the topics below. Then write an introduction, the pros, the cons, and your conclusion (about 250 words).
• The mobile phone
• Travelling the world in your 20s
• Adult children living at home

Subject: ## Email – a good thing or a bad thing?

In recent years email has become an increasingly important means of communication. However, in my opinion, like most things it has both advantages and disadvantages.

On the plus side:

• First of all, email is easy. All you need is the appropriate software on your computer. There are no stamps to stick and no trips in the freezing cold to postboxes.

• A second point is that email is fast. No matter where you're sending your message, whether it's to the next street or to the other side of the planet it takes only seconds to reach its destination. Nowadays, whenever I send regular mail (or snail mail as email users call it), I can't believe that it's actually going to take days to reach its destination. How primitive!

• Email is not only fast, it is also cheap. Unlike long distance telephone calls, you pay no more for messages sent from the US to London, Ohio, or London, Ontario, or London, England.

• Also, email messages are easily stored. Because they're electronic, saving an email message you've received (and calling it back up again later) is a breeze.

• In addition to this, email is environmentally friendly because being electronic, it saves natural resources such as paper.

• Last but not least, email is practically universal. Even my great aunt in Galashiels, Scotland is using it these days.

On the minus side:

• Firstly, email is impersonal. Unlike when face to face or in telephone conversations, it's difficult to get across subtle meanings in email prose with no visual or voice clues.

• Secondly, it can be argued that email is in fact too easy. You can write a message in a few seconds and send it off with one click. And once sent, you can't get back a message that may have been written in a fit of irritation or anger.

• Another point is that email security is lax. As your email message makes its way to its destination, it has to pass through other, public, systems. Anyone with the right technical know-how can intercept it without you knowing.

• Although, as stated above, it is an advantage that email messages are easily stored, this can also be a disadvantage. If you say nasty things about your boss in a message, a saved copy can come back to haunt you in the future.

• A final and very important point is that email can take over your life. Because it is so easy you start getting more and more correspondence, and you end up spending most of your day reading and responding to floods of messages.

Overall, however, to my mind the pros of email easily outweigh the cons, and email is a good thing. It has transformed the world of communication in largely beneficial ways, and alongside text messaging, is now a major way of keeping in touch.

1 What's your favourite town or city? Why do you like it? Which parts of it do you particularly like? Work with a partner and tell them about it.

2 Do the words in the box describe something positive, negative, or neutral?

Do they refer to a person, a place, or food? Or more than one?

> lively   dash around (v)   shabby   dull
> brand-new   snoring   a down-and-out
> cosmopolitan   pedestrianized   buzz (v)
> trendy   boutiques   packed   flock (v)
> mouth-watering aromas   a magnet

3 Read the description of Soho. Which parts of Soho do the pictures show?

4 Work with your partner and decide where you could divide the text into paragraphs. What is the purpose of each paragraph? Think of a heading for each one and compare them with others in the class.

5 The description is part fact and part opinion. Find examples of both.

6 <u>Underline</u> examples of relative clauses and participles.

7 Write a description of your favourite part of town (about 250 words). Use the paragraph plan to help you.

Paragraph 1: General / personal impressions
Paragraph 2: Its history
Paragraph 3: Its character
Paragraph 4: Conclusion and/or final anecdote

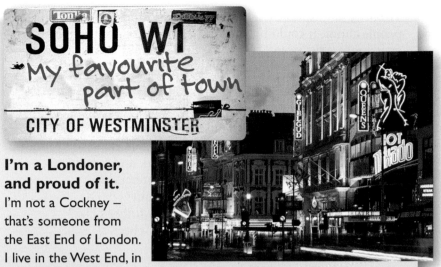

SOHO W1
My favourite part of town
CITY OF WESTMINSTER

I'm a Londoner, and proud of it.
I'm not a Cockney – that's someone from the East End of London. I live in the West End, in Soho, which is right in the centre, and includes Piccadilly Circus, Shaftesbury Avenue, and Leicester Square. It's my favourite part of town. So why do I like it so much? It is always lively and colourful, with people dashing around, going about their business, which is mainly honest but not always. Some of the streets may be a bit shabby but life in Soho is never dull. There's a surprise round every corner – maybe a brand-new night club that wasn't there last week, a snoring down-and-out sleeping in a doorway, or a celebrity being pursued by paparazzi and fans. A sense of history pervades Soho. The name is derived from a hunting call, 'So-ho', that huntsmen were heard to cry as they chased deer in what were the royal parklands. It has been a cosmopolitan area since the first immigrants, who were French Huguenots, arrived in the 1680s. They were followed by Germans, Russians, Poles, Greeks, and Italians. More recently there have been a lot of Chinese from Hong Kong. Gerrard Street, which is pedestrianized, is the centre of London's Chinatown, and buzzes all year round, but especially at the New Year celebrations in February. Many famous people have lived in Soho, including Mozart, Karl Marx, and the poet T.S. Eliot. It has a reputation for attracting artists, writers, poets, musicians, and people in the media. Shaftesbury Avenue is in the heart of London's theatre land, and there are endless clubs, pubs, trendy boutiques, and of course, restaurants. A large part of the Soho experience is to do with food. Soho is packed with continental food shops and restaurants. Mouth-watering aromas are everywhere, from first thing in the morning till late at night. Soho is a genuine 24/7 part of town. Piccadilly Circus is like a magnet for young people. They flock from every corner of the world to sit on the steps under the statue of Eros, celebrating the freedom and friendship of youth. My mother, who was a Cockney, used to say that if you wait long enough at Piccadilly Circus, you'll meet everyone you've ever known!

1 Think of *any* aspect of your life that you would like to tell other people about. It could be your job, a hobby, a person, a place, a special occasion, a news event. Write some notes about it. Ask and answer questions about it with a partner.

2 **T 9.13** Read and listen to someone talking about a man called Christopher and answer the questions.

1 What is the speaker's relationship to Christopher?
2 Why is he called 'Cheap Christopher'? What does 'stingy' mean?
3 What do you learn of Christopher's work and family?
4 Name some of the stingy things Christopher does.
5 What's the stingiest thing he has ever done?
6 What did he use to give his mother on Mother's Day?
7 What is the speaker's opinion of Christopher?
8 What does his wife say?

3 Now read the talk carefully and answer the questions.

1 Underline the phrases that introduce each paragraph. Why are these words used?
2 Underline *all* the questions in the text. These are *rhetorical questions*. What does this mean? Why are they used?
3 Find examples of the speaker giving his personal opinion.
4 Practise reading aloud the first paragraph with a partner.

Preparing your talk

4 Think of a title for the notes you made about your topic. Write a talk using these guidelines. Try to include some rhetorical questions.

1 Give the title:
   The title of my talk is …
2 Introduce your topic:
   I want to talk about X because …
   Today I'll be talking about X because …
3 Give some background:
   Let's start with some background. …
   I've always been interested in …
   As you all probably know, …
4 Hit your first point:
   First, …
   What happened was this, …
5 Move to new points:
   I'd now like to turn to …
   Moving on,
   Another thing is …
6 Conclude:
   Finally, I'd like to say …
   Thank you all very much for listening to me.
   Are there any questions?

5 Mark pauses and words you want to stress. Practise reading it aloud to a partner. Give your talk to the class. Answer any questions.

Cheap Christopher

The title of my talk is 'Cheap Christopher'. That's what everyone calls my cousin. Why do they call him that? Well, simply because he's so stingy. He gets everything on the cheap. He's the stingiest person I've ever met and that's why I want to talk about him today.

Let's start with some background. Christopher is intelligent. He's a part-time journalist and he's not at all poor. I think he makes about $50,000 a year. He's married with two children, and his wife has a good job, too. So why is Christopher so stingy?

First, let me tell you just how stingy he is. He never spends money on himself. He never buys new clothes. He gets them second-hand from thrift stores for about $5 an item. He never eats out in restaurants. When his work colleagues invite him out to lunch, he stays in his office and says he's expecting a phone call. He hardly ever uses his car. He says he can live on $10 a week. Can you believe that?

Another thing, Christopher never, ever invites friends to dinner, but he doesn't feel guilty about accepting their invitations. Do you know what he says? He says that they invite him to dinner just to have someone interesting to talk to.

All these things are pretty bad, but in my opinion the stingiest thing he's ever done is this. He went to a friend's wedding without a present. He just took some wrapping paper and a card saying 'Love from Christopher' and put it on the table with the other presents. Afterwards he got a thank-you letter from the bride. She obviously thought she'd misplaced the present.

The obvious question is 'why is he so stingy?' I asked him about it. He said, 'I've always been stingy.' When he was a child, he'd never buy his mother flowers on Mother's Day. He'd give her a bouquet from her own garden.

Finally, I'd like to say that Christopher may be the world's stingiest guy, but I still like him. Why, you may ask? Well, he's my cousin, and besides, he's got a lot of other good qualities, like his sense of humor. His wife doesn't seem to mind that he's so cheap. She says he's just being 'careful with his money'.

1 You have looked at letters and emails in Units 1, 2, and 5. Are the following statements about **informal** letters and emails true or false? (Some are part true.)

1 You can begin with *Dear Rob*, *Hi Rob*, or just *Rob*.
2 Use contracted forms such as *won't*, *I've*, and *couldn't*.
3 The way you end the letter depends on how well you know the person.
4 You can end with *Goodbye*, *Bye for now*, *Cheers!*, *All the best*, *Best of wishes*, *Take care*, *Yours*, or *Love*.
5 Sign or write your full name, and print it out underneath.
6 If you have forgotten to write something important, you can add it at the bottom with PS, for example, *PS Say Hi to Ellie! Tell her I'll be in touch*.

2 Are these statements about **formal** letters and emails true or false? (Some are part true.)

1 If you know the person's name, you can begin with *Dear Mr Brown*, *Dear Robert Brown*, *Dear Brown*, *Dear Mr Robert Brown*, or just *Brown*.
2 If you're writing to a woman, begin with *Dear Ms Black*.
3 If you don't know their name, you can begin with *Dear Sir* or *Dear Madam*.
4 Avoid contracted forms except *doesn't*, *don't*, or *didn't*.
5 If you begin with *Dear Sir* or *Dear Madam*, end with *Yours faithfully* or just *Yours*. If you begin with the person's name, end with *Yours sincerely*.
6 Sign or write your full name.

3 Read the letter from Keiko to her friend, Amber Jones. Which parts sound too formal? Replace them with words on the right.

4 Write an informal letter to another student in the class (about 250 words). Ask a few questions about the other person's life, and then give some news about yourself. Invite the other person out, and give some suggestions for a time and place to meet.

4-2 Nagayama 3-chome
Tama-shi, Tokyo 206

Dear Ms Jones

How are things with you? I trust you and your family are in good health, and that you benefited from an enjoyable holiday in France. I went to the mountains for a few days with several acquaintances. Please find enclosed a photo of us at an ancient temple. Hope you like it.

I was most delighted to hear that you are coming to Japan in the near future! You didn't specify the exact dates. I would be grateful if you could supply them to me. I will do my utmost to ensure I have some time free in order to be able to accompany you around Tokyo. I can assure you that there is a lot to see and do here. We'll have lots of fun! The shops here are of a very high standard, too, so we'll no doubt end up buying excessive quantities of clothes!

In conclusion, I'm obliged to finish now. It's time for bed! Please contact me soon. I look forward to hearing from you.

Yours sincerely

Keiko

PS Please give my sincere regards to your parents. Tell them I miss them!

Believe me,
had a great time
It's great news
hope
say when exactly
can't wait to hear
Anyway
Please let me know
Hi Amber!
get in touch
loads of
so I can show
soon
say hello
Love and best wishes
absolutely fantastic
a few friends
we're bound to
I'll do my best to make sure
I have to
I'm sending you
all well

1 Think of something that you looked forward to for a long time that finally happened.

- What was the occasion or event? Why did you want it so much?
- Did you have to make preparations for it? If so, what were they?
- What actually happened?
- Did it live up to your expectations or not?

Write some notes and then tell your partner about it.

2 Read these lines from Larry's story and reconstruct it with a partner.

> Larry's dream to fly aeroplanes /
> bought twenty balloons / a garden chair
> / packed a few sandwiches and an air
> pistol / cut the rope / floated around /
> the winds were blowing / a British
> Airways pilot at 3,500 metres /
> a helicopter / a TV reporter

3 Read the full story and compare it with yours. Match these five headings with the correct paragraphs.

- ☐ **Serious problems**
- ☐ **Preparing for take-off**
- ☐ **Down to earth with a bump**
- ☐ **Larry and his dream**
- ☐ **Flying high**

4 Read the story again and complete it with a correct linking word or expression from the box.

first of all	Finally	Eventually	Next
However	All day long	Then, one day	
By this time	until	As soon as	
Immediately	Fortunately, just at that moment	
Unfortunately	in order to	so	because

5 Use your notes from exercise 1 and write your story (about 250 words).

6 Read each other's stories and ask and answer questions about them.

Larry follows his dream

1 Larry was a truck driver, but his lifetime dream was to fly aeroplanes.

(1)_____ he would watch the fighter jets criss-crossing the skies above his back garden and dream about the magic of flying. (2)_____, he had an idea. He drove to the nearest hardware shop and bought twenty large balloons and five tanks of helium. (3)_____, they were not normal brightly-coloured party balloons but heavy one-metre weather balloons used by meteorologists.

2 Back in his garden, (4)_____, Larry used a rope to tie a chair to his car door. (5)_____ he tied the balloons to the chair and inflated them, one by one. (6)_____, he packed a few sandwiches and a bottle of Coke, loaded an air-pistol, and climbed on to the chair. His plan was to float up lazily into the sky to about sixty metres, and then to pop a few balloons (7)_____ descend to earth again.

3 His preparations complete, Larry cut the rope. (8)_____, he didn't float up, he shot up, as if he had been fired from a cannon! Not to sixty metres, but up and up and up, (9)_____ about 3,500 metres. If he had popped any balloons at this height, he would have plummeted to earth, (10)_____ he just had to stay up there, floating around and wondering what to do.

4 (11)_____, night was falling and things were getting serious. Winds were blowing Larry out to sea. (12)_____ an amazed British Airways pilot spotted him and radioed the airport saying he'd just seen a man with a gun, sitting on a garden chair at 3,500 metres. (13)_____ a helicopter was sent to rescue him, but it wasn't easy (14)_____ the wind from their rotor blades kept pushing the home-made airship further away. (15)_____, they managed to drop a line down from above, and pulled him to safety.

5 (16)_____ he was on the ground he was arrested. A TV reporter shouted, 'Hey mate, why did you do it?' Larry looked him in the eye, and said, 'A man's got to follow his dreams'.

1 Who are the most influential people in the world today? And in the past? Share ideas as a class.

2 Compare the two texts about Michelangelo. Work with a partner and find differences in the way the same information is presented.

Find examples of how emphasis is added by:

1 Changes of word order.
2 Changes of words.
3 Sentences that begin with *It was …* and *What … .*
4 The use of *this* to refer back.

Which text sounds better? Why?

3 Rephrase these sentences in different ways to make them more emphatic.

1 I love my grandfather's kind, wrinkly smile.
   What I love about …   *The thing I love about …*
   What I love about my grandfather is his kind, wrinkly smile.
   The thing I love about my grandfather is his kind, wrinkly smile.

2 They don't understand the President's policies.
   It's the President's policies …   *What they …*

3 The softness of Norah Jones' voice makes it special.
   What makes …   *It's the …*

4 I admired Mother Teresa's courage.
   What I admired about …   *It was …*

5 The way Pele could head a football was amazing.
   What was …   *What amazed me …*

4 Research the career of someone you consider influential, a sportsperson, artist, singer, actor, writer or business person.

Using some of the structures for adding emphasis, write (about 250 words) about:

- their early life
- how their career grew
- why he/she is/was a person of influence
- the high points of their professional life

MICHELANGELO (1475–1564)

TEXT A

1 Michelangelo had a great influence on the world of art. He was a sculptor, an architect, a painter, and a poet.

2 He was born near Arezzo, but he considered Florence to be his home town. He loved the city's art, architecture, and culture.

3 He concentrated on sculpture initially. He began to carve a figure of David from a huge block of marble in 1501. He finished it in 1504, when he was 29.

4 Pope Julius II asked him to paint the ceiling of the Sistine Chapel later. He worked at this every day for four years from 1508 till 1512. He lay on his back at the top of high scaffolding.

5 He designed many buildings. His greatest achievement as an architect was his work at St Peter's Basilica. Its revolutionary design is difficult to appreciate nowadays.

6 Michelangelo belongs to a small group of artists such as Shakespeare and Beethoven, who have been able to express humanity's deepest experiences through their work.

TEXT B

1 Michelangelo, sculptor, architect, painter, and poet, had a tremendous influence on the world of art.

2 Although he was born near Arezzo, it was Florence that he considered to be his home town. What he loved above all about the city was its art, architecture, and culture.

3 Initially, he concentrated on sculpture. In 1501 he began to carve a figure of David from a huge block of marble. This he finished in 1504, when he was 29.

4 Later, he was asked by Pope Julius II to paint the ceiling of the Sistine Chapel. To do this, every day for four years, from 1508 till 1512, he worked lying on his back at the top of high scaffolding.

5 He designed many buildings, but it was his work at St Peter's Basilica that was his greatest achievement as an architect. What is difficult to appreciate nowadays is its revolutionary design.

6 There is a small group of artists such as Shakespeare and Beethoven, who, through their work, have been able to express the deepest experiences of humanity. Michelangelo belongs to this group.

Tapescripts

UNIT 1

T 1.1

1 How long has Max been at summer camp?
Just two days.
2 Is he having a good time?
No, not really. He's feeling very homesick.
3 Is this his first time at summer camp?
No, it's not. He's been once before. Last year he went to Pine Trees.
4 Did he like it at Pine Trees?
Oh, yes he did, very much.
5 Why was that?
Because they did things like archery and mountain biking.
6 What's he doing tomorrow?
He's making pancakes.
7 Why does he want his cell phone?
Because all the other kids have theirs.

T 1.2

1 How long has Sophie been in New Zealand?
Nearly a week.
2 How long was she in Australia?
Three weeks.
3 Who is she travelling with?
Catherine.
4 Why does she like New Zealand?
Because it's smaller and cooler than Australia.
5 Why did she like Kangaroo Island?
Because of the wildlife. She saw some platypus there.
6 What's their car like?
It's OK – the lights work and it has a big glove box – but it sometimes makes strange noises.
7 Which wildlife has she seen already?
She's seen dolphins, whales, and enormous albatrosses.
8 Where are they going next?
They're heading up the west coast.
9 Why is she sending Rob photos?
So that he won't forget what she looks like.

T 1.3

1 A Are you being served, sir?
B Oh, -er, just looking, thank you.
2 I've heard that she's been seeing a lot of Patrick recently.
3 I'll be seeing Bill this afternoon – I'll tell him the good news then.
4 Apparently, he was overtaking on a bend at 70 mph when they stopped him.
5 I hadn't seen her since she was a little girl, and she'd changed beyond all recognition.
6 Nobody will listen to him. He's the kind of guy who isn't believed by anyone.
7 I haven't been told yet if I've got it. I'll be told in writing sometime next week.
8 Do you have any idea which address it was sent to?

T 1.4

1 A At weekends I often don't bother getting up 'til lunchtime.
B Absolutely! Why bother if you don't have to?
2 A My parents have never had a cross word in all their married lives.
B Really? Mine are at it all the time.
3 A I don't think I'll ever master this DVD player.
B Well, don't ask me. I can't even find the on/off button.
4 A I was saying to a friend just the other day that I hadn't seen you for ages.
B I know. How long has it been?

5 A I hate Mondays because nothing ever goes right on a Monday.
B Just Mondays, eh? Aren't you the lucky one!
6 A I'd just arrived home last night when I realized I'd left my briefcase on the bus.
B Well, you won't see that again.
7 A I was just getting ready to go out this morning when my grandmother rang for a chat. It's so frustrating!
B I know, and you feel really bad if you say it's not a good time.
8 A I've been told that our teacher wears purple pyjamas in bed!
B Who on earth told you that?!
9 A In my very first English lesson I was taught to introduce myself and say 'hello'.
B I was taught to say 'the cat runs after the mouse' and stuff like that – useful, uh?!
10 A The reason I'm learning English is because it's spoken all over the world.
B True. But isn't Chinese spoken by more people?

T 1.5

1 A Heard about Jane and John splitting up?
B No! Really? I always thought they got on really well.
A Apparently not. John's been seeing his ex-girlfriend.
2 A Leaving already? What's wrong?
B I just have a headache, that's all.
3 A Failed again? How many times is that?
B OK, OK. There's no need to rub it in! They say the *best* drivers fail three times.
4 A Sorry I'm late. Been waiting long?
B No, I've just arrived myself. Got caught in traffic.
5 A Doing anything interesting this weekend?
B Yeah, if you call housework interesting. I've just *got* to tidy my flat this weekend.
6 A Like the car! When did you get it?
B We've had it a while actually. Second-hand, you know.
7 A Bye, Jo! See you later.
B Yeah. I'll be round about eight!
8 A Just coming! Hang on!
B Get a move on, or we'll go without you!
9 A Want a lift? Hop in.
B Great. Can you drop me in the centre?
10 A Seen Jim lately?
B No, I haven't. I wonder what he's up to at the moment.

T 1.6 A long-distance phone call

D Hello?
K Dad! It's me, Kirsty.
D Kirsty! How are you? How's it all going?
K I'm fine, but still a bit jet-lagged.
D I can imagine. What exactly is the time difference over there?
K It's nine hours ahead. I just can't get used to it. Last night I lay awake all night and then today I nearly fell asleep at work in the middle of a meeting.
D You poor thing. And what's work like?
K It's early days but, I think it's going to be really good. It's a big company but everybody's being so kind and helpful. I've been trying to find out how everything works.
D And what about Tokyo? What's it like? Have you seen much of the city yet?
K I've seen a bit. It just seems such a big, busy city. I don't see how I'll ever find my way round it.
D I know. Big cities can seem really strange and frightening at first. Is it anything like London?
K No, it's nothing like London. It's like nowhere else I've ever been – masses of huge buildings,

underground shopping centres, lots of taxis and people – so many people – but it's so clean. No litter on the streets or anything.
D And where are you living? What kind of accommodation have you got?
K Well, for the time being I've been given a tiny apartment, but it's in a great part of town.
D What do you mean 'for the time being'? Will you be moving somewhere else?
K That's right. I won't be living here for long. I'll be offered a bigger place as soon as one becomes available, which is good 'cos this one really is tiny, but at least it's near to where I'm working.
D How do you get to work then? Do you walk?
K Walk! You're kidding. It's not *that* close. It's a short subway ride away. And the trains come so regularly – it's a really easy journey, which is good 'cos I start work very early in the morning.
D It all sounds really interesting but are you enjoying yourself?
K Again it's too early to say. I think I really will be enjoying it all soon. I'm sure it's going to be a great experience. It's just that I miss everyone at home so much.
D Oh, we miss you too, very much. Make sure you email us regularly – it's the best way to keep in touch.
K I will. I promise. And you email me back with all your news. I just love getting news from home. Give everyone my love. Bye.
D Bye sweetheart. It's been great talking to you.

T 1.7

1 A I'm going away on business for two weeks. Do you think you could possibly water my house plants for me?
B No problem. I'd be glad to. I'll keep an eye on your whole flat if you like.
A That would be great.
B Don't worry, I know how house-proud you are. I'll make sure everything stays clean and tidy.
A I'll do the same for you any time, you know.
B Thanks.
2 A Julie, have you heard? Anna's just been made managing director of the UK branch of her firm, so she's coming back from the States!
B Oh, that's great news. Let's give her a spectacular homecoming party when she gets back. Hmmm. She's certainly the career girl of the family.
A Doing really well, isn't she?
B I know and I'm happy for her. Me? I'm just a housewife. Four kids, home-made cakes and home-grown vegetables!
A And how *are* my wonderful grandchildren?
3 A We're having a house-warming party on the 12th. Can you come?
B Yes, you bet. We'd love to! But I didn't know you'd moved.
A Yeah, two weeks ago. It's much bigger than the old one. Huge kitchen and three big bedrooms.
B Sounds great.
A Yeah. Mind you, there's much more housework to do!
B That's a drag!
4 A Hey, you going to Carly's on Saturday?
B I dunno.
A It's a free house. It'll be great.
B Cool. Where are her parents then?
A Carly says they're visiting her grandma – she's sick and housebound so they have to go and help.
B OK. Count me in. I'll be there.

1 I'm going away for two weeks. Do you think you could possibly water my house plants for me?
2 Don't worry, I know how house-proud you are. I'll make sure everything stays clean and tidy.
3 Let's give her a spectacular homecoming party when she gets back from New York.
4 Me? I'm just a housewife. Four kids, home-made cakes and home-grown vegetables!
5 We're having a house-warming party on the 12th. Can you come? I'll give you our new address.
6 Mind you, with it being much bigger, there's much more housework to do!
7 Her grandmother's sick and housebound so they have to go and help.

T 1.9 Things I miss from home

Andrew
Well, the thing I miss most when I'm away from home is definitely listening to the radio, and the way I get round this, particularly when I go away for two, three or four months or something, is to take a small short wave radio that I found and take great trouble to tune in this short wave radio to get an English language station, something like the World Service. And I'm there, waving the aerial around and twiddling the knob, and trying to find the correct kind of station, but then suddenly when it all comes in, and you can hear it, it's great, it really makes me feel like I'm back home, back in my bedroom tuning into weird programmes on wonderful subjects really.

Helen
When I'm away from home for any length of time, something that I really have to have with me is my hair straighteners, … erm … I can't bear to wake up in the morning and be without them, because my hair is most unruly, and I would feel very uncomfortable having gone out without straightening my hair beforehand, so I have to take those with me whenever I stay with friends or go on holiday.

Gabriele
When I'm away for a little bit longer, … erm … what I do miss are my two cats and I do take a photo of them. That sounds very silly but I like to see them from time to time.

Paul
Erm … if I'm away from home for a while, what I usually miss most is my bed. I like a good solid bed. Er … in particular what I find I miss if I'm in a hotel is a pillow that I like. I do find that hotels have this incredible knack of providing pillows that you just can't sleep with – there always seems to be two pillows on the bed and if you use one it's never enough, and if you use both of the pillows, your head seems to be just stuck up in the air – so I have thought of taking a pillow with me but that seems a bit excessive. Erm … but again connected with sleep, one thing I always do take with me is ear plugs. I find they're absolutely invaluable, if you're not sure where you're going to be in a hotel and if it's very noisy, as long as you're quite used to sleeping with ear plugs … er … they can be wonderful 'cause you don't need to worry about traffic and people making a lot of noise in the next room.

Sylvia
Well, when I'm away from home … erm … there are several things I miss, the usual ones, my children of course, and a good cup of tea … erm … but something I realize I do miss is, is the news, and it's not, it's not that other countries don't have any news, but I'm very attached to a particular news programme and a particular presenter, and if they're not around to tell me the news, I can't quite believe it. It's very odd – doesn't happen with papers, I'm happy to read another paper but on the telly I like to see, I like to see a familiar face and … erm … the same background colours and it's all very reassuring, even if he's telling something dreadful. But what do I take … erm … with me? I always travel with a bag of snacks, … erm … I don't know why, because I'm terr… er … I'm just terrified of, of being hungry while I'm travelling and not finding anything I want to eat. Gosh, I didn't, I didn't think I was so fussy – there you go!

Chris
I think the thing I miss most when I go away for an extended period, on holiday or whatever … er … especially if I go away abroad is probably Sunday morning, and by that I really mean a lazy Sunday morning when I can get up fairly late, wander down to the newsagent's, buy the newspaper, come back with a croissant and make a big pot of coffee, and spend … er … at least the morning and maybe a large part of the day just sitting around reading the paper, drinking coffee and relaxing.

T 1.10

1 A Great to see you. Come on in.
   B I was just passing and thought I'd drop in.
2 A Excuse me, don't I know you from somewhere?
   B No, I don't think so.
3 A What d'you mean you're not coming?
   B Well, I just don't feel up to going out tonight.
4 A I think I'll have the chocolate mousse. What about you?
   B Let me see. No, actually, I don't think I'll bother with dessert.
5 A My flatmate can't make it to your party.
   B Really! That's a drag. I was hoping to meet her.
6 A How come you're not having a holiday this year?
   B We just can't afford it.
7 A You'll make yourself ill if you carry on working at that pace.
   B That's as maybe but I have to get this finished by Friday.
8 A I've got you the last two tickets for the show.
   B Fantastic! I knew you'd swing it for us.

T 1.11 See p15

T 1.12 See p153

T 1.13

1 A Excuse me, don't I know you from somewhere?
   B Actually, I don't think so.
   A Weren't you at Gavin's party last week?
   B Not me. I don't know anyone called Gavin.
   A Well, someone who looked just like you was there.
   B Well, that's as maybe but it certainly wasn't me.
   A I am sorry!
2 A Tony! Hi! Great to see you.
   B Well, I was just passing and I thought I'd drop in and say 'hello'.
   A Come on in! Have a drink!
   B You're sure? You're not too busy?
   A Never too busy to talk to you.
   B Thanks Jo. It'd be really nice to have a chat.
   A Fantastic! Let me take your coat.

UNIT 2

T 2.1 Marco Polo 1254–1324

Marco Polo was the first person to travel the entire 8,000 kilometre length of the Silk Route, the main trade link between Cathay (China) and the West for over two thousand years. He was born in Venice, the son of a merchant. In 1271, when he was 17, he set off for China. The journey took him four years. His route led him through Persia, Afghanistan, and Mongolia. He travelled by boat, but mainly on horseback, and he frequently got lost. He was met by the emperor Kublai Khan. He was one of the first Europeans to visit the territory, and he travelled extensively. He went over mountain ranges, down rivers, and across deserts. He stayed in China for seventeen years. When he left, he took back a fortune in gold and jewellery. He arrived back home in 1295. He wrote a book called *The Travels of Marco Polo*, which gave Europeans their first information about China and the Far East.

Tommy Willis, backpacker in Asia
Tommy Willis is in Fiji. He's on a nine-month backpacking trip round south-east Asia. He flew into Bangkok five months ago. Since then, he's been to Vietnam, Hong Kong, South Korea, and Japan. He's visited royal palaces and national parks in South Korea, and climbed to the summit of Mount Fuji in Japan. He's been staying in cheap hostels, along with a lot of other young people. 'I've met a lot of really great people, but it hasn't all been easy,' said Tommy. 'I've had diarrhoea a few times, and I've been pickpocketed once. I've also been mugged, which was really scary.' Apart from that, his only worry is the insects. He's been stung all over his body. He's been travelling mainly by public transport – bus, train, and ferry, but when he's been able to afford it, he's also taken the occasional plane. He's looking forward to taking things easy for another week, then setting off again for Australia. 'Once you've got the travel bug, it becomes very hard to stay in the same place for too long,' he said.

T 2.2

He's been stung all over his body.
He's visited royal palaces.
He's been staying in cheap hostels.
I've been pickpocketed and mugged.
I've met a lot of really great people.
He's been to Vietnam and Japan.

T 2.3

1 When and where was he born?
   In 1254 in Venice.
2 How long did it take to travel to China?
   Four years.
3 How long did he stay in China?
   For seventeen years.
4 What did he take back to Venice?
   Gold and jewellery.
5 What was his book called?
   The Travels of Marco Polo.
6 How long has he been away from home?
   For five months.
7 Which places has he been to?
   Thailand, Vietnam, Hong Kong, South Korea, and Japan.
8 Where's he been staying?
   In cheap hostels.
9 How many times has he had diarrhoea?
   A few times.
10 Has he been pickpocketed?
   Yes, once.

T 2.4

1 **Alan**
They are … one of the most eerie … and -er strange experiences you can possibly have. The first time I saw them, they appeared as a kind of shimmering curtain, over the top of a ridge of mountains, and they went from a greeny colour to a kind of purply red colour. And they just stayed there. The second time I saw them, it was the most amazing sight because they were right above our heads, and they covered the whole of the sky. The other interesting thing is that -er not everybody hears it, but they sometimes make a sound, a kind of -er buzzing noise. It was a real sense of wonder and awe. I just kind of sat there with my mouth hanging open, just feeling kind of small.

2 **James**
You start at the bottom of the valley, and slowly make your way up the hill, -er about a seven-hour hike until you get to a camp. Then you get up very early the next morning, about four o'clock, in order

to get there for the sunrise. You walk for an hour or so, and suddenly you reach this point where you're looking down on this ancient city, just as the sun is breaking through the clouds. It's the most extraordinary sight. And you walk around in the total silence of a city that's more than five hundred years old. At that point it's invaded by thousands of tourists, and -er it's time to go.

3 Willow
We got up about five o'clock in the morning. We went to the site, and set off. Because you're floating with the wind, there is no breeze on you, and it really was like ... flying like a bird. You could look down on everyone, and they were all so small, like ants. It was just amazing, and so silent. And we landed about seven o'clock, and suddenly we were back with the rest of civilization. It was just the most beautiful experience.

T 2.5

1 When you go for a job interview, it's important to make a good impression.
2 I think we're all getting tired. Can I make a suggestion? How about a break?
3 A lot of research has been done into the causes of cancer.
4 I think the director is basically doing a good job. He's reliable, he's honest, and he gets results.
5 I'd like to make it clear right now that I am totally opposed to this idea.
6 Right. I think we should make a start and get down to business.
7 I don't mind if we go now or later. It makes no difference to me.
8 Could you do me a favour and lend me some money till tomorrow?

T 2.6

1 I'm so thirsty. I could do with a cup of tea.
2 We've bought an old flat. We're going to do it up over the next few years.
3 I think we should do away with the monarchy. They're all useless. And expensive.
4 I could never do without my personal assistant. She organizes everything for me.

T 2.7

1 Thieves broke into the castle and made off with jewellery and antique paintings.
2 Jake's parents buy him loads of toys. They're trying to make up for always being at work.
3 What do you make of the new boss? I quite like him.
4 You didn't believe his story, did you? He made the whole thing up.

T 2.8 Tashi Wheeler – girl on the move

I = Interviewer, T = Tashi
Part one
I Now, travelling. Erm ... when did you start travelling?
T When I was eight months old.
I And where did you go?
T Erm I think we did a lot of South ... yeah we did a lot of South East Asia when I was younger. And Galapagos Islands, Philippines, and stuff like that.
I And your first memories ... OK, eight months, you started, but you presumably don't ...
T ... don't remember.
I What are your first memories of travelling?
T Erm ... airports. Erm ... what else? Beaches. It was a lot in Asia at the time, so it was always hot. Big fruit drinks, and ... I don't know, lots of bus rides.
I Was there a time at which you sort of felt 'Yeah, I quite enjoy this travelling', or was it ...? It sounds almost a bit of a chore, the way you describe it at the moment.
T No, it was never a chore. I always really enjoyed it. I think I was quite comfortable. Mum used to say that when I was two years old she just put me down and I just ran off. And she wouldn't see me

and then someone would pick me up and bring me back. I was quite happy fitting in everywhere.
I What do you think were your, your best memories of travelling? I mean, what can you actually remember that still stands out years on?
T From when I was much younger?
I Yes.
T Erm ... Africa, when I think I was around eight, or nine. We had ... we went on safaris there, and got chased by an elephant, had lion cubs jumping around the ... erm ... safari bus, monkeys swinging off the ... erm ... rear-view mirrors, and things. So that was ... and trekking in Nepal is something I'll always remember. The getting up at like four in the morning and looking over all the mountains, and then just walking all day, talking to porters, and coming into villages, and all the kids running out and seeing you, and things. There's lots of amazing experiences.

T 2.9 Part two

I And when you were on these travels, I mean, did your Dad sort of have a notebook, and he'd be sort of stopping everywhere ...?
T Constantly.
I ... and writing detailed notes of everywhere?
T Yeah, he's always got pen and paper and three or four guidebooks and other people's guidebooks and so on.
I And that must have made travelling a lot slower for you as a family.
T Oh, no. He's hectic, Dad. He's ... We land in a country, his feet hit the ground, and he takes off. We don't stop for two seconds. He gets up and goes out before we get up, comes back, gets us up, takes us to breakfast, we rush around all the sights, see everything, stop for one drink here, lunch somewhere else, dinner somewhere else, after dinner drink somewhere else, takes us back to the hotel and he goes out again, and goes on all night.
I Amazingly exhausting!
T Ah, it is! It's really exhausting! It got to a point where me and my brother ... what we really liked about travelling for a while was sitting at home watching movies and getting room service. That was quite exciting and different for us.
I This raises the question, of course, travel broadening the mind, as ... as ... is often said. Do you think it does?
T Yeah, definitely. I don't think you can travel and not have your mind broadened. We saw everything, we ran around, and it was hectic, but at the same time, you knew it was an experience while you were doing it, especially as you got older. And you value it. And still do.

T 2.10 Part three

I I was going to say, we've talked a bit about, you know, when you were really young. What about as you got older? I mean, how did the sort of experience and feel of it change, as you became say a teenager, and ... mid-teenage years and so on?
T You always wanted to stay home, summer holidays. I mean, just before you go away ... there'd be all your friends having parties and holidays and things, and you'd want to stay and hang out. But at the same time you knew you were doing something different, and everyone's always asking you about where you've been, and what you're doing, so you know you ... it's a privileged situation, and you're lucky to have it.
I Did that make it easier for you socially, or ... or not so easy?
T Erm ...
I Being different in that way, in that you'd travelled sort of more than anyone, really, hadn't you?
T I think it had its pros and cons. I think for a number of years, especially around probably thirteen to sixteen, I felt backward, I think, 'cos I didn't really know how to get along with kids my age and my own culture and country and stuff. Erm ... just from travelling for so long in places,

countries, cultures or whatever, where you can't talk to boys, or you can't look at people in a certain way, or you don't wear certain clothing, or something. And I think ... I don't know ... just the adjusting back and forth constantly did make it a little awkward. The kids at school seemed to be cool, and they had things going on, watch TV, and this programme was good, and I was never up to date with all that stuff, so I was constantly being pulled out of it and brought back. But at the same time, I did have that, like I'd seen things, I knew things, and stuff – just a broader view of life I guess.
I There is a view of travelling that you become a kind of world citizen, and the world is your home.
T Melbourne's definitely my home. But I do feel comfortable anywhere, particularly in Asia, I don't know ... I think I'm a real ... I just feel like I'm coming home when I go back to Asia. And after living for a year in Paris, I love going back there, but it's not really my home, I guess. No, Melbourne is definitely my home.
I Is there anywhere you fe... don't feel comfortable?
T Erm ... I haven't found that place yet! But you never know, I might. I haven't been everywhere.
I Your mother's not so long ago written a book about travelling with children, hasn't she? Is travelling ... would ... is that, is that something you'd sort of advocate, travelling with children? Would you travel with ... will you travel with your own children?
T Yeah, definitely. I think ... I mean ... it's a time where your ideas, your personality is being formed, and I think ... it can only benefit you. Really. I think it's something ... And you don't have as much time to do these things when you're older, so try to fit as much of it in as you can when you're younger. Definitely.
I So you'll continue travelling yourself, will you, do you think?
T I hope so. I really can't handle being in one place for too long. I get very itchy-footed.

T 2.11

1 How's your steak? Is it OK?
2 We were all going on holiday to Spain next week. We were really looking forward to it, but my father's been quite ill so we had to cancel the holiday.
3 A Has Ann had the baby yet? It must be due any time now.
  B Oh, yes. Haven't you heard? She didn't have one baby. She had three! Tom's the father of triplets!
4 Mind your head as you come through this door. It's very low.
5 Do be careful. That bowl's really heavy.
6 Did you know that they eat horse-meat in some countries? And snails. And pigs' feet.
7 Look! Isn't that Peter over there, sitting on his own?
8 Sarah told me that you hated me. She said that you never wanted to see me ever again!
9 I saw Julie yesterday.
10 Tomorrow's test has been cancelled!

T 2.12

1 A How's your steak? Is it OK?
  B Mmm! It's absolutely delicious! Just the way I like it.
2 A We were all going on holiday to Spain next week. We were really looking forward to it, but my father's been quite ill, so we had to cancel the holiday.
  B Ah! What a shame! You must be so disappointed!
3 A Has Ann had the baby yet? It must be due any time now.
  B Oh, yes. Haven't you heard? She didn't have one baby. She had three! Tom's the father of triplets!
  A Wow! That's unbelievable! How amazing! Triplets! That'll keep them busy!

4 A Mind your head as you come through this door. It's very low.
  B Ouch! That really hurt!
  A I told you! Well, it isn't bleeding, but you'll have a nice bruise.

5 A Do be careful. That bowl's really heavy.
  B Whoops! Sorry about that! I dropped it! Don't worry. I'll get you a new one.

6 A Did you know that they eat horse-meat in some countries? And snails. And pigs' feet.
  B Yuk! That's disgusting! You wouldn't catch me eating that!

7 A Look! Isn't that Peter over there, sitting on his own?
  B Hey, Peter! Come over here and sit with us. Let's have a chat.

8 A Sarah told me that you hated me. She said that you never wanted to see me ever again!
  B Uh? That's nonsense! What a stupid thing to say! You know it's not true.

9 A I saw Julie yesterday.
  B Oh, really? How interesting! I haven't seen her for ages. How is she?

10 A Tomorrow's test has been cancelled.
  B Phew! What a relief! Thank goodness for that! I hadn't done any revising for it at all.

T 2.13 See p25

T 2.14

1 I've just won $25,000 on the lottery!
2 Let's have a long coffee break!
3 Maria, you wrote 'at Rome' instead of 'in Rome'.
4 We were stuck in a traffic jam for four hours!
5 Look at the state of the kitchen! It hasn't been cleaned for weeks!
6 Rain, rain, rain.
7 The teacher told us to learn the dictionary for homework!
8 We hadn't heard from our daughter for a month, then she phoned last night.
9 My sister says it's possible to learn French in three months!
10 Yesterday I got a tax bill for $20,000.

UNIT 3

T 3.1

1 A Did you read that story about the guy who went over the Niagara Falls?
  B No. What happened to him? Did he die?
  A No, he survived, amazingly enough.
  B Really? But I suppose he was wearing some kind of protection.
  A That's the incredible thing. He was just wearing ordinary clothes. He just jumped in, fell down 180 feet, and somehow managed to avoid hitting the rocks.
  B That's amazing! What did he do it for?
  A Apparently he just did it for a dare. He'd been talking about doing it for ages. His friends had bet him he wouldn't do it.
  B What a crazy guy!
  A You're not kidding. The strange thing is, before he jumped, people around him said he'd been smiling.
  B Wow! How weird!

2 A There was this story the other day about … this woman mountain climber …
  B Uh huh. What about her?
  A Well, she was stuck on top of a mountain, and she only managed to escape by sending text messages.
  B Gosh! Where did this happen?
  A In the Swiss Alps, I think. She was climbing with a partner. They'd been climbing for three hours when they got trapped in a terrible storm.

  B You're kidding!
  A No. But they built a shelter or something, and they hid in that.
  B Then what happened?
  A She started sending text messages to friends in London, and one of them sent a text back saying that the mountain rescue teams in Switzerland had been contacted.
  B Uh huh.
  A They tried to find them, but the weather was too bad – storms and everything.
  B Oh, no!
  A Anyway, they were rescued the next night, and now they're safe and sound.
  B Thank goodness for that!

3 A I was reading in the paper the other day about a schoolboy who hacked into the United States military computers.
  B No! Really? How old was he? 17? 18?
  A Actually he was only 14.
  B How did he do it?
  A Well, he'd developed his own software program, and he'd been using this to download films and music from the Internet.
  B I don't get it. What's that got to do with the US military?
  A Well, he'd figured that if he broke into these powerful military computers, he could use them to download stuff even faster, so he wasn't really trying to get to their secrets.
  B Oh, I see. I bet they were worried, though.
  A They were. They got in touch with Scotland Yard, and this boy was tracked down to his house in North London.
  B And he's only 14! They should give him a job!

T 3.2

He was wearing ordinary clothes.
He'd been talking about doing it for ages.
His friends had bet him he wouldn't do it.
She was climbing with a partner.
They were rescued the next night.

T 3.3

This is the six o'clock news.
Ten workers have been rescued from an accident 400 feet beneath the streets of London. They had spent the past 36 hours trapped underground. They had been digging a tunnel for a new Underground line when the roof collapsed. Sixty men managed to escape immediately, but two were fatally injured. Last night the ten men were recovering in hospital. An investigation into the cause of the accident is due to start tomorrow.

T 3.4

Three children who had been missing for two days have been found safe and well. The three ten-year-olds, two boys and a girl, disappeared after school on Wednesday. Police had issued photographs of the three, and had been searching nearby houses. They were eventually spotted by a neighbour, who alerted the police. They said they had slept out in a garden shed for a dare, and hadn't realized the concern they had caused.

T 3.5 Books and films

Paul
Certainly one of my favourite films is *Witness*. It's the one starring Harrison Ford, where he plays a detective who's investigating a murder that an Amish child has witnessed, and he has to protect the child and to do that at one point he has to go and spend some time living with the Amish community. Now the Amish community are that religious group … erm … in America who live a very old-fashioned lifestyle. They have no modern gadgets and no modern technology because their religion doesn't allow it. Now, Harrison Ford plays this very tough, hard-nosed city cop and there are some wonderful scenes where his values and culture really clash with

this very peaceful Amish community. It's also, it has a love story in it because he falls in love with the boy's mother, who's Amish. It's a very, very intense and passionate love story, and it's a thriller because it deals with police corruption, and it's unbearably tense and the build up towards the end is incredible. It really, really does have you on the edge of your seat.

Kate
I don't know if I'd say this is my favourite book, but this is certainly a book that made … erm … quite an impression on me. The book is called … erm … *The Secret History* and it's by Donna Tartt, and … erm … without actually giving away entirely what happens in the story, … erm … *The Secret History* is about a group of students and it's all about somebody's desire to belong to a group. And in fact the group of students … erm … do something really, really terrible. Erm … they are involved in a murder and you know right from the beginning of the novel that this is going to happen and so you would think that there isn't any element of suspense because you know that somebody's going to die and you have some idea about how they're actually going to die, but in fact … erm … the whole story's very, very claustrophobic. You feel sort of trapped inside the group and trapped inside their situation. It's completely compelling to read. It's not a comfortable read but it was about 600 pages long and I read it in about a week … erm … and I lived and breathed this book over that week. Erm … I would recommend it to anybody who wants to read something that psychologically is really dramatic.

T 3.6 The money jigsaw

I = Interviewer, R = Rachel

I Well and one of those girls, Rachel Aumann, is on the line now as we speak. Good morning to you, Rachel.
R Good morning.
I Erm … extraordinary, this. You saw these bits of bank notes just blowing in the wind?
R Yeah, it was … erm … like really out of the ordinary. We were just walking to school and there's ripped up notes flying all over the floor. And then we traced it to like a bin, so that's where the … the big bag was full of them.
I How big a bag?
R Erm …
I Like a bin bag or something?
R No, actually, not that big … erm … it's about, I think it was like a Sainsbury's bag, like one of those.
I And it was just jammed full of torn-up banknotes, what fivers and tenners and that sort of thing?
R Yeah, just fives, tens, twenties.
I And how little were the pieces?
R Erm … some were bigger than stamp sizes.
I That small though?
R Yeah, some were smaller.
I And so what did you do? You took them to the police or something?
R Erm we, we had to go to school so we went to school and then … erm … after school we were playing outside around … erm … like on the same road and … erm … when the police arrived we were, we went over then and started talking to them and telling them when we found it.
I And they took them away at that stage, did they?
R Yeah.
I And then what happened?
R Erm … they kept them for like a long time 'cos there's a certain amount of months that they have to keep them before you, they can give them back.
I Right.
R And I think they went to the Royal Bank of England and to Scotland Yard and … erm … when … erm … they said yeah, it's real money … erm … they gave it back and we put it together.

I You say you put it together, but tiny bits of bank notes it must have taken you forever to do ... I mean, what a jigsaw puzzle!

R Yeah it's taken ages 'cos it's been about a year and we still haven't finished.

I So how many have you got left now then?

R Erm ... we have all the fives to do and just a few twenties but the tens are all finished.

I Extraordinary! Is it ... how much time do you spend doing this?

R Erm ... well when we first got it we did like half an hour, an hour a day but then as like time passed we just slowly like died down and didn't do as much.

I But I'm trying to picture you doing this. What do you do, do you stick bits of sellotape or something, or do you stick them onto a piece of paper or what?

R Well you have to get, you get the two serial numbers and ... erm ... then you have to get like a little bit from the middle of the note and so once you've got that, you just put sticky tape on the back of them so that they all stay together and put it in a bag.

I Good heavens! And you're going to carry on doing it, eh?

R Yeah, hopefully.

I £1200 so far?

R Erm ... yeah.

I And how much do you reckon you will be worth at the end of it all?

R Erm ... I think we we if stick to it we could probably get about £2,000.

I Well, I think that you've earned every penny of it, Rachel. Thank you very much.

R Thank you.

T 3.7

A Jade's got a new boyfriend.
B A new boyfriend? Good for her!
A Apparently, he lives in a castle.
B Does he? How amazing!
A Yes. She met him in Slovenia.
B In Slovenia? That's interesting.
A Unfortunately, he can't speak much English.
B Can't he? I thought everyone could these days!

T 3.8   See p33

T 3.9

1 **A** Sam wants to apologize.
  B Does he?
  A Yes. He's broken your mother's Chinese vase.
  B My mother's Chinese vase? Oh, no!
2 **A** We had a terrible holiday.
  B Did you?
  A Yes. It rained all the time.
  B Did it?
  A Yes. And the food was disgusting!
  B Was it? What a drag!
3 **A** I'm broke.
  B Are you? How come?
  A Because I just had a phone bill for £500.
  B £500? Why so much?
  A Because I have a girlfriend in Korea.
  B Do you? How interesting!
4 **A** It took me three hours to get here.
  B Did it?
  A Yes. There was a traffic jam ten miles long.
  B Ten miles long? That's awful!
  A Now I've got a headache!
  B Have you? Poor darling. I'll get you something for it.
5 **A** I'm on a mountain, watching the sun set.
  B Are you?
  A Yes. And I've got something very important to ask you.
  B Have you? What is it? I can't wait!
  A You'd better sit down. I'd like to marry you.
  B Marry me? Wow!

UNIT 4

T 4.1

1 Oh dear! It's not that I *dislike* him, I just don't *love* him. How can I tell him I don't want to marry him without hurting his feelings? Trouble is, I actually fancy his best friend!
2 There's this group of lads you see – they're always chasing me and I don't think it's for fun. But I can't tell my mum and dad – if they find out, they'll go to the head teacher and complain and that would make everything much worse.
3 How do you tell someone when they look awful? That dress doesn't suit her at all. But I don't know how to tell her. She obviously thinks she looks great in it.
4 Me and Emma are going clubbing, but I daren't tell my Dad – he'd kill me. I've got an important exam next week and I haven't done a thing for it. I haven't a clue when I'll be back.
5 I know I'm not really ill. But it's a beautiful day and I don't want to sit in a stuffy office all day. I'm off to play golf. I never have days off usually.
6 I don't care who it is. I had a late night and I feel really rough this morning. Tell them I'm in an important meeting and I don't want be disturbed at the moment.

T 4.2

1 Who did she give it to?
2 What do you want to have a word about?
3 Who did you dance with?
4 What do you need it for?
5 Who did you get it from?
6 Who did you buy it for?
7 What are you thinking about?
8 Where do you want a lift to?

T 4.3   See p36

T 4.4

1 **A** Don't you like ice-cream?
  B No. I know it's weird, but I never have done. Not even vanilla.
2 **A** Don't you like learning English?
  B No, actually, I don't. I think it's really difficult.
3 **A** Don't you like your neighbours?
  B Well, they're all right, but they make a lot of noise.
4 **A** Haven't you ever been abroad?
  B Not really. I went to Scotland once, but that's not really abroad, is it?
5 **A** Haven't you got a TV at home?
  B No. We must be the only people in the whole world without a telly.
6 **A** Isn't it Tuesday today?
  B Yeap. It follows on from Monday.
7 **A** Isn't this your pen?
  B No, it isn't, actually. Mine's blue. That's black.
8 **A** Didn't you go to the States last year?
  B You bet. All down the east coast from Boston to Florida.
9 **A** Aren't you going to the races next weekend?
  B Uh huh. And I bet I'll lose a fortune. Hey ho!

T 4.5   My mate Norman

Part one
My mate Norman's a funny guy. He's an insomniac, he's dyslexic, and he's an atheist. He's single, unemployed, and lives all alone in a tiny one-roomed flat without even a pet for company. Also he's vegetarian and teetotal. He's -er pretty anti-social, actually.

Part two
I went round to see him last Sunday. As I walked up the drive, his dog started barking. His wife answered the door, and she called for Norman to come downstairs and join us in the living room. He was in a bad mood because he'd overslept that morning

and he'd been late for church. He also had a bit of an hangover, which he told me was the result of a wild party that they'd had at his house the night before. All his friends from his office were there. They'd had a barbecue in the garden with steaks and burgers. One of his favourite pastimes is doing crosswords, and while he was talking to me, he was doing one of those big puzzles from the newspaper.
'So how are you, Norman?' I asked him.
'KO, mate, KO. How about you?'
Anyway, as I said, Norman's an insomniac, dyslexic, atheist. So the joke is that he lies awake all night wondering about the existence of dog. Get it?

T 4.6   My most memorable lie

1 **Andrew**
Well, one lie I can remember from when I was younger was when, with a friend in the basement of my house, we were playing pool, 'cos we had a pool table down there, and decided to smoke our first cigarettes, these fantastic gold-filtered cigarettes, I remember – quite expensive – and halfway through the second or third cigarette, my dad came home, who was very anti-smoking, and we stubbed out our cigarettes and pushed them through a kind of grate underneath the window and he found them about a day later and he asked me if these, you know, if I knew what these cigarette stubs were all about, if I'd been smoking, and I completely denied all knowledge of these cigarettes and in fact pool, and the basement, and everything else.

2 **Paul**
I have one memory of regularly lying as a child and ironically it was to a priest, which sounds a bit alarming, but ... erm ... I was brought up Catholic and from the age of seven you had to go to confession every week and confess your sins and when you're that age, ... erm ... first of all you're not quite sure what a proper sin is, and also you just can't remember, and every week you had to go in and, and tell the priest some sins that you'd committed, so of course it's, it's quite common that what you end up doing is just making things up ... erm ... you say, 'I swore and I stole some biscuits from the pantry in the kitchen ...' and bizarrely what you end up doing is lying to the priest so that you've got something to say in your confession.

3 **Carolyn**
I can think of a, a time recently when I had to tell a white lie which was ... erm ... basically when a friend of mine got married. Erm ... it, they actually got married in America because his wife's American, so I didn't go to the wedding but they, they were showing me the photos and ... erm ... basically she looked absolutely awful she had a really horrible dress on that really did nothing for her figure and didn't suit her at all and just looked much older than she really is and quite frumpy, but ... erm ... yes obviously you can't say that when you see someone's wedding pictures, so I said 'that's really pretty, you look really lovely'. I felt really horrible as a result.

4 **Kiki**
One lie I can remember telling was when I lost a necklace that my grandmother had made for me especially – it had a 'K' on it. And I know where I lost it, I lost it at a party because ... erm ... I was having a very good time and wasn't taking care of it and I lied and told her it had been stolen in a robbery we had at our house. And to this day I've never told her what happened to it. But sometimes when she mentions things like 'Ooh I should get you another one', ... er ... it comes back to me.

5 **Sean**
The first lie I can really remember ... erm ... was – when I was at school. I must have been about five or six years old and I was in the playground and I was just about to get into a fight and ... erm ... the only way I could think of defending myself was to say ... erm ... 'You can't hit me, I go to judo lessons'. Erm ... and I don't know where it came from, I'd never done

judo in my life and ... erm ... I wasn't even sure what judo was, but people left me alone ... erm ... because they thought I did judo. Erm ... but then people started to take an interest, they asked me where I went, and when the lessons were, how much they cost, and ... erm ... eventually somebody's mother rang my mother to get details of, of these judo lessons, which was when I had to admit that it was all, it was all a lie and ... erm ... it was a bit embarrassing really.

6 Kate
I do remember ... erm ... possibly the first time I, I told a lie as a child because it had some rather unpleasant consequences ... erm ... this happened when I was about ... er ... maybe four or five years old, and I had been ... erm ... playing with the dressing-up box that we had in our children's playroom, which was an enormous box full of wonderful ... erm ... clothes, and you could be a princess, you could be a soldier, you could be whatever, whatever you found in the dressing up box. And I was playing with our pet cat, and I put him in the box, and I left him there, and I shut the lid for hours and hours and hours and – I was four or five, I forgot about him – and I went off and did something else and didn't think any more of it, and when my mother asked after the cat, ... erm ... struck with horror, I lied and, and said that I hadn't seen him, and I hadn't played with him, and I probably said 'and I didn't put him in the dressing-up box' because my mother went and found him, and I do remember telling this lie because I was spanked for it.

T 4.7

1 A Gary's a really successful businessman.
   B Yeah, but he's a complete failure as a family man. He never sees his children.
2 A My grandad's so generous he gives me £20 every time I see him.
   B Lucky you! My grandad's famous for his meanness. A fiver every birthday, *if* he remembers.
3 A Well, Henry, I'm pleased there's been some improvement in your behaviour this term ... but sadly your work has got worse.
   B Didn't I do OK in the test then?
4 A You're not going bungee-jumping! It sounds really dangerous.
   B No, honestly, it's safe enough as long as you're careful.
5 A Our teacher is always criticizing us. I feel useless.
   B I know – it's not fair, he should give us more encouragement if he wants us to work hard.

T 4.8

1 A What a boring party!
   B You're right, it wasn't exactly an exciting evening.
2 A I don't know about you, but I thought the holiday was awful.
   B Well, it wasn't the most fun I've had.
3 A I can't believe how mean Jane is!
   B Mmmm, I suppose she's not famous for her generosity.
4 A That was one helluva difficult exam! I couldn't do a thing.
   B Too right, I've seen easier papers.

T 4.9

1 I'm sorry to bother you, but could you possibly change a ten-pound note?
   Have you got change for a ten-pound note?
2 Where's the station?
   Could you tell me where the station is, please?
3 A This is a present for you.
   B For me! Oh, how kind! You shouldn't have, really. Thank you so much.
   C This is a present for you.
   D Thanks.

4 A Can you come to a party on Saturday?
   B No, I can't.
   C Can you come to a party on Saturday?
   D Oh, what a pity! I'm already going out, I'm afraid.
   C Oh well, never mind!
   D But, thanks for the invitation anyway.
5 A Excuse me! Do you mind if I sit down here?
   B No, not at all.
   C Is anyone sitting here?
   D No.
6 A Can you give me a hand? I need to carry this box upstairs.
   B OK, if you like.
   C I wonder if I could possibly ask you a favour? Would you mind helping me with this box?
   D No, not at all.

T 4.10 See p43

T 4.11

1 A Do you think you could give me a lift to the station?
   B I'm terribly sorry, I can't. I have to be at work by 8.30. I'll order you a taxi, though.
2 A Could you possibly help me find my glasses? I can't find them anywhere.
   B Sorry! I'm afraid I have to dash or I'll miss the bus. I'm hopeless at finding things anyway.
3 A Hi! Listen, would you like to come round for a meal tomorrow evening? I'm cooking Chinese.
   B Oh, I'd love to, but I'm afraid I'm already going out.
   A Oh, what a shame! Another time perhaps.
4 A Would you mind lending me your dictionary?
   B I would if I could but I'm afraid I forgot to bring it with me today. Sorry.
5 A Hi, it's Susan here. Could I ask you a big favour? I wonder if you could look after my dog next week? I'm going on holiday.
   B I'm terribly sorry, Susan, but I can't. I'd love to have Molly, you know I adore dogs, but I'm going away myself for a few days.
6 A Do you happen to know where the toilet is?
   B Sorry. I'm afraid I've no idea. Ask the guy serving drinks, he'll know.
7 A Would you like me to help you with this exercise? I think I know the answers.
   B That's really kind of you but I want to try and work it out for myself. Thanks anyway.
8 A Excuse me. Would you mind *not* whistling?
   B I'm sorry. I didn't realize I was.
   A That's OK.

T 4.12

A = Anna, B = Ben, H = Henry
B Kim! Hello! Great to see you. Come on in. Let me take your coat.
Kim Thanks very much. Oh, these are for you.
A What lovely flowers! How kind of you! Thank you so much. Now, I don't think you know Henry! Let me introduce you. Henry, this is Kim.
H Hello, Kim. Nice to meet you. I've heard a lot about you.
Kim Oh, I hope it was all good!
H Where exactly are you from, Kim?
Kim Well, I'm Canadian. I was born in Saskatoon but I've been working in the US for the last couple of years.
H That's interesting. And what are you doing in London?
Kim Work, I'm sorry to say. Actually, I'm on my way to Amsterdam for a conference, and I thought I'd stop over in London to see Anna and Ben. We used to work together in New York.
H And how do you find London, Kim? Is it like home, or is it very different?
Kim Well, it's very different from Saskatoon and New York! I know London quite well, actually, I always love it here.

B Now, Kim. What would you like to drink?
Kim Oh, could I have a beer? No, sorry, I'll have a glass of red wine, if that's OK.
B Right. I'll just get that for you.
Kim Thanks.
A Right, everybody. Dinner's ready. Come and sit down. Kim, can you sit next to Henry?
Kim Yes, of course.
B Has everyone got a drink? Cheers, everybody!
Kim Cheers! It's great to be here.
A Kim, help yourself. Would you like some Parmesan parsnips?
Kim Parmesan parsnips? I don't think I've ever had them. What are they?
A Well, they're parsnips coated in Parmesan cheese and roasted. Would you like to try some?
Kim Well, I'd love to but I'd better not – cheese doesn't always agree with me.
B Another glass of wine, perhaps?
Kim No, I'm alright, thanks very much. But d'you think I could have a glass of water?
B Yes, of course. Sparkling or still?
Kim Just tap water would be fine. That's great Thanks a lot.
A Well, *bon appetit* everyone!

UNIT 5

T 5.1

1 I did my A-levels a few months ago, and I've just got my results. Fortunately, they're good, so I'm going to study psychology at Bristol University. The course lasts three years.
2 It's Saturday tomorrow, so I'm going to see the football with my boy and some mates. Oxford United are playing Bristol Rovers. It'll be a great game. Kick-off is at 3 o'clock, so we'll have a beer or two before the match.
3 Marie's having a baby soon, so we're both very excited. The baby's due in five weeks. If it's a boy, we're going to call him Jamie. And if it's a girl, she'll be Hatty.
4 What am I doing tomorrow, you say? Well, it's Thursday tomorrow, so I'll be doing what I always do on a Thursday. My daughter will come to see me, she'll be bringing the little 'uns, and we'll all have a cup of tea and a good old chat. And I'll bake a cake. A sponge cake with jam in it. They like that.
5 At the moment I'm packing, because tomorrow I'm going to France for a year. I'm going to study literature at the Sorbonne. My plane leaves at 10.30. My mum and dad are taking me to the airport. I have absolutely no idea how I'm going to carry all this lot.
6 Well, I work in the City. In the next few years I'm going to be even more successful. I hope I'll be earning twice what I'm getting now. I've set myself this goal. Before I'm twenty-five I'll have made a million.

T 5.2

1 She's going to study psychology.
   It lasts three years.
2 He's going to a football match.
   The match starts at 3.00.
3 Because they're going to have a baby.
4 Her daughter and grandchildren will be visiting.
   They'll have a cup of tea and a chat.
5 Because she's going to France for a year.
   Her mother and father are taking her.
6 He's going to be successful. He'll be earning a lot of money. He'll have made a million pounds before he's twenty-five.

T 5.3

1 Which university is she going to?
2 Who's he going to the match with? Who's playing?
3 What are they going to call the baby?
4 What sort of cake is she going to bake?
5 What time does her plane leave?
6 How much will he be earning?

T 5.4

1 I'm very excited. I'm going to see all my family this weekend.
  I don't know if I have time to come this evening. I'll see.
2 So you're off to the States for a year! What are you going to do there?
  I'm sure you will pass your exams, but what will you do if you don't?
3 I'll come with you if you like.
  I'm coming with you whether you like it or not.
4 Your school report is terrible. What are you going to do about it?
  What are you doing this evening?
5 I've had enough of her lazy attitude. I'm going to give her a good talking to.
  I'm giving a presentation at 3.00 this afternoon. I'm scared stiff.
6 John! Peter is leaving now. Come and say goodbye.
  The coach leaves at 9.00, so don't be late.
7 I'll see you outside the cinema at 8.00.
  I'll be seeing Peter this afternoon, so I'll tell him your news.
8 You'll have seen enough of me by the end of this holiday.
  I'm going to make a success of my life. You'll see.

T 5.5

This is your captain speaking. Good morning, ladies and gentlemen. Welcome on board this British Airways flight to Rome. In a very short time we'll be taking off. When we've reached our cruising speed of 550 miles per hour, we'll be flying at 35,000 feet. Our flight time today is two and a half hours, so we'll be in Rome in time for lunch. The cabin crew will be serving refreshments during the flight. If you need any assistance, just press the button and a flight attendant will come to help you.
(Near the end of the flight)
In a few moments' time, the crew will be coming round with duty-free goods. We will also be giving out landing cards. When you have filled them in, place them in your passport. They will be collected as you go through passport control. In twenty minutes' time we will be landing at Leonardo da Vinci airport. Please put your seats in the upright position. You are requested to remain seated until the plane has come to a complete standstill. We hope you will fly again soon with British Airways.

T 5.6

1 Do you think you'll ever be rich?
  I hope so.
  I might one day.
  It's possible, but I doubt it.
  I'm sure I will.
  I'm sure I won't.
2 Are you going out tonight?
  Yes, I am.
  I think so, but I'm not sure.
  I might be.
3 Do you think the world's climate will change dramatically in the next fifty years?
  I don't think so.
  I hope not.
  Who knows? Maybe.

T 5.7

1 The wedding took place in an old country church. It was lovely, but it was miles away. It took ages to get there.
2 My son's buying cigarettes, but I'll soon put a stop to that. I won't give him any more pocket money.

3 Please don't take offence, but I don't think your work has been up to your usual standard recently.
4 I told you that boy was no good for you. You should have taken my advice and had nothing to do with him.
5 The older you get, the more you have to learn to take responsibility for your own life.
6 My boss is putting pressure on me to resign, but I won't go.
7 I tried to get the teacher's attention but she took no notice of me at all.
8 Children never say 'Thank you' or 'How are you?' to their parents. They just take them for granted.

T 5.8

1 The shop takes on a lot of extra staff every Christmas.
2 The lecture was too complicated, and the students couldn't take it all in.
3 My business really took off after I picked up six new clients.
4 You called me a liar, but I'm not. Take that back and say sorry!

T 5.9

1 Put some music on. Whatever you want.
2 That article about factory farming has really put me off eating chicken.
3 Could you put away your clothes, please. Your room's a total mess.
4 Put your cigarette out! You can't smoke in here.

T 5.10 The reunion

A = Alan   S = Sarah
S Hello. 267890.
A Hello. Is that Sarah?
S Speaking.
A Hi, Sarah. It's Alan, Alan Cunningham.
S Alan! Hi! How are you? How are things?
A OK, yeah, not too bad, thanks. And you? How's the family?
S Oh, we're surviving! Busy, busy, busy, but what's new?
A Tell me about it! Listen, I'm phoning about our reunion ...
S Oh, yes? On the fourteenth, right? Friday night. I can't wait. I'm really looking forward to it.
A Have you any ideas where we can meet? A restaurant somewhere?
S Well, what do you fancy? Indian? A Chinese? There's that really good Chinese we used to go to in Claypath.
A Oh, yes. What's it called?
S The Lotus Garden.
A That's right. Now, I'm driving from the Midlands, so I'll be coming into Durham from the M1. Where can I park?
S There's a car park bang opposite the restaurant.
A That's great. I'll be leaving about 3.00 in the afternoon, so I should be in Durham about 5, 6 o' clock depending on the traffic.
S Where are you staying?
A In The County. What about you?
S Oh, that's good. I'm staying in The Three Tuns, just down the road. We can meet up for a drink.
A Sounds great! How are you getting there?
S By train. It's direct from Leeds, so it's easy. The journey takes less than an hour. I'm getting the 17.05. Why don't I come to The County at about 6.30? I'll see you in the bar.
A All right. That sounds great. Will you phone James, or shall I?
S Erm ... No, don't worry. I'll phone him.
A OK. So I'll see you in the bar of The County on the fourteenth. I presume there's only one.
S Well, it's not that big. I'm sure we won't lose each other!
A True. OK. See you then.
S About 6.30.
A That's it. Bye.
S Bye. Take care.

T 5.11 The reunion

J = James   S = Sarah
J Hello. Simpson's Travel Agents.
S Hello, James. This is Sarah Jackson. How are you?
J Sarah! Hello! How lovely to hear from you!
S Sorry to disturb you at work.
J Oh, don't worry. I'm only too pleased to be interrupted. How's everything with you?
S Oh, fine. Have you got a lot on at the moment?
J Well, it's our busy time of year. Still, I mustn't complain.
S That's right. Business is business! Anyway, James, I spoke to Alan yesterday, you know, about our get-together in Durham on the fourteenth, and I'm just ringing to let you know what's happening.
J Great!
S We've decided to meet in the Lotus Garden, the er ... Chinese restaurant ...
J You mean the one in Claypath?
S Yes.
J Where we all used to go?
S Yeah.
J Oh.
S Why? Is that no good?
J Er ... it closed about three years ago.
S Oh, dear. Are you sure?
J Uh huh. Absolutely. But it doesn't matter. There's the other one, the Kwai Lam.
S Now where's that? I've forgotten.
J It's on the corner of Saddler Street.
S Oh, great. OK. Now, how are you coming from Sunderland?
J Well, I'm so close. I'll be catching the bus. The office closes at 6.00, and I'll go straight to the bus station.
S So you'll be there at about ... what? Seven?
J Yeah, something like that.
S Well, look. Why don't we see you in the Kwai Lam? I'm meeting Alan in The County before that, because we both get in earlier than you.
J OK. I'll phone Alan and sort it all out.
S Great. What about if we see you in the Kwai Lam between seven and half past? How does that sound?
J Fine. That'll give me enough time, I'm sure. Shall I phone and book a table?
S Good idea. By the way, where are you staying that night?
J I'm going to phone a friend of mine to see if he can put me up for the night.
S Oh, lovely! Well, we'll see you on the fourteenth, then, around 7.15.
J In the restaurant, that's it. And you know where it is, don't you?
S Yeah, yeah, I've got it. Bye, now, James.
J Bye, Sarah. Thanks for phoning.

T 5.12

1 A Hello. The Regent Hotel. Kathy speaking. How can I help you?
  B Hello. I was wondering if I could book a room ...

2 A Hello.
  B Hello, Pat. It's me, Dave.
  A Dave! Hi! How are things?
  B Not bad. Busy, busy, busy, but life's like that. How's everything with you?
  A Oh, you know, we've all got the flu, and Mike's away on business, so I've got to do the lot. School, shop, kids, cook, clean. It's great! What are you up to?
  B This and that ...
  A How's your mother, by the way?
  B She's a lot better, thanks. Really on the mend.

3 Welcome to National Phones. To help us deal with your call more efficiently, please select one of the following options.
  For customer services, press 1. To query a bill, press 2. To request a brochure, press 3.
  To return to the beginning of this menu, press the hash key. To speak to an operator, please hold.

A Hello. TVS Computers. Samantha speaking. How can I help you?
B Good morning. Could I speak to your customer services department, please?
A Certainly. Who's calling?
B This is Keith Jones.
A (*pause*) I'm afraid the line's busy at the moment. Will you hold?
B Yes, please.
A (*pause*) OK. It's ringing for you now.
B Thank you.
C (*ring, ring*) Hello. Customer services.
B Hello. I was wondering if you could help me ...

T 5.14

A So, Barry. It was good to talk to you. Thanks very much for phoning.
B My pleasure. By the way, how's your golf these days? Still playing?
A No, not much. I just don't seem to find the time these days. Anyway, Barry ...
B What a shame! You used to enjoy it so much.
A It's true. Right, Barry. I must fly. I'm late for a meeting.
B OK. Don't want to keep you. So, you'll give me a ring when you're back, right?
A I certainly will. And you'll send me a copy of the report?
B It'll be in the post tonight.
A That's great, Barry. Have a good weekend!
B Same to you, too! Bye, Andy.
A Bye, Barry.

UNIT 6

T 6.1 Jamie Oliver

At only 28, Jamie Oliver is now an extremely successful and well known chef, with his own acclaimed restaurant in the centre of London. He has made quite a few TV series, written four books, and still does a large number of live shows a year. He doesn't have many free days now. How did he make it big?
Well, his rise to fame and fortune came early and swiftly. By the age of eight he had already started cooking at his parents' pub. It was an easy way to earn a little pocket money! After a couple of years in catering college, and a little time spent in France, he started working in restaurants. He worked under a few famous chefs in London, before he was spotted by a TV producer at 21, and his life changed.
Even though he had hardly any experience, he had a lot of enthusiasm for cooking, and was very natural in front of the camera. His first TV programme featured him zipping around London on his scooter buying ingredients and cooking for his friends, all to a rock and roll soundtrack. The recipes were bare and simple – they didn't involve complicated cooking techniques and used lots of fresh ingredients and herbs. It attracted a completely new audience that previously didn't have any interest in food programmes. Jamie Oliver became an overnight success.
So what's his recipe for success? 'A little bit of luck, a little bit of passion, and a little bit of knowledge!' he says.

T 6.2

1 'How much money have you got in your pocket?'
  'About twenty euros.'
2 'How many cups of coffee do you drink a day?'
  'It depends. I have milky coffee for breakfast, sometimes another mid-morning, then maybe one or two, black, after lunch and dinner.'
3 'How many times have you been on a plane?'
  'About five or six.'
4 'How much time do you spend watching TV?'
  'A couple of hours a night, just before I go to bed, I suppose.'

5 'How much sugar do you have in your coffee?'
  'Just half a spoonful in white coffee, and none in black.'
6 'How many pairs of jeans do you have?'
  'Three. A black pair, a blue pair, and an old pair I wear when I do dirty jobs like cleaning the car.'
7 'How many books do you read in one year?'
  'I honestly don't know. Ten? Fifteen? I read most when I'm on holiday.'
8 'How much homework do you get a night?'
  'Too much! About two hours, maybe? It depends.'
9 'How many English teachers have you had?'
  'Er ... let me see ... about ten, I guess.'
10 'How many films do you watch a month?'
  'One or two in the cinema, and one or two on television.'

T 6.3

1 There's no need to rush. We've got masses of time.
2 She's got bags of money. I think she inherited it.
3 We've got heaps of food for the party. Don't buy any more.
4 When my daughter comes back from university, she always brings piles of washing.
5 I can't see you today. I've got tons of things to do.
6 There were millions of people at the sales. I couldn't be bothered to fight my way through them.

T 6.4 Six radio adverts

1 **S = Sarah M = Mummy**
Sarah is five, and this is her favourite play shirt. It's pink, with fluffy yellow ducks. Sarah loves her play shirt.
  S It's my favourite.
And she wears it to play in the garden.
  S Look what I've found, Mummy!
And you wash it at low temperature. And she wears it to play in the garden.
  S Mummy! Look what I've made!
And you wash it. And she wears it to play in the garden.
  M Sarah! What on earth ... ?
And after a while, the dirt builds up, so the pink isn't quite as pink, and the yellow ducks aren't as fluffy. New System Sudso Automatic can help. Its advanced formula can remove ground-in dirt even at low temperatures. So the pink stays very pink, and the fluffy yellow ducks are happy again. Wash ...
  S Mummy! Look what I've made!
... after wash ...
  S Look what I've found, Mummy!
... after wash ...
  M Sarah! Don't you dare bring that in here!
New System Sudso Automatic. It's all you could want from a powder.

2 **A** 'Ere, Bill! Just ... just watch this. Look! Look at that car trying to park!
  B Ooh! You're joking! Ooh-ooh! Now that just has to be a woman driver. It must be.
  A It's gotta be. 'Ere, do you want some help, love? Hey, look! Look at her now! Look! Look!
  B I don't believe it! She's just whacked that GTI! Are you all right, darling?
  A It's a bloke.
  B Bloke. Oh. It was a tight space, though, wannit, eh? [Oh, yeah.] Really.
  A Yeah, that space, very tight space. Yeah.
  B Complicated.
Since men are responsible for 81% of parking offences and 96% of dangerous driving offences, why should women have to pay the same for car insurance? At Swinton, we have access to policies with up to 20% reductions for women. For a competitive quote, contact your local branch, or Freefone Swinton on 0800 600 700.

3 **C = Child D = Daddy**
  C Daddy! Daddy! Today I did a painting of you! And I got two stars! And Miss Lewis says I was the best in class!
  D You're a very naughty girl!

  C Why daddy?
  D Don't argue with your father, young lady! Now, go to your room ...! It's no use crying about it. Go on! Go on! Get out!
Wednesday's UEFA Champion's League night. Manchester United – Bayern Munich. 7.30. ITV 1. Do not disturb.

4 **D = Daughter F = Father**
  D Well, Dad. I've decided which new car I'm getting.
  F It's all right for some. When I was your age ...
  D ... you counted yourself lucky to have a bike. And that was second-hand.
  F Now, well, that's where you're wrong, Miss Smartypants. I was going to say that when I was twenty-two. I couldn't even have afforded to insure a new car.
  D Neither can I.
  F Well, don't expect me ...
  D ... and I don't have to. 'Cos all new Ford Escorts now come with one year's free insurance, for anyone between 18 and 80. Which rules you out, anyway.
See your Thames Ford dealer now, as offer ends soon. Free insurance, subject to age and status.
  F Just like your mother. Always have to have the last word.
  D No I don't.

5 Hi, this is Sue. Please leave a message.
  Hi Sue. Met you last night. Just wondering if you –er want to meet up sometime. Erm, I'm going away soon, so maybe it could be soon. Er, don't want to sound too keen. Not that I'm not keen, 'cos I am. Well, you know, within reason. Anyway, maybe lunch, or maybe just a drink? Not that you shouldn't do lunch, I mean you're not, you're not fat –er, you're not fat at all actually, you've got a great, –erm ... Not that that's important, it, it's personality that counts. Erm, anyway ...
Have a break. Have a Kit Kat.

6 **P = Priest T = Tony**
  P Er–hem! Everyone! Welcome! We're gathered here today, in the presence of others, to marry Tony and Helen. Helen, do you take Tony to be your husband? Just nod. Tony, do you take her?
  T I w...
  P Lovely rings. Oop! Leave it! Leave it! Kiss! Lovely. Husband and wife. Wife, husband. Right. You're married. Jolly good. I'm outa here.
Come to IKEA after work. But don't rush! We're open till 10 p.m. weeknights.

T 6.5

a	'export	ex'port
b	'import	im'port
c	'decrease	de'crease
d	'increase	in'crease
e	'progress	pro'gress
f	'record	rec'ord
g	'refund	re'fund
h	'produce	pro'duce
i	'permit	per'mit
j	'transport	trans'port
k	'insult	in'sult
l	'protest	pro'test

T6.6

1 Scotland imports a lot of its food from other countries. Its exports include oil, beef, and whisky.
2 I'm very pleased with my English. I'm making a lot of progress.
3 Ministers are worried. There has been an increase in the number of unemployed.
4 But the number of crimes has decreased, so that's good news.
5 How dare you call me a liar and a cheat! What an insult!
6 There was a demonstration yesterday. People were protesting about blood sports.

7 He ran 100m in 9.75 seconds and broke the world record.
8 Don't touch the DVD player! I'm recording a film.
9 Britain produces about 50% of its own oil.

T 6.7

a	'refuse	re'fuse
b	'present	pre'sent
c	'minute	min'ute
d	'desert	de'sert
e	'content	con'tent
f	'object	ob'ject
g	'invalid	in'valid
h	'contract	con'tract

T 6.8

1 A refuse collector.
2 An unidentified flying object.
3 A desert in northern Africa.
4 Presents!
5 The contents pages.
6 con'tent   mi'nute
  'contract   re'fuse
  in'valid

T 6.9

1 A Mike! Long time no see! How are things?
  B Good, thanks, Jeff. Business is booming. What about yourself?
2 A I'm afraid something's come up, and I can't make our meeting on the 6th.
  B Never mind. Let's go for the following week. Is Wednesday the 13th good for you?
3 A What are your travel arrangements?
  B I'm getting flight BA 2762, at 18.45.
4 A Could you confirm the details in writing?
  B Sure. I'll email them to you as an attachment.
5 A They want a deposit of 2½ percent, which is £7,500, and we ... the two ... thousand ... ge ... t...
  B Sorry, I didn't quite get that last bit. What was it again?
6 A I'll give you £5,250 for your car. That's my final offer.
  B Great! It's a deal. It's yours.
7 A I don't know their number offhand. Bear with me while I look it up.
  B No worries. I'll hold.
8 A OK. Here's their number. Are you ready? It's 0800 205080.
  B I'll read that back to you. Oh eight double oh, two oh five, oh eight oh.
9 A So what's your salary, Dave? 35K? 40K?
  B Hey! Mind your own business! You wouldn't tell anyone yours!
10 A Have you applied for that job?
  B There's no point. I'm not qualified for it. I wouldn't stand a chance.

T 6.10   See p61

UNIT 7

T 7.1

1 If I were you I wouldn't wear red. It doesn't suit you.
2 Is it OK if I make a suggestion?
3 You're allowed to smoke in the designated area only.
4 I'll be able to take you to the airport after all.
5 You are required to obtain a visa to work in Australia.
6 It's always a good idea to make an appointment.
7 You're bound to pass. Don't worry.
8 You aren't permitted to walk on the grass.
9 I didn't manage to get through, the line was engaged.
10 I refuse to discuss the matter any further.

T 7.2   See p62

T 7.3

1
A What the ... where d'you think you're going?
B What d'you mean?
A Well, you're not allowed to turn right here.
B Who says it's not allowed?
A That sign does mate. 'No Entry', you ought to be able to read that.
B It's impossible to see.
A You'd better get your eyes tested, you had. You're not fit to be on the roads.

2
A Promise not to tell anyone!
B I promise.
A It's really important not to tell a soul.
B Trust me. I won't say a word.
A But I know you. You're bound to tell someone.
B Look. I really am able to keep a secret, you know. Oh, but is it OK if I tell David?
A That's fine. He's invited too of course. It's just that Ben and I want a really quiet affair. It being second time around for both of us.

T 7.4

A I think you should swallow your pride and forgive and forget.
B Never! I will not.
A You'll have to in the end. You can't ignore each other forever.
B I might forgive him but I can never forget.
A It must be possible to talk it over, and work something out. You must for the sake of the children.
B Oh dear! I just don't know what to do for the best.

T 7.5

A I don't know if I can come this evening.
B But you must. You said you would.
A Yeah, but I can't go out on weekday evenings. My parents won't let me.
B You could tell them that you're coming over to my house to do homework.
A I can't. Somebody will see me and tell them.
B We'll have to cancel the match then. Lots of kids can't come to practice in term time.

T 7.6   Exciting news

R Hello?
M Rick, Rick is that you? I've got to talk to you.
R Miranda, hi! Why all the excitement?
M Well, can you remember that competition I entered, just for a laugh, a few weeks ago?
R Yes, I can. I remember you doing it in the coffee bar. It was the one in the *Daily Sun*, wasn't it? Didn't you have to name loads of capital cities?
M Yeah, that's it. You've got it. Well, get this, I've *won*! I came first!
R Never! I don't believe it! What's the prize?
M A trip to New York.
R You must be kidding! That's brilliant. For how long?
M Just three days – but it's three days in the Ritz Carlton, of all places!
R Well, you should be able to do quite a lot in three days. And the Ritz Carlton! I'm impressed! Doesn't that overlook Central Park?
M Yes, it does.
R I thought so. Not that I've been there, of course.
M Well, you can now.
R What do you mean? How would I ever be able to?
M Well, it's a trip for two and I'd really love it if you would come with me. Will you?
R You can't be serious? You know I'd love to! But why me? Surely you should be taking David?
M Haven't you heard? David and I have split up.
R Oh, I'm sorry! I didn't know. When did this happen?
M Well, a couple of weeks ago. We haven't been getting on well for ages.
R Well, what can I say? How could I possibly refuse an offer like that?
M You'll come then?
R I certainly will.

T 7.7   An arranged marriage

I = Interviewer, P = Pratima
I How old were you when you met your husband, Pratima?
P Mmm ... I was just sixteen.
I Were you still at school?
P No, I'd left school but I was having private tuition at home, to prepare me for some exams.
I And your father arranged your marriage? Is that right?
P That's right.
I Could you tell me how he did that?
P Well, he looked around for a suitable husband. He asked friends and relatives if they knew anyone, and found out about their education, their background and ... er ... most importantly the family's background. He managed to get a lot of information about them, you know.
I And how long did this take?
P Not too long in my case, but you know ... er ... sometimes a father can see up to a hundred men before he chooses one. For my sister, my elder sister he saw over one hundred men before ...
I He saw how many? Goodness! It must take up a lot of time.
P Yes, it can be difficult to decide but for me he saw only two ... er ... one in the morning and one in the afternoon and ... er ... he chose the second one.
I What a day! Can you tell me about it?
P Yes ... well, in the morning the first man was very wealthy, and he was well-dressed and ... er ... had good manners but ... er ... he hadn't had a good education.
I Ah. And the other one?
P Well, he wasn't terribly wealthy, but he was well-educated and he came from a good background ... er ... his family owned a village and were like princes. He was 22 and studying law.
I And this one your father chose?
P That's right. I think he thought money wasn't everything – for my father education was more important and anyway, if a man is well-educated, he will earn in the end. Actually, Shyam, that's my husband's name, Shyam didn't want to get married at all but his father had told him he must ... so ... er when he came to my house to meet my father, he was very badly-dressed because he hoped my father would refuse him. But luckily for me, my father did like him, and ... er ... he had to say yes.
I He had to?
P Oh yes, he had promised his father.
I And what about you? Did you meet both men?
P Yes, I met them that day. First my family spoke to them and then they called me in and we ... er ... we spoke for four ... four or five minutes.
I And did you prefer the second?
P Well, actually I wasn't sure. I left it to my father.
I You must trust him a lot!
P Oh, yes.
I So what happened next?
P Well, after a while, there was a special day when I went to meet his family and his family came to meet mine. It was ... er kind of an engagement party. But we – you know – Shyam and me, we used to be on the phone every day and we'd meet regularly but always we had to have a chaperone. And after ten months we got married.
I And how long have you been married?
P Nearly twenty-five years now.
I And ... it's been a successful marriage? Your father made a good choice?
P Oh ... yes, of course and we have two beautiful sons. They're twenty-two and seventeen now.
I And will you arrange their marriages?

P Oh yes. My husband is planning them now. He's been asking families for some time already and ...
I And your sons want it?
P Well, Krishna, he's the eldest, he's OK about it – he's studying hard and hasn't got the time to meet girls but ...
I Yes, what about the youngest? Ravi, isn't it?
P Yes ... er, well actually, Ravi's not so keen. It might be difficult to persuade ...
I But you still believe that the system of arranged marriages is a good one?
P Oh yes, I do, of course I do – but you know it depends on a lot ... er ... especially on the family choosing the right person. But one main reason, I think it does work, is that the couple enter the marriage not *expecting* too much – if you see what I mean. Actually, you know, there are many more divorces between couples who thought they were marrying for love. You know, my mother ... er ... she had to marry at thirteen but she's still happily married nearly fifty years later. Of course, nowadays thirteen is considered too young but you know ... times change.
I Yeah, that's very true. Thank you very much indeed, Pratima.

T 7.8

1 They went where?
2 You got home when?
3 You paid how much?
4 You met who?
5 He did what?

T 7.9

1 A I'm absolutely dying for a drink.
  B Yes, my throat's a bit dry, I must say.
2 A His family are pretty well off, aren't they?
  B You can say that again! They're absolutely loaded!
3 A You must have hit the roof when she told you she'd crashed your car.
  B Well, yes, I was a bit upset.
4 A I think Tony was a bit rude last night.
  B Too right! He was totally out of order!
5 A I can't stand the sight of him!
  B I must admit, I'm not too keen on him either.
6 A He isn't very bright, is he?
  B You're not kidding. He's as thick as two short planks.
7 A I'm fed up with this weather! It's freezing.
  B I suppose it *is* a bit chilly.
8 A Well, that was a fantastic holiday!
  B Yes, it was a nice little break, but all good things must come to an end.
9 A I'm knackered. Can we stop for a rest?
  B OK. I feel a bit out of breath, too.
10 A They're obviously madly in love.
  B Yeah, they do seem to get on quite well.

T 7.10 See p69

T 7.11

1 A Is that a new watch? I bet that cost a bit.
  B A bit!? It cost a fortune!
2 A It's a bit chilly in here, don't you think?
  B You can say that again! I'm absolutely freezing!
3 A These shoes are rather nice, aren't they?
  B They're *gorgeous*! I want them!
4 A Can we stop at the next service station? I could do with something to eat.
  B Me too. I'm starving! I didn't have breakfast this morning.
5 A I think those two like each other, don't you?
  B *Like's* the wrong word. They're obviously crazy about each other.
6 A I bet you were a bit upset when your team lost.
  B Me? Upset? I only cried myself to sleep!

 UNIT 8

T 8.1 Jumbolair – home of jet pilot John Travolta

Welcome to JUMBOLAIR, Florida – the world's only housing estate where the super-rich can commute to work by jet plane from their own front doors. Jumbolair's most famous resident is Hollywood film star John Travolta, whose $3.5 million mansion is big enough to park a row of aeroplanes, including a Gulfstream executive jet, a two-seater jet fighter, and a four-engined Boeing 707, previously owned by Frank Sinatra. Travolta holds a commercial pilot's licence, which means he is qualified to fly passenger jets. He can land his planes and taxi them up to his front gates. His sumptuous Florida home, which is built in the style of an airport terminal building, is the ultimate boys' fantasy house made real. As well as the parking lots for the jets, there is a heliport, swimming pool and gym, stables for 75 horses, and of course a 1.4-mile runway. Family man Travolta, who lives with wife Kelly, daughter Ella Bleu, and aptly named son Jett, flies daily from his home when filming. Walking out of his door and into the cockpit, he is airborne in minutes. His neighbours, most of whom share his love of aviation, don't seem to mind the roar of his jets. They say that it's nice to meet a superstar who isn't full of his own importance. 'He's just a regular guy, very friendly', says one neighbour.

T 8.2

1 The area of London I like best is Soho.
2 My father, who's a doctor, plays the drums.
3 The book that I'm reading at the moment is fascinating.
4 Paul passed his driving test first time, which surprised everybody.
5 People who smoke risk getting all sorts of illnesses.
6 I met a man whose main aim in life was to visit every capital city in the world.
7 The Channel Tunnel, which opened in 1995, is a great way to get from England to France.
8 What I like best about work is the holidays.
9 A short bald man, seen running away from the scene of the crime, is being sought by the police.

T 8.3

1 A How did you do in the maths test?
  B Oh! Don't ask! It's too awful.
  A Oh, dear. What did you get?
  B Twenty-two per cent. I came last and I thought I was going to do really well.
2 A How was your holiday?
  B Great, thanks. Just what we needed.
  A Did you do much?
  B Not a lot. We just sat by the pool, read books, and took it easy for two whole weeks. Absolute bliss.
3 A Have you heard about Dave and Maggie?
  B No. Tell me, tell me!
  A Well, last week they went to a party, had this huge row in front of all these people and ... .
  B Did it get physical?
  A Oh yeah! Maggie shoved Dave into a flowerpot, told him to get lost and went off with another bloke!
  B What! I'm amazed! I just can't believe Maggie'd do such a thing. It doesn't sound like her at all.
4 A Come on in. You must be shattered!
  B Oof, I am. I've been travelling for the past thirty hours and I haven't slept a wink.
  A I know – I can never sleep on a plane, either. Just sit down, take it easy and I'll get you a drink.
5 A How's the new job going?
  B Good, thanks, very good – but it's quite difficult. I'm having to deal with so many new things. Still, I'm enjoying it all.
  A Mmm – I know what you mean.
  B It's great to be doing something that's so satisfying, and meeting so many people from abroad.
  A Absolutely.

6 A So, anyway, just to end the perfect evening, I had to walk back home because I'd lost the car keys and I didn't have any money for a taxi. I didn't get home until three in the morning.
  B That's the funniest thing I've heard for ages. Poor you. Sorry I'm laughing.
  A Well, I'm glad you think it's so funny – I didn't think it funny at the time.
7 A There is just nothing good on TV tonight!
  B What about that wildlife programme?
  A D'you mean the one about the life of frogs?
  B Yeah – does it look any good?
  A You're kidding. It looks absolute rubbish.
8 A What's the matter with you?
  B Oh my gosh – I've just put my foot right in it.
  A What d'you mean?
  B Well, I was talking to that lady over there and I asked her when her baby was due, and ... er ... she told me she wasn't pregnant.
  A Oh, no! That's awful!

T 8.4

Lost in her thoughts, a beautiful, young woman was sitting in her country garden, watching a bee lazily going from rose to rose gathering honey.

T 8.5

1 Exhausted after a hard day's work, a balding, middle-aged man wearing a crumpled suit, and carrying a briefcase, walked slowly along the road that led from the station to his home, pausing only to look up at the night sky.
2 Peter, who's very wealthy, has a huge, sixteenth century farmhouse, surrounded by woods in the heart of the Devon countryside.
3 Ann Croft, the world famous actress, who married for the sixth time only last month, was seen having an intimate lunch in a London restaurant with a man who was definitely not her husband.
4 The two-week holiday in Mauritius, which we had looked forward to so much, was a complete and utter disaster from start to finish.
5 A ten-year-old boy, walking home from school, found an old, battered, leather wallet filled with £5,000 in £50 notes in the High Street.

T 8.6 Simone

Well, it was when I was living in Cairo and ... erm ... it was in the middle of the summer, so, was it, it was extremely hot, – between 40 and 45 degrees centigrade, and ... erm ... stupidly we decided to go dancing and ... er ... we went to this night club and we must have danced for hours and hours, ... erm ... and it was very hot inside the night club and we were sweating profusely, ... erm ... and ... er ... by the time we came out it was about 5 o'clock in the morning, and we decided, 'Ooh wouldn't it be a great idea to go to the pyramids to see the sunrise!' So we jumped in a taxi, and the taxi was also quite stuffy and hot, ... erm ... and we must have been starting to dehydrate at this point. Anyway, we got to the pyramids – and ... erm ... the sun was just starting to come up. And in, in Egypt, as soon as the sun comes up, the temperature rises dramatically, ... erm ... but we were so excited at seeing the pyramids that we decided just to, to go and walk and see. At this point, ... erm ... a man approached us and asked us if we wanted to borrow his motorbike, or hire his motorbike, ... erm ... and so we said yes. So my friend and I, we jumped onto the motorbike and raced out into the desert – only to find after about ten, fifteen minutes, that the motorbike was ... erm ... rather old and suddenly it broke down. So we were miles from anywhere and ... erm ... had to push this motorbike to, to get back. I was the one at the back pushing the motorbike and of course ... erm ... I was using lots of energy, I was, ... erm ... losing a lot of fluid and, ... erm ... it was getting hotter and hotter. Anyway, we ended up having to walk back, ... erm ... to, to the village to give the motorbike back to the man. And by this time we were rather fed up and tired and very hot, so we decided to go home. By the time we got home, ... erm ... I did start to feel a bit strange, I had a bit of a headache and ... erm ... I decided to go to, straight to bed. Anyway, I woke up about half an hour later, feeling rather confused, and sick, a bit nauseous and ... er ... I realized that ... erm ... my brain wasn't working properly and that in fact I probably had ... erm ... heat exhaustion. Anyway, it was a, it wasn't very pleasant, and –er, ah, it was a lesson in what not to do in ... er ... in such temperatures. I've never done that again. I always carry my rehydration salts with me.

T 8.7 Anna

The time that I was very, very cold ... erm ... was a time when I was working in Russia, in a small town in central Russia and ... er ... I was going to see some friends who lived on the outskirts of the town, and they were worried about me getting lost and they said that they'd come to the tram stop to meet me. But I wanted to be independent, so I, I told them 'don't be silly, of course I'll find it'. And on the day of, of the visit, ... erm ... it was very, very cold, it might have been minus thirty, but it might have been colder than that and ... er ... it, it was so cold that at some of the tram stops and bus stops there were bonfires lit – special street fires ... erm ... to keep people warm and I think it was a day when the schools were closed, when the children didn't go to school because it was so cold. So I put on all the clothes that I had – all the scarves and jumpers, and, and I took the tram to the outskirts of the town where my friends lived and it was right, right way out to the end of the line and I, I got off the tram, which was heated, ... erm ... into this cold white world. And ... erm ... it was, it was so cold that if you ... when you breathed in, little balls of ice formed in your nostrils, you, you had to keep your ... erm ... a scarf over your mouth and nose. About a minute, two minutes after getting off the tram my, my ... er ... feet and hands were already hurting they were so cold. So I was walking around, trying to find the, the flat, but it was completely anonymous this, this landscape ... erm ... and there were these huge snow-covered white blocks, these buildings, fifteen or sixteen floors, but they all looked exactly the same and I couldn't find the name of the, the street either, and it was very, very quiet and the, the tram had gone. Er ... and I began, actually, to get very frightened because I was feeling so, so cold. Erm ... my feet and hands had, had gone beyond hurting almost, I couldn't feel them any more. Erm ... it was quite difficult to breathe because of the icy scarf over my mouth and nose, ... erm ... and I, I just couldn't find where, where they lived, and I asked an old lady the way but my Russian wasn't good enough, she didn't understand me. And I was beginning to really, seriously panic, when suddenly in the distance I, I saw my friends. They'd come to find me and ... erm ... they took me home.

T 8.8

1 We went dancing in temperatures of over 40°C, which was rather a stupid thing to do.
2 My friends were worried I'd get lost, which was understandable.
3 We visited the pyramids at sunrise, which was just amazing.
4 My nostrils actually froze, which is hard to believe.
5 This motorbike broke down in the desert, which was no laughing matter.
6 The old lady didn't understand a word I said, which is hardly surprising because my Russian's lousy.

T 8.9

1 A Did you get very wet in that shower?
  B Shower! It was a downpour. We're absolutely soaking!
2 A I bet you were quite excited when your team won.

B Excited! We were absolutely thrilled!
3 A I thought she looked rather silly in that flowery hat, didn't you?
  B Silly! She looked absolutely ridiculous!
4 A Come on, nobody'll notice that tiny spot on your nose.
  B They will, I just know they will! It's absolutely enormous!
5 A I thought the last episode of *Friends* was absolutely hilarious.
  B Mmm. I wouldn't say that. It was quite funny but not hilarious.
6 A Len left early. He wasn't feeling well.
  B I'm not surprised. When I saw him this morning he looked absolutely awful!

T 8.10 See p76

T 8.11 See p76

T 8.12 A night at the Oscars

I am absolutely amazed and delighted to receive this award. I'm truly grateful to all those wonderful people who voted for me. *Red Hot in the Snow* was an absolutely fantastic movie to act in, not only because of all the brilliant people involved in the making of it, but also because of the fabulous, thrilling, and often extremely dangerous locations in Alaska. None of us could have predicted that it would be such a huge success. My special thanks go to Marius Aherne, my excellent director; Lulu Lovelace, my gorgeous co-star; Roger Sims, for writing a script that was both fascinating and hilarious, and last but not least to my marvellous wife, Glynis, for her priceless support. I absolutely adore you all.

T 8.13

1 A Hello. Could I make an appointment for our golden retriever, Molly?
  B Sure. What seems to be the problem?
  A Well, she's gone off her food, which is most unusual for her, and she has no interest in going out for walks. She just lies around all day long.
2 A What have we got here?
  B Some old carpet, a washing machine that doesn't work anymore, and a whole load of cardboard.
  A Right, well the carpet can go in there, and all old electrical appliances go over there.
3 A Hello. I'd like to open a savings account, please.
  B Are you a student?
  A Yes, I am.
  B Well, we have a couple of special accounts for students. One allows you 24 hours a day access, and pays 3% interest. Another requires one week's notice for withdrawals and pays 3.5% interest. For both accounts you need a minimum of one hundred pounds, but we can offer overdraft facilities ...
4 A Yes, please. How can I help you?
  B Yeah, I've got a few money problems.
  A Mmm huh.
  B You see, I've fallen behind with my rent, about three months, and they're threatening to cut off the electricity.
  A Because you haven't paid the bills?
  B Yeah, right. And I keep getting all these credit card demands, and I just don't know what to do. I just can't cope any more ...
5 A Hello, can I help you?
  B Yes, please. I'm trying to get some quotations to move all my stuff from a house in the south-west of England up to Scotland. Do you go as far as that?
  A Oh, yes, madam. We will deliver anywhere in the world. Now whereabouts are you in the south-west?
  B Not far from Bristol, and we're moving to Edinburgh in a couple of months time ...

UNIT 9

T 9.1 An email to a friend

Dear Sally
I'm sending this through Friends Reunited. Do you remember me? We used to go to Allendales School together. You were the first person I got to know when I started there.
We used to sit next to each other in class, but then the teachers made us sit apart because we were always giggling so much.
I remember we'd go back to your house after school every day and listen to music for hours on end. We'd get all the Beatles records as soon as they came out. Once we ate all the food in your fridge and your mother was furious.
Do you remember that time we nearly blew up the science lab? The teacher went crazy, but it wasn't our fault. We used to call him 'Mickey Mouse' because he had sticky-out ears.
I still see Penny, and she's still as mad as ever. We meet up every now and again, and we'll always end up chatting about old times together. She's always talking about a school reunion. So if you're interested, drop me a line.
Looking forward to hearing from you.
Your old schoolmate
Alison Makepeace
PS I'm not used to calling you Sally *Davies*! To me, you're still Sally *Wilkinson*!

T 9.2

we used to go to school together
we used to sit next to each other
we were always giggling so much
we'd go back to your house
we used to call him 'Mickey Mouse'
I'm not used to calling you Sally *Davies*

T 9.3

1 I got on very well with my mother. She was my best friend, still is. We had to get on, really. Dad left when I was three. I used to tell her everything, well, nearly everything. And she'd talk to me very openly, too. Sometimes she'd say to me 'Don't go to school today. Stay with me'. And we'd go out shopping or, or something like that. It's a wonder I had any education at all, the number of days I missed from school.
2 I don't remember much about my childhood. My wife's always asking me questions like -erm 'When you were a boy, did you use to ...?', and I reply 'I don't know. I can't remember'. We didn't ... er ... really we didn't use to talk very much, we weren't very close, or if we were, we didn't show it. I remember I used to have my hair cut every Friday. My father was in the army, and he had a thing about short hair, so every week he'd take me to the hairdresser. I had the shortest hair in the school. I used to hate it. And him.
3 I'm not a very tidy person, but my mother's very house-proud, so she's always telling me to pick things up and put them away, and do this and do that. She'll go on for hours about 'Cleanliness is next to godliness' – that just makes me want to scream. My father isn't like that at all, he's much more laid back. I think he's just learned to blank out my mother.
4 I have very fond memories of my childhood. To me it represented security. We used to do a lot together as a family. I remember walks, and picnics, and going for car rides on a Sunday afternoon. Every Friday when my Dad came home, he'd bring us each a treat, just something little. My mother used to say he was spoiling us, but why not? It didn't do us any harm.

T 9.4

1 A You don't like your new teacher, do you?
  B Not a lot, but we're getting used to her.

---

2 **A** How can you get up at five o'clock in the morning?
  B No problem. I'm used to it.
3 **A** How come you know Madrid so well?
  B I used to live there.
4 **A** How are you finding your new job?
  B Difficult, but I'm getting used to it bit by bit.
5 **A** Do you read comics?
  B I used to when I was young, but not any more.
6 **A** You two argue so much. How can you live together?
  B After twenty years' marriage we're used to each other.

T 9.5 **A teacher I'll never forget**

1 Alan
I was very fortunate in high school to have erm ... one particularly good teacher for a subject called -er social studies, which incorporates history and erm ... geography. And I think the thing that made this teacher so good was that he not only had a terrific sense of humour but he also had an ability to control the class in such a way that we always paid attention when he wanted us to pay attention, but he could always get us to laugh at the same time. So he had a way of kind of being very fluid in his teaching style. And erm ... he'd, he'd do crazy things like ... -er you know, sometimes he'd stand on a desk and recite a poem, or he'd erm ... he'd draw funny pictures on the blackboard. But I never, never forget him. His name was Mr Sparks, which I think is a fantastic name for a teacher, anyway. And -er he'd stand at the front of the class ... he had this kind of -er ... he had a sort of, of a funny er ... short, pointy beard, and glasses and er ... this kind of greying, slicked back hair ... and erm he'd, he'd stand there and look at us with a, an imperious look on his face, and then tell a joke! He'd just make us all laugh!

2 John
I had a teacher at school who was just awful. He taught French and German, and his name was Colin Tivvy. I'll never forget that name. It sends shivers down my spine just to hear it. It wasn't that he was a bad teacher. In fact he used to get very good results. It was the way he got those results. He taught out of pure fear. All the kids were scared stiff of him, so you'd do his homework first and best, because the last thing you wanted was to make a mistake. If you made a mistake, in homework or in class, you had to write it out one hundred times that night. He'd been a soldier in the army, and he'd worked as an interrogator, and that was just how he taught. We had to stand in a line outside his classroom, and when he was ready, he'd shout 'Get in, men!', and we'd all march into class. And as the lesson went through, he'd pace up and down the classroom, and er ... he used to wear those kind of shoes that didn't make a noise, you know? And the worst feeling in the whole world was when you knew he was just behind you. You were waiting for a smack on the back of the head. But the worst was when he picked you up by the hairs on the back of your neck. That hurt!

3 Lizzie
The teacher I remember most from schooldays was ... erm ... a teacher called Miss Potts. She was a history teacher and I was about thirteen or fourteen years old. We were all very interested in fashion, and Miss Potts used to wear the most amazing things to come in to teach – so she was a very memorable teacher. Every day we'd be asking ourselves 'What's she gonna wear today?' She'd wear blue tights with red skirts and very red jumpers, and very bright red lipstick and she'd come teetering into the classroom on very high heels and we thought she looked wonderful. But the very best thing about Miss Potts was the way, in fact, she taught history – it's what makes her most memorable. She not only brought history to life, but she made it seem dead easy. She didn't just act it out for us, ... erm ... but the way she described the characters from history made us feel as

if we knew them and, and sometimes instead of writing essays we would do cartoon strips ... erm ... of the, of the different tales from history and we loved it. She was a brilliant, brilliant teacher. It's interesting 'cos I think another teacher who was called Miss Potts would probably have been called 'potty' or ... er ... given such a name as that, but there was something about her that we respected so much that ... er ... she just never had a nickname.

4 Kate
My favourite is called Mr Brown. We call him Brownie, but not to his face. We wouldn't dare. He's my PE teacher, and he's great. He'll joke and make fun of you, but never in a horrible, nasty way. And we like to pull his leg, too. He's bald, poor guy, totally bald, but when it's his birthday, we'll ask him if he wants a comb or a brush, or something like that. But there's a line we all know we can't cross. We have a lot of respect for him as a teacher, and he treats us totally fairly, but he also keeps his distance. He never tries to be one of us, oh no! If a teacher ever tries to be, you know, a teenager like us, same music, same clothes, same jokes, it just doesn't work. But there's another side to Brownie. He's also head of discipline in the school, so whenever a student you know ... misbehaves or cheeks a teacher, they get sent to Mr Brown and he scares the pants off them. And when he shouts, boy he is absolutely terrifying. No one, but no one, messes with Mr Brown.

T 9.6

Theme tune to *Friends*

T 9.7

1 I like her because she's so different from the others. She thinks differently, she behaves differently. She'll say the craziest of things in the most serious way.
2 I like him because he's so cute and so amazingly self-centred. He's so uncomplicated. What you see is what you get. So charmingly dumb and unsophisticated.
3 I can't stand her because she's so fussy and uptight. She has to have control over everything and everybody. And she screeches.
4 He really annoys me because he's so hopeless with women. But he's so funny. He uses his humour and sarcasm as a defence mechanism to get out of difficulty. How he ended up with Monica I'll never know.
5 She's my favourite because she's incredibly good-looking. She's a bit scatty, she's always losing things. She's a real daddy's girl. She was so popular at school.
6 He's my favourite because he's always falling in love with the wrong woman. He's the coolest of the non-cool crowd. He's so sensible, his parents think he can do no wrong, but he's always getting into trouble.

T 9.8

where nose mail break through sent

T 9.9 See p84

T 9.10

Customer Waiter! I'm in a hurry. Will my pizza be long?
Waiter No, sir. It'll be round.
Teacher You missed school yesterday, didn't you Johnny?
Johnny No, sir. Not a bit.

What's the difference between a sailor and someone who goes shopping?
One goes to sail the seas, the other goes to see the sales!

What's the difference between a jeweller and a jailer?
One sells watches and the other watches cells.

What sort of crisps can fly?
Plain crisps.

Why was the doctor angry?
Because he had no patients!

What did the sea say to the beach?
Nothing. It just waved.

What's black and white and red all over?
A newspaper.

What do you get when 5,000 strawberries try to go through a door at the same time?
Strawberry jam!

T 9.11

1 Vicky
If you ask me, this is a terrible idea. Firstly, it would be an infringement of individual freedom. Secondly, another way of saying fast food is convenience food, and that means it really suits the kind of lifestyle of people today. Another thing is that it would be a tax on people who are less well off. Personally, I don't eat in these places, but that's not the point. The point I'm trying to make is that people should be allowed to eat what they want.

2 Al
To tell you the truth, I haven't really thought about it. I suppose the problem is that we don't know what's in these burgers and pizzas. As far as I'm concerned, people can do what they want. I don't see what's wrong with that. Actually, I'm seeing a friend for lunch and we're going to have a burger. There's that new place just opened, you know, down by the square. It's supposed to be quite good. Anyway, as I was saying, I don't really feel strongly one way or the other.

3 Beth-Anne
If you want my opinion, I think this is a really good idea. There are far too many people who have a terrible diet, and they just go to the nearest hamburger joint and fill themselves up with rubbish. Basically, it's laziness. As I understand it, they just can't be bothered to buy fresh food and cook it. But the main point is that fast food, or junk food, is too cheap. If it was taxed, people would think twice before buying. What really worries me is that the next generation is going to have so many problems with kids being overweight.

T 9.12

If you ask me ...
Another thing is that ...
That's not the point.
The point I'm trying to make is that ...
To tell you the truth ...
I suppose the problem is that ...
As far as I'm concerned ...
Anyway, as I was saying ...
If you want my opinion ...
As I understand it ...
But the main point is that ...
What really worries me is that ...

T 9.13 See p120

 UNIT 10

T 10.1

1 She must have been very rich.
2 I had to do my homework.
3 I couldn't sleep because of the noise.
4 They can't have been in. There were no lights on.
5 I thought that was Jane but I might have been wrong.
6 You should have seen a doctor.

T 10.2

A You know that prehistoric man, the one they discovered in Italy years ago ...

B You mean that guy in the Alps?

A Yeah, that's the one. He's supposed to be about five thousand years old. They've done all sorts of tests on him, you know DNA tests and things, to find out about his life.

B What was he? Some sort of hunter?

A Well, they aren't sure. He could have been a hunter, or he could have been some kind of shepherd, you know, looking after his sheep up in the mountains. The mystery is 'What was he doing up there?' He might have just got lost for all we know.

B It must have been cold up there. How did he keep warm?

A I suppose he lived in a cave and wore stuff like animal furs. They reckon he fell asleep sheltering from a snowstorm, so he may have died from cold and starvation. He shouldn't have gone up so high without the right ... you know, protective clothing.

B I wonder what they did for food five thousand years ago. They hunted wild animals, didn't they, with -erm arrows and axes and things?

A Yeah, I guess they ate a lot of meat, and, and berries and fruit. They might even have grown crops, you know, like cereals to make bread.

B No, they can't have been that clever. I bet they didn't know how to do that. I'd have thought they just ate meat, you know, like -erm, like carnivores.

A Who knows? Maybe these tests will tell us. I don't suppose they got around much. It would have been too difficult.

B I'm sure. I wouldn't have thought they travelled much at all. I bet they stayed in the same area. How old was he when he died?

A They think he was maybe forty to forty-five, which must have been quite old in those days.

B I've bought the magazine *New Scientist*, so we can read all about the results.

A Well, you needn't have bothered. I've downloaded them from the Internet. Let's have a look at them.

T 10.3

1 What was he?
He could have been a hunter, or he could have been a shepherd.
2 What was he doing in the mountains?
He might have been looking after his sheep, or he might have got lost.
3 Where did he live? What did he wear?
He must have lived in a cave.
He must have worn animal furs.
4 How did he die?
He may have fallen asleep.
He may have died of cold and starvation.
5 Was it a good idea to go so high?
He shouldn't have gone so high on his own.
He should have worn protective clothing.
6 What did he eat?
He must have eaten a lot of meat and berries.
They might have grown crops like cereals to make bread.
They can't have grown crops.
I'd have thought they just ate meat.
7 Did they travel much?
I wouldn't have thought they travelled much at all.
They must have stayed in the same area.
8 How old was he when he died?
He could have been between forty and forty-five.
That must have been quite old in those days.

T 10.4

1 I *did* tell you about Joe's party. You can't have been listening.
2 Thanks so much for all your help. I couldn't have managed without you.
3 Flowers, for me! That's so kind, but really you shouldn't have.
4 Come on! We're only five minutes late. The film won't have started yet.
5 I don't believe that Kathy's going out with Mark. She'd have told me, I know she would.

6 We raced to get to the airport on time, but we needn't have worried. The flight was delayed.
7 We've got a letter here that isn't for us. The postman must have delivered it by mistake.
8 You shouldn't have gone swimming in such rough sea. You could have drowned!

T 10.5

Hello.
Oh, it's you.
We're all right, no thanks to you. Why are you ringing?
What do you mean, next Saturday? What about next Saturday?
Already! Is it the second Saturday of the month so soon? Yes, I suppose it is. All right, then.
Where are you thinking of taking them? The children always pester if they don't know, especially Daniel.
The zoo! Again! Can't you think of anything else? They hated it last time. Nicky did, anyway.
That's not what she told me. Anyway, that's up to you. What time are you going to pick them up?
OK. I'll have them ready. By the way, when they come home after a day with you, they're always filthy. Can't Alison wash their clothes?
Well, she has enough time to go shopping and have lunch with her friends, from what the kids have told me.
All right! I don't want to argue about it.
I'll tell them you rang. Bye.

T 10.6

Hello.
This is Jeremy Brook speaking.
Sorry – Janice who?
I'm sorry. I don't think I know anyone by that name.
On holiday? Did we? When was that?
In Greece! Of course! I remember! You're the American girl who was in the next room. That was years ago! How are you?
I'm fine. What a surprise! What are you doing? Where are you?
Here? What are you doing here?
Erm ... well ... I'd love to, but erm ... well, it's not very convenient, actually.
Yes, I know I said that, but that was a long time ago, and erm ... our flat isn't that big, and ...
Yes, I am. I got married last year.
Well, I'm glad you understand. I'm sorry to let you down. I'd have liked to help, but you see what I mean.
Well, maybe we could meet for a drink er ... you know, for old times' sake?
No, no, I suppose you're right. Well, it was nice to hear your voice again. Enjoy your trip round Europe.
Thanks. Bye, Janice. Same to you.

T 10.7

1 **A** That exam was totally impossible!
  B You can say that again! I couldn't answer a single question. I'm bound to have failed.
2 **A** You might as well apply for the job, even though you're too young.
  B Yes, why not! After all, I've got nothing to lose. You never know, I might be just the person they're looking for.
3 I know I shouldn't have eaten a whole tub of ice-cream but I just couldn't help it. I feel as fat as a pig now.
4 **A** I'm going to tell her exactly what I think of her.
  B I wouldn't do that if I were you. You've no idea how she'll react. It could get really nasty.
5 **A** You might have told me that Jackie and Dave had split up! I felt really stupid when I asked Jackie where they were going on holiday.
  B Sorry! I thought you knew. Everybody else does.

6 **A** I think you should forget all about her and move on.
  B Believe me, I would if I could. But I just can't get her out of my mind. I think it must be love.
  A Oh no!
7 **A** You should have been here yesterday! You'd have died laughing!
  B Why? What was so funny?
  A Well, Pedro was imitating the teacher, and he was so good, and then the teacher walked in!
8 **A** Then I found out that Annie's been going out with ... guess who? Dave!
  B Huh! I could have told *you* that. It's common knowledge. Where have you been?
9 I'd known this guy for five minutes when he asked me to marry him! I just couldn't believe it! Maybe he does the same to every girl he meets.
10 **A** I could do with a break.
  B Me, too. I'm dying for a coffee. It feels like this lesson's been going on for ages.

T 10.8

Jim, who ran away from his nurse, and was eaten by a lion

There was a boy whose name was Jim;
His friends were very good to him.
They gave him tea, and cakes, and jam,
And slices of delicious ham,
And read him stories through and through,
And even took him to the zoo –
But there it was the dreadful fate
Befell him, I now relate.
You know – at least you ought to know,
For I have often told you so –
That children never are allowed
To leave their nurses in a crowd;
Now this was Jim's especial foible,
He ran away when he was able,
And on this inauspicious day
He slipped his hand and ran away!
He hadn't gone a yard when – bang!
With open jaws, a lion sprang,
And hungrily began to eat
The boy: beginning at his feet.
Now just imagine how it feels
When first your toes and then your heels,
And then by gradual degrees,
Your shins and ankles, calves and knees,
Are slowly eaten, bit by bit.
No wonder Jim detested it!
No wonder that he shouted 'Hi!'
The honest keeper heard his cry,
Though very fat, he almost ran
To help the little gentleman
'Ponto!' he cried, with angry frown
'Let go, sir! Down, sir! Put it down!'
....
The lion having reached his head
The miserable boy was dead!
When nurse informed his parents they
Were more concerned than I can say: –
His mother, as she dried her eyes,
Said, 'Well – it gives me no surprise,
He would not do as he was told!'
His father, who was self-controlled
Bade all the children round attend
To James' miserable end,
And always keep a-hold of nurse
For fear of finding something worse.

T 10.9

1 **A** How's the new job?
  B OK, but I'm still getting used to it. My boss seemed very strict at first, but underneath it all she's very kind and generous. She understands the retail business very well, so she knows what she's doing.
2 **C** Can you help me to fix my computer? I can't open any of my files.
  D Listen, you'd better accept the fact that your computer is ancient. It's been about to stop

working for years. You can get a new one for about £500 these days.

C Are you joking?

D No, I'm perfectly serious.

3 E Pat's been unbearable lately. That promotion has made her feel more important than she is. She's been shouting at everyone. She's always spoken in a harsh and unkind way, but now she's upsetting everyone.

F I know. I'll have to talk to her honestly and openly.

T 10.10

1 A How's the new job?

B OK, but I'm still finding my feet. My boss seemed very strict at first, but underneath it all she's got a heart of gold. She has a very good head for the retail business, so she knows what she's doing.

2 C Can you give me a hand to fix my computer? I can't open any of my files.

D Listen, you'd better face the fact that your computer is ancient. It's been on its last legs for years. You can get a new one for about £500 these days.

C Are you pulling my leg?

D No, I'm perfectly serious.

3 E Pat's been unbearable lately. That promotion has gone to her head. She's been shouting at everyone. She's always had a sharp tongue, but now she's upsetting everyone.

F I know. I'll have to have a heart-to-heart talk with her.

UNIT 11

T 11.1

1 It's raining *again*. I wish it wasn't.

2 I'm not going out tonight. I wish I was.

3 There's nothing good on TV. I wish there was.

4 I don't like my job. I wish I did.

5 My boyfriend and I split up last week. I wish we hadn't.

6 I know he won't call me. I wish he would.

7 I feel really depressed. I wish I didn't.

8 I can't talk to anyone about it. I wish I could.

T 11.2

1 A No, I can't possibly go out tonight. I shouldn't have gone out last night.

B Come on – we had a great time. It was one helluva party!

A I know it was.

B So, when's your exam?

A Tomorrow, 9 o'clock. If only I hadn't left all my revision 'til the last minute.

B I wouldn't worry if I were you. You know you always do OK.

A There's always a first time.

B Good luck anyway.

2 A If only we could just fly off to that island.

B That would be fantastic. I'd sit on a beach and read all day.

A I'd just sleep forever. I can't remember a full night's sleep.

B Yeah. Sometimes I wish I'd never had kids. I mean, not really, but ...

A I know what you mean. No – you can't have an ice cream. I said NO!

3 A Oh boy! What would you give to drive one of those?!

B Which one would you choose if you had the money?

A That's one big 'if'! But ... mmm ... ... er ... if I won the lottery, I'd buy the Aston Martin.

B I wouldn't – I'd go for the Ferrari.

A In your dreams.

---

4 A Brilliant shot Charlie! Well-done!

B Don't you wish you still played football dad?

A Me? No. I was never any good. But *you* could have been a brilliant player if you'd wanted.

B Nah! I wasn't as good as Charlie. Aaah – oh nearly! YES!!

A Yeah, he'll go far.

5 A Look, I know I shouldn't have parked here but I was only gone two minutes.

B I've already written the ticket.

A Surely you could cancel it if you wanted? It was literally one minute.

B One minute, two minutes. You can't park here, it's as simple as that.

A But I just had to dash into the chemist to collect a prescription for my sick grandmother. Supposing you cancelled it just this once?

B I don't care what you were doing. I can't cancel a ticket – it's more than my job's worth. You've got two weeks to pay.

T 11.3

Well, Carrie and I were holidaying in Vanuatu in the South West Pacific It's really beautiful there and –er and one day we went for a walk and saw this piece of land for sale. It was on a cliff overlooking a bay and you can imagine – the views were absolutely fantastic. We just fell in love with it. We had to have it – so we bought it there and then, and the next day signed up an architect to design our dream holiday home. That evening we celebrated with rather a lot of champagne and in the middle of the night we were fast asleep when suddenly we were thrown from our beds, the room was shaking – it was the biggest earthquake that had ever hit the region. But worse was to come because next morning when we drove out to check our newly bought land, we found that the whole cliff had fallen into the sea. It was a tragedy for us. We lost every cent we had, and our marriage never really recovered.

T 11.4

1 A Would it be OK if I left bit early today? I have a dental appointment.

B No problem. Just tell Janet to cover for you.

2 A How's it going?

B OK. If all goes well, -er we should be finished by Friday. Er, we've just got to put the finishing touches to the doors and windows.

3 A If you knew what I know, you'd never go out with him again.

B You're just jealous.

4 A Could I have a word with you if you've got a minute?

B Yeah, of course but I'm in a bit of a rush.

A Er, it's about that pay rise I was promised.

5 A Aren't you helping Jackie organize her wedding?

B I am. It's a nightmare. If anything went wrong, I'd never forgive myself.

6 A Win? What do you mean? If you ask me, they don't stand a chance.

B Don't you think so? They've been playing much better recently.

A Come on. They haven't won a match for months.

7 A We arrived on the Tuesday and ...

B It was a Thursday not a Tuesday if I remember rightly.

A Oh Tuesday, Thursday – the day doesn't matter. I'll just never forget the blue of the water and the white of the sand.

8 A Well, if the worst comes to the worst, we can always postpone it for a day or two.

B I'd rather not. I've just got a bit of a headache. The sea air will do me good.

A OK, if you're sure.

9 A You haven't made much progress, if any at all.

B What d'you mean? I've written five hundred words.

A Yeah, but you have to write ten thousand.

---

10 A I don't think much of Nancy's new boyfriend. He's really cold and arrogant.

B Actually, I don't think he's cold or arrogant. If anything, he's a bit shy.

A Shy?! You wouldn't say that if you'd seen him at Ned's party!

T 11.5

1 In any relationship you have to be prepared to give and take. You can't have your own way all the time.

2 I didn't buy much at the shops. Just a few odds and ends for the kids. Socks for Ben and hairbands for Jane.

3 I don't want to hear any ifs and buts. Just finish the job as soon as you can.

4 It's difficult to explain the ins and outs of the rules of cricket. It's so complicated.

5 'What have you got me for my birthday?' 'You'll have to wait and see.'

6 'Oh, no! The Burtons are coming for lunch! I hate their kids!'
'I'm sorry, but you'll just have to grin and bear it. It's only for an hour or so.'

7 OK, you can have it for £90. That's my final offer, take it or leave it.

8 Britain has lots of faults, of course, but by and large, it's a pleasant place to live.

T 11.6 See p157

T 11.7 **I'll see you in my dreams**

Well, my story, I suppose it's ... erm ... in the supernatural category, which is stra... (*Oh yeah*) ... erm ... exactly, strange for me because I'm a very down-to-earth person. I'm basically quite sceptical when people tell weird and wonderful stories. But there is just one occasion when something very weird and inexplicable happened to me. Erm ... it was when I was at university, a long time ago, and I had a girlfriend, and the first time I stayed at her house we stayed in separate bedrooms, because it was in the less pes... permissive times (*uh hum*) and I had this incredibly vivid dream. You know sometimes when you wake up and you're not sure what's more real (*Yeah, yeah I do*) the dream or what's around you. It was like that. Erm, there was nothing very momentous happened in the dream, but in the main part of it I was walking along a street in the town where I originally come from, and I bumped into my girlfriend unexpectedly, and we stood in the street and we kissed and everyone was looking, and it was just a really strange atmosphere. (*laughs*) Right? (*Yeah*.) And I was lying there, in bed, and I was just thinking how incredibly vivid this dream was, I could just remember every detail of, of the scene. And then my girlfriend came in with a cup of tea for me. And she walked in the door and said 'wow I had this really strange dream last night'. And I just felt uneasy already, ... erm ... and I suppose it was ... like an experience of *déjà vu*, (*Yeah go on, go on*) which I'd never had before. I just knew what she was going to say, it felt like that, and she went on to describe the dream that she'd had and it was *exactly* the same as the dream I'd had (*Wow, that's w... that's really weird!*). It was, and she said how incredibly vivid it was, and then she looked at me and said 'what's wrong?' (*laughs*) because I, I must have looked very, very shocked. And I asked her to describe the street where we were ... er ... and where we'd been standing there kissing. And she described the shop we were standing in front of, (*yeah*) and she said it was a stationer's shop. Erm ... she remembered that, selling pens and paper, and stuff like that, which is exactly right. Erm ... and I was feeling pretty cold and shivery by this time. (*I bet you were.*) Well, the really spooky part is that of course I knew it was the town I'd grown up in, but at this point she'd never been there, (*laughs*) so she didn't know the town at all (*Well, that's amazing!*) and yet she was describing it very accurately. And I was... I was kind of obsessed by this point. I wanted to make sure it wasn't just a similar street and I drew this little map of the street and asked her to describe things, and she put loads of details onto it ... erm ... like she could say exactly where the traffic lights and the pedestrian crossing was. So, I don't know, it must have been my dream in a way because only I knew the town, but somehow I must have transmitted it to her. It's just inexplicable. (*How clever of you!*) Well, I did – I saw a TV programme ... er ... last year ... erm ... in which they said that it, it's called 'dream telepathy', and they say it's not that unusual in dreams (*Well I've never heard of it before.*). Haven't you? Well, it's never happened to me since, and to be honest, I, I can't say I'd want it to, because it was, it was actually strangely very disturbing. (*Well it sounds like it!*)

T 11.8

1 **A** I could kick myself. As soon as I'd handed it in, I remembered what the answer was.
   B Oh, I hate it when that happens! But do you think you've still passed?
2 **A** I don't believe it! I've spent all morning trying to send this, and all I get is 'Ooops! Your message wasn't sent. Try again later'.
   B What a pain! Have you tried ringing the computer helpline?
3 **A** These instructions don't make any sense to me at all. If you can follow them, you're a genius.
   B Don't ask me! This flatpack stuff is a nightmare! I had exactly the same trouble trying to put up a bedside table.
4 **A** It's not fair. I'd been looking forward to watching it all day and then the phone goes and rings!
   B Typical! And who was it? Anyone interesting?
5 **A** How many times do I have to tell you? Take them off *before* you come into the house!
   B Give me a break! I was in a hurry. Anyway, they're only a *bit* muddy.
6 **A** This has gone beyond a joke. You promised you'd deliver it by Tuesday at the latest. Now you're saying next month!
   B I'm awfully sorry, sir. I'm afraid there's nothing I can do about it. It's out of my hands.
7 **A** I went away to think about it, and of course, when I went back it had been sold. I wish I'd just bought it there and then.
   B It's such a shame. It would have gone so well with your white jeans.
8 **A** What a waste of time! Ten minutes listening to music and 'All our lines are busy. Thank you for waiting'.
   B I know, it drives me mad. But worse still is that you *never* get to speak to a real person anyway!

T 11.9 See p101

UNIT 12

T 12.1

My grandfather, who's a widower, used to be a judge and when he retired the year before last, he decided to go on a sea cruise. He enjoyed the cruise very much indeed. He sailed all round the world and it sounded like a great experience. Anyway, the most interesting thing about this cruise was that he met an attractive, American widow – I think she's pretty rich as well. She comes from California. Well, my grandfather invited her to have dinner with him and they got on really well with one another. And would you believe it, my grandfather fell in love? No kidding! He says you can find love at any age, and the next thing *we* knew he'd asked her to marry him. Apparently, they were married by the captain of the ship. It's so romantic. The whole family's amazed, but we're all very happy for him 'cos he's been rather lonely since my grandmother died. I just hope I find love one day, like Grandpa.

T 12.2

1 I don't like cereal for breakfast.
2 Do any of your friends like dancing?
3 What are the people in your class like?
4 I just sent my nephew £10 for his birthday.
5 Did you know Bob's training to be a vet and he doesn't even like animals.
6 Isn't your mother Scottish?
7 What do you think the most important thing in life is?
8 I bet you've told loads of girls that you love them.
9 It's very kind of you to offer but I can't take your car. You might want to use it this afternoon.
10 There was quite a crowd at your birthday party, wasn't there?

T 12.3

1 **A** I don't like cereal for breakfast.
   B Well, would you like an egg? A boiled egg and some toast?
2 **A** Do any of your friends like dancing?
   B What d'you mean *any*? *All* my friends like dancing. We go every Saturday night.
3 **A** What are the people in your class like?
   B They're great. Every person in my class is really friendly. We all get on really well together.
4 **A** I've just sent my nephew £10 for his birthday.
   B Well, I have five nieces, I gave £10 to each one for Christmas. Cost me a fortune.
   A I only have the one nephew at the moment. Thank goodness.
5 **A** Did you know Bob's training to be a vet and he doesn't even like animals?
   B I'd have thought that a love of animals was vital for a vet.
   A Me too. I think it's 'cos he wanted to be a doctor but he failed the exams.
6 **A** Isn't your mother Scottish?
   B In fact *both* my parents are Scottish. My father was born in Glasgow but he moved to London when he was eighteen.
7 **A** What do you think the most important thing in life is?
   B I think love is everything. If you can find true love you'll be happy forever.
8 **A** I bet you've told loads of girls that you love them.
   B This time it's different. The love I have for you is forever. I've never felt like this before.
9 **A** It's very kind of you to offer but I can't take your car. You might want to use it this afternoon.
   B Look, I have *two* cars. Borrow either one, I don't mind. I probably won't be using either anyway.
10 **A** There was quite a crowd at your birthday party, wasn't there?
   B Yeah, it was great to see everyone and I think they all had a good time.

T 12.4

1 What's that song you're singing?
2 Look at this ladybird on my hand!
3 Did you hear that storm in the middle of the night?
4 Mmm! These strawberries are delicious!
5 Take those dirty shoes off! I've just cleaned in here.
6 I can't stand this weather. It's really getting me down.
7 Who was that man you were talking to this morning?
8 Do you remember when we were young? Those were the days!
9 Children have no respect for authority these days, do they?

T 12.5

1 **A** What was the meal like?
   B It was revolting, every bit as bad as you said it would be.
2 **A** Did you apologize to all the guests?
   B Each and every one of them. I felt I had to.
3 **A** They didn't all pass, did they?
   B All but three did. Seventeen out of twenty, that's not bad.
4 **A** Sorry, I only have 50p on me.
   B Don't worry. Every little helps you know.
5 **A** When do you think you'll get there?
   B All being well, we should be there about six.
6 **A** Do you fancy a quick pint?
   B If it's all the same to you, I'd rather not.

T 12.6

1 **Bernie Danziger**
Personally, I'm just happy to be alive. I have this enormous appetite to get what I can out of life. I know it sounds corny but after all that I've been through I just appreciate each day. Er – every single day I have with my wife and kids is much more than I thought I'd have a few years ago. It all started in my 20s – I began to feel very run-down and being a sporty person it was clear something wasn't quite right. Anyway, I had some tests and when the results came through, the doctor walked into the room and I just knew from his face that it was something awful. .. ... er ... I'd been diagnosed with a rare liver disease and he told me that if I didn't have a transplant, I'd be dead in 18 months. I went into denial. You see, I'd recently married and our baby son had just been born and I couldn't bear the thought of him being fatherless. Anyway, I had the transplant and at first everyone was full of optimism but in fact it ... the transplant failed to take and ... er ... ... from elation I was plunged again into despair. I had to wait for a suitable match, a suitable donor to be found – it was torture, not only for me, but for my whole family. This time though, after the operation I knew immediately it would be OK. It felt different. Eventually I started working again. These days the only thing that makes me unhappy is meeting people who don't realize what a gift life is – they just take all they have for granted. I could never do that. The birth of our daughter a year ago was for me just the icing on the cake.

2 **Hayley**
I = Interviewer H = Hayley
I Teenagers get a bad press, don't they?
H I know and I think it's just so unfair – you watch telly or read the papers and it's all kids getting kicks from drugs and booze and stuff.
I So what do you and your friends get your kicks from?
H Well, of course we like going out and having good times. We go clubbing and stuff ...
I And drinking?
H Well, actually, most of us just get off on dancing. I just lose myself when I'm dancing I ...
I D'you have a boyfriend?
H Not at the moment. Life's simpler that way. I'm really happier without one. You have a boyfriend and all they ever want to do is watch football, play football, talk about football. Boring! I have really good times with my girlfriends. We do things and have proper conversations.
I So what do you talk about? Boys?
H OK, yeah sometimes. But loads of things. Honestly, my best times are evenings chatting with my girlfriends.
I Do any of them have boyfriends?
H Oh yeah. Some girls have to have boyfriends. You know what I mean.
I What do you mean?
H Well, you know, they don't feel good about themselves unless they have a boyfriend in tow. It's all they want to talk about ... ugh ...
I And you don't like that?
H Absolutely. I think it's pathetic. I want to feel I

can do things for myself, by myself, before I tie myself to one person. I had a boyfriend for three years when I was fifteen – yeah he was lovely but you can't have a relationship for life that begins when you're fifteen.

I Some people do.

H Mmm ... not these days. I want to see the world, meet lots of people, get a good career before I settle down.

I Sounds exciting. Good luck with it all.

3 **Tony**

The kind of things that get me down are part political and part physical. I suppose like a lot of old, well or older, people, I think the world has gone to pot. All these politicians come and go, but they don't make any difference, they all sound the same, they, they make promises and then break them. Not like politicians when I was younger, I can tell you. And then, on the physical side, I don't have the energy I used to have. I'm exhausted by tea-time. I always seem to have aches and pains somewhere – knees, hip, shoulder, back. Best thing I ever did was take early retirement. Honestly! It was like buying my life back. Suddenly I could do what I wanted. The first thing we did, Lizzie and me, was move to the country. We have a fantastic cottage by the sea in Devon, and we love taking our dog, Bonnie, for walks on the beach, or the cliffs, or the estuaries. We have quite a big garden, and there, there is no better feeling for me than spending the whole day outside. I like to, to walk round it in the early morning, listening to the birds, and smelling the fresh, early-morning air. I planted an orchard a year or so ago, and that's coming on well, and -er Lizzie and I are quite content just to potter in the vegetable patch, or cut the grass, or weed the flower beds. Having said that, we often go out for lunch with friends, or we have friends come and stay with us for the weekend, and of course they need entertaining with some good food and wine! Lizzie's the food expert, and -er I look after the wine. One of my favourite moments is, is to, –er just sit out on the terrace in the evening and, and watch the sunset, with a good book in one hand and a glass of wine in the other.

4 **Tommy**

I = Interviewer   T = Tommy

I So what makes you happy, Tommy?

T Mmmm ... er ... my *best* thing is to go to Bigbury Beach.

I Oh, where's that?

T It's where the sea is.

I Nice. What do you do there?

T I play ... I play with my brother in the rock pools and we have buckets and spades and when the tide's in we go on the sea tractor and ...

I A sea tractor? What's that?

T You know, it's when the tide comes in and you can't get to the island, so you go on the sea tractor. It's got big, big wheels, hugest wheels ever.

I Bigger than you?

T Yeaah. THIS BIG. You have to climb up the steps at back, at the back to get on it.

I Wow! And it goes through the water to the island?

T Yeah. I like it. It costs 60p.

I Is that right? It sounds great, Tommy, and going on the sea tractor makes you happy. So what makes you unhappy?

T ... er ... ... er ... I think it's – it's – I think it's when birds die.

I When *birds* die!?

T Yeah, I don't like it.

I Have you *seen* birds die?

T Yeah, our cat got one in the garden and it was dead and it made me sad.

I Ah, I see. That *is* sad when a cat catches a bird.

T Yeah and I saw it lying on our path. I didn't like it.

T 12.7

1 **A** I can't believe it. I failed again.
  B Never mind. You'll have better luck next time.

A But that was the second time.
  B They say the best drivers pass on the third try.

2 **A** Come on! Get up! Get a life!
  B What'd'you mean?
  A Well, it's high time you did something other than watch TV soaps all day.
  B Like what?
  A I dunno. Travel, see the world. See life.
  B Boring.
  A I give up. Be a couch potato if that's what you want.

3 **A** Oh no! We've missed it. It must have left dead on time.
  B I thought we might just get it.
  A What do we do now? There isn't another until 1 o'clock.
  B That's nearly two hours to kill!
  A More shopping?
  B Not on your life. I'm shopped-out! Let's just get a coffee. There's a café on platform 1.

4 **A** How's it going?
  B Well, they've finished at last but not before time – only four weeks late.
  A And how much is it all going to cost?
  B We haven't had the final bill yet.
  A Well, you can bet your life it'll be more than they estimated.
  B I know. We *were* going to have the kitchen decorated as well, but enough's enough for the time being.

5 **A** How come Dave has such a cushy life? He never seems to do any work.
  B Didn't you know? He won the lottery.
  A You're kidding! I had no idea. I do the lottery every week and never win a thing.
  B Me neither. That's life.

T 12.8 **That's Life**

That's life, that's what people say.
You're riding' high in April,
Shot down in May.
But I know I'm gonna change that tune,
When I'm back on top in June.
That's life, funny as it seems.
Some folks get their kicks,
Steppin' on dreams;
But I don't let it get me down,
'cause this ol' world keeps spinnin' around.
I've been a puppet, a pauper, a pirate,
A poet, a pawn and a king.
I've been up and down and over and out
And I know one thing:
Each time I find myself flat on my face,
I pick myself up and get back in the race.
That's life, I can't deny it,
I thought of quitting,
But my heart just won't buy it.
If I didn't think it was worth a try,
I'd roll myself up in a big ball and die.

T 12.9

1 **A** Did you see the match last night?
  B No, but apparently it was a good game. We won, didn't we?
  A Actually, it was a draw, but it was really exciting.

2 **A** What do you think of Claire's new boyfriend?
  B Personally, I can't stand him. I think he'll dump her like all the rest. However, that's her problem, not mine.
  A Poor old Claire! She always picks the wrong ones, doesn't she? Anyway, we'll see soon enough.

3 **A** I don't know how you can afford to buy all those fabulous clothes!
  B Hopefully, I'm going to get a bonus this month. My boss has promised. After all, I did earn the company over £100,000 last year. Basically, I deserve it.

4 **A** She said some terrible things to me. I hate her!
  B All the same, I think you should apologize to her. If you ask me, you lose your temper too

easily. You're being very childish. It's time you both grew up!

A What?! I never thought I'd hear you speak to me like that.
  B Honestly, I'm not taking sides. I just think you should make up.

5 **A** So, Billy. You say that this is the last record you're ever going to make?
  B Definitely.
  A But surely you realize how upset your fans are going to be?
  B Obviously, I don't want to hurt anyone, but basically I'm fed up with pop music. I'd like to do something else. Ideally, I'd like to get into films.

Grammar Reference

UNIT 1

▶ 1.1 The tense system

There are three classes of verbs in English: auxiliary verbs, modal verbs, and full verbs.

1 Auxiliary verbs

The auxiliary verbs are *be*, *do*, and *have*.

be

1 *Be* is used with verb + *-ing* to make continuous verb forms.
You're lying. (present)
They were reading. (past)
I've been swimming. (present perfect)
We'll be having dinner at 8 o'clock. (future)
You must be joking! (infinitive)

2 *Be* is used with the past participle to make the passive.
These books are printed in Hong Kong. (present)
Where were you born? (past)
The car's been serviced. (present perfect)
The city had been destroyed. (past perfect)
This work should be done soon. (infinitive)

do

1 *Do/does/did* are used in the Present Simple and the Past Simple.
Do you smoke? (question)
She doesn't understand. (negative)
When did they arrive? (question)

2 *Do/does/did* are used to express emphasis when there is no other auxiliary.
I'm not interested in sport, but I do like tennis.
'If only she had a car!' 'She does have a car!'
'Why didn't you tell me?' 'I did tell you!'

have

Have is used with the past participle to make perfect verb forms.
Have you ever tried sushi? (present)
My car had broken down before. (past)
I'll have finished soon. (future)
I'd like to have met Napoleon. (infinitive)
Having had lunch, we tidied up. (participle)

---

have and have got

1 *Have* and *have got* are both used to express present possession.

Do you have
Have you got | any brothers or sisters?

Yes, | *I do. I have*
| *I have. I've got* | two brothers.

2 *Have to* can be replaced with *have got to* for present obligation.

Do you have to
Have you got to | go now?

Yes, | *I do. I have to*
| *I have. I've got to* | catch the bus.

3 Only forms of have (not have got) are used in all other tenses.
I had my first car when I was nineteen.
I've had this car for two years.
I'll have a strawberry ice-cream, please.
I'd had three cars by the time I was twenty.
I'd like to have a dog.
He loves having a sports car.

---

4 *Have* (not *have got*) is used in many expressions.

have breakfast	have a bath
have a party	have a good time
have fun	have a word with someone

5 *Have got* is generally more informal. It is used more in spoken English than in written English. However, they are often interchangeable.
Have with the *do/does* forms is more common in American English.

Other uses of auxiliary verbs

1 In question tags.
It's cold today, isn't it?
You don't understand, do you?
You haven't been to China, have you?

2 In short answers. *Yes* or *No* alone can sound abrupt.
'Are you hungry?' 'No, I'm not.'
'Do you like jazz?' 'Yes, I do.'
'Did you have a nice meal?' 'Yes, we did.'
'Has she seen the mess?' 'No, she hasn't.'

3 In reply questions. These are not real questions. They are used to show that the listener is paying attention and is interested. They are practised on p33 of the Student's Book.
'The party was awful.' 'Was it? What a pity.'
'I love hamburgers.' 'Do you? I hate them.'
'I've bought you a present.' 'Have you? How kind!'

2 Modal auxiliary verbs

These are the modal auxiliary verbs.

can	could	may	might	will	would
shall	should	must	ought to	need	

They are auxiliary verbs because they 'help' other verbs. They are different from *be*, *do*, and *have* because they have their own meanings.
He must be at least 70. (= probability)
You must try harder. (= obligation)
Can you help me? (= request)
She can't have got my letter. (= probability)
I'll help you. (= willingness)
(Ring) That'll be the postman. (= probability)
Modal auxiliary verbs are dealt with in Units 5, 7, 9, 10, and 11.

3 Full verbs

Full verbs are all the other verbs in the language.

run	walk	eat	love	go	talk	write

The verbs *be*, *do*, and *have* can also be used as full verbs with their own meanings.
Have you been to school today?
I want to be an engineer.
I do a lot of business in Russia.
The holiday did us a lot of good.
They're having a row.
Have you had enough to eat?

▶ 1.2 English tense usage

English tenses have two elements of meaning: time and aspect.

Time

1 The time referred to is usually obvious.
English people drink tea. (all time)
Shh! I'm watching this programme! (now)

I'll see you later. (future)
I went out with Jenny last night. (past)

2 Sometimes a present tense form can refer to the future.
I'm going out tonight. (Present Continuous for near future)
The train leaves at 10.00 tomorrow. (Present Simple for a timetable)
If you see Peter, say hello from me. (Present Simple in a subordinate clause)

3 Sometimes a past tense form can refer to the present.
I wish I could help you, but I can't.
This use of unreal tense usage is dealt with in Unit 11.

The simple aspect

1 The simple aspect describes an action that is seen to be complete. The action is viewed as a whole unit.
The sun rises in the east. (= all time)
When I've read the book, I'll lend it to you. (= complete)
She has red hair. (= permanent)
He always wore a suit. (= a habit)
It rained every day of our holiday. (= the whole two weeks)
This shop will close at 7.00 this evening. (= a fact)

2 Remember the verbs that rarely take the continuous. This is because they express states that are seen to be permanent and not subject to frequent change.

Verbs of the mind	know	understand	believe	think	mean
Verbs of emotions	love	hate	like	prefer	care
Verbs of possession	have	own	belong		
Certain other verbs	cost	need	contain	depend	

3 The simple aspect expresses a completed action. For this reason we must use the simple, not the continuous, if the sentence contains a number that refers to 'things done'.
She's written three letters this morning.
I drink ten cups of tea a day.
He read five books while he was on holiday.
Simple tenses are dealt with further in Units 2, 3, and 5.

The continuous aspect

1 The continuous aspect focuses on the duration of an activity. We are aware of the passing of time between the beginning and the end of the activity. The activity is not permanent.
I'm staying with friends until I find a flat. (= temporary)
What are you doing on your hands and knees? (= in progress)
I've been learning English for years. (And I still am.)
Don't phone at 8.00. We'll be eating. (= in progress)

2 Because the activity is seen in progress, it can be interrupted.
We were walking across a field when we were attacked by a bull.
'Am I disturbing you?' 'No. I'm just doing the ironing.'

3 The activity may not be complete.
I was writing a report on the flight home. (I didn't finish it.)
He was drowning, but we saved him. (He didn't die.)
Who's been drinking my beer? (There's some left.)

4 The action of some verbs, by definition, lasts a long time, for example, *live*, *work*, *play*. The continuous gives these actions limited duration and makes them temporary.
Hans is living in London while he's learning English.
I'm working as a waiter until I go to university.
Henman has been playing well recently. Maybe he'll win Wimbledon.

5 The action of some other verbs lasts a short time, for example, *lose*, *break*, *cut*, *hit*, *crash*. They are often found in the simple.
I lost all my money. *I've crashed your car. Sorry.*
She's cut her finger. *He hit me.*
In the continuous, the action of these verbs seems longer or habitual.
I've been cutting the grass. (= for hours)
He was hitting me. (= again and again)

Note
We cannot say a sentence such as *I've been crashing your car* because it suggests an activity that was done deliberately and often.
Continuous tenses are dealt with further in Units 2, 3, and 5.

The perfect aspect

The perfect aspect expresses two ideas.

1 The action is completed before another time.
Have you ever been to America? (= some time before now)
When I arrived, Peter had left. (= some time before I arrived)
I'll have finished the report by 10.00. (= some time before then)

2 The exact time of the verb action is not important. The perfect aspect refers to indefinite time.
Have you seen my wallet anywhere? I've lost it. (= before now)
We'll have arrived by this evening. (= before this evening)
The exception to this is the Past Perfect, which *can* refer to definite time.
I recognized him immediately. I had met him in 1992 at university.
Perfect tenses are dealt with further in Units 2, 3, and 5.

Active and passive

1 Passive sentences move the focus of attention from the subject of an active sentence to the object.
Shakespeare wrote Hamlet in 1599.
Hamlet, one of the great tragedies, was written in 1599.

2 In most cases, *by* and the agent are omitted in passive sentences. This is because the agent is not important, isn't known, or is understood.
My car was stolen yesterday.
This house was built in the seventeenth century.
She was arrested for shoplifting.

3 Sometimes we prefer to begin a sentence with what is known, and end a sentence with what is 'new'. In the passive, the 'new' can be the agent of the active sentence.
'What a lovely painting!' 'Yes. It was painted by Canaletto.'

4 In informal language, we often use *you* or *they* to refer to people in general or to no person in particular. In this way we can avoid using the passive.
You can buy anything in Harrods.
They're building a new airport soon.

5 There are many past participles that are used more like adjectives.
I'm very impressed by your work.
You must be disappointed with your exam results.
I'm exhausted! I've been on my feet all day.
Passive sentences are dealt with further in Unit 3.

UNIT 2

Introduction to the Present Perfect

1 Many languages have a past tense to refer to past time, and a present tense to refer to present time. English has these, too, but it also has the Present Perfect, which relates past actions to the present.

2 The use of the Past Simple roots an action in the past, with no explicit connection to the present. When we come across a verb in the Past Simple, we want to know *When?*

3 The use of the Present Perfect always has a link with the present. When we come across a verb in the Present Perfect, we want to know how this affects the situation now.

4 Compare these sentences.
I lived in Rome. (But not any more.)
I've lived in Rome, Paris, and New York. (I know all these cities now.)
I've been living in New York for ten years. (And I'm living there now.)

*She's **been married** three times.* (She's still alive.)
*She was **married** three times.* (She's dead.)
***Did** you **see** the Renoir exhibition?* (It's finished now.)
***Have** you **seen** the Renoir exhibition?* (It's still on.)
***Did** you **see** that programme on TV?* (I'm thinking of the one that was on last night.)
***Did** you **enjoy** the film?* (Said as we're leaving the cinema.)
***Have** you **enjoyed** the holiday?* (Said near the end of the holiday.)
*Where **have** I **put** my glasses?* (I want them now.)
*Where **did** I **put** my glasses?* (I had them a minute ago.)
*It **rained** yesterday.* (= past time)
*It's **been snowing**.* (There's snow still on the ground.)

Present Perfect Simple and Continuous

See the introduction to the perfect aspect and the continuous aspect in Unit 1. These tenses have three main uses.

1 Unfinished past

The verb action began in the past and continues to the present. It possibly goes on into the future, as well.

*We've **lived** in this house for twenty years.*
*Sorry I'm late. **Have** you **been waiting** long?*
*I've **been** a teacher for five years.*
*I've **been working** at the same school all that time.*

Notes

- There is sometimes little or no difference between the simple and the continuous.

  *I've **played*** | *tennis since I was a kid.*
  *I've **been playing*** |

- The continuous can sometimes suggest a more temporary situation. The simple can sound more permanent.

  *I've **been living** with a host family for six weeks.*
  *The castle **has stood** on the hill overlooking the sea for centuries.*

- Certain verbs, by definition, suggest duration, for example, *wait, rain, snow, learn, sit, lie, play, stay*. They are often found in the continuous.

  *It's **been raining** all day.*
  *She's **been sitting** reading for hours.*

- Remember that state verbs rarely take the continuous.

  *I've **known** Joan for years.* *I've been knowing
  How long **have** you **had** that car?* *have you been having
  I've never **understood** why she likes him.* *I've never been understanding

2 Present result

The verb action happened in the past, usually the recent past, and the results of the action are felt now.

*You've **changed**. What **have** you **done** to yourself?*
*I've **lost** some weight.*
*I've **been doing** some exercise.*
*I'm covered in mud because I've **been gardening**.*

In this use, the simple emphasizes the completed action. The continuous emphasizes the repeated activities over a period of time.

Notes

- Certain verbs, by definition, suggest a short action, for example, *start, find, lose, begin, stop, break, die, decide, cut*. They are more often found in the simple.

  *We've **decided** to get married.*
  *I've **broken** a tooth.*
  *I've **cut** my finger.*

  In the continuous, these verbs suggest a repeated activity.

  *I've **been stopping** smoking for years.*
  *You've **been losing** everything lately. What's the matter with you?*
  *I've **been cutting** wood.*

- The use of the simple suggests a completed action.

  *I've **painted** the bathroom.*

The use of the continuous suggests a possibly incomplete action.

*I'm tired because I've **been working**.* (Finished? Not finished?)
*Someone's **been drinking** my beer.* (There's some left.)

- The continuous can be found unqualified by any further information.

  *I'm wet because I've **been swimming**.*
  *We're tired because we've **been working**.*
  *'Why are you red?' 'I've **been running**.'*
  The simple sounds quite wrong in this use.
  *I've swum. *We've worked. *I've run.

- Sometimes there is little difference between the Past Simple and the Present Perfect.

  Where | *did you put* | *my keys?*
  | *have you put* |

- American English is different from British English. In American English, these sentences are correct.

  Did you hear the news? The President resigned!
  Did you do your homework yet?
  Your father just called you.
  I had breakfast already.

3 Indefinite past

The verb action happened at an unspecified time in the past. The actual time isn't important. We are focusing on the experience at some time in our life.

***Have** you ever **taken** any illegal drugs?*
*She's never **been** abroad.*
***Have** you ever **been flying** in a plane when it's hit an air pocket?*

Note

- Notice these two sentences.

  *She's **been** to Spain.* (At some time in her life.)
  *She's **gone** to Spain.* (And she's there now.)
  The first is an example of indefinite past.
  The second is an example of present result.

UNIT 3

Narrative tenses

Past Simple and Present Perfect

See the introduction to the perfect aspect and the simple aspect on p141. The Past Simple differs from all three uses of the Present Perfect.

1 The Past Simple refers to **finished past**.
   *Shakespeare **wrote** plays.* (He's dead.)
   *I've **written** short stories.* (I'm alive.)

2 There is **no present result**.
   *I **hurt** my back.* (But it's better now.)
   *I've **hurt** my back.* (And it hurts now.)

3 It refers to **definite past**.

   *I **saw** him* | *last night.*
   | *two weeks ago.*
   | *on Monday.*
   | *at 8.00.*

   Compare this with the indefinite adverbials found with the Present Perfect.

   *I've **seen** him* | *recently.*
   | *before.*

   *I haven't **seen** him* | *since January.*
   | *yet.*
   | *for months.*

   I've | *never* | *seen him.*
   | *just* |

Note

Even when there is no past time adverbial, we can 'build' a past time in our head.

Did you have a good journey? (The journey's over. You're here now.)
Thank you for supper. It was lovely. (The meal is finished.)
Where did you buy that shirt? (when you were out shopping the other day.)

Past Simple

The Past Simple is used:

1 to express a finished action in the past.
   Columbus discovered America in 1492.

2 to express actions which follow each other in a story.
   I heard voices coming from downstairs, so I put on my dressing-gown and went to investigate.

3 to express a past state or habit.
   When I was a child, we lived in a small house by the sea. Every day I walked for miles on the beach with my dog.

This use is often expressed with *used to*.

We used to live ...
I used to walk ...

See Unit 9 for more information on *used to*.
See Unit 11 for information on the Past Simple used for hypothesis.

Past Continuous

See the introduction to the continuous aspect on p141.
The Past Continuous is used:

1 to express an activity in progress before and probably after a time in the past.
   I phoned at 4.00, but there was no reply. What were you doing?

2 to describe a past situation or activity.
   The cottage was looking so cosy. A fire was burning in the grate, music was playing, and from the kitchen were coming the most delicious smells.

3 to express an interrupted past activity.
   I was having a bath when the phone rang.

4 to express an incomplete activity in the past.
   I was reading a book during the flight. (But I didn't finish it.)
   I watched a film during the flight. (the whole film)

5 to express an activity that was in progress at every moment during a period of time.
   I was working all day yesterday.
   They were fighting for the whole of the holiday.

Notes

• The Past Simple expresses past actions as simple, complete facts. The Past Continuous gives past activities time and duration.
   'What did you do last night?'
   'I stayed at home and watched the football.'
   'I phoned you last night, but there was no reply.'
   'Oh, I was watching the football and I didn't hear the phone. Sorry.'

• Notice how the questions in the Past Continuous and Past Simple refer to different times.
   When we arrived, Jan was ironing. She stopped ironing and made some coffee.
   What was she doing when we arrived? She was ironing.
   What did she do when we arrived? She made some coffee.

Past Perfect

See the introduction to the perfect aspect and the continuous aspect on p141.
The Past Perfect is used to look back to a time in the past and refer to an action that happened before then.

She was crying because her dog had died.

I arrived to pick up Dave, but he had already left.
Keith was fed up. He'd been looking for a job for months, but he'd found nothing.

Notes

• The continuous refers to longer actions or repeated activities. The simple refers to shorter, complete facts.
   He'd lost his job and his wife had left him. Since then he'd been sleeping rough, and he hadn't been eating properly.

• The Past Perfect can refer to definite as well as indefinite time.
   I knew his face immediately. I'd first met him in October 1993. (= definite)
   I recognized her face. I'd seen her somewhere before. (= indefinite)

Past Perfect and Past Simple

1 Verbs in the Past Simple tell a story in chronological order.
   John worked hard all day to prepare for the party. Everyone had a good time. Even the food was all right. Unfortunately, Andy upset Peter, so Peter left early. Pat came looking for Peter, but he wasn't there.
   It was a great party. John sat and looked at all the mess. He felt tired. It was time for bed.

2 By using the Past Perfect, the speaker or writer can tell a story in a different order.
   John sat and looked at all the mess. It had been a great party, and everyone had had a good time. Even the food had been all right. Unfortunately, Andy upset Peter, so Peter left early. Pat came looking for Peter, but he'd already gone.
   John felt tired. He'd been working all day to prepare for the party. It was time for bed.

Note

For reasons of style, it is not necessary to have every verb in the Past Perfect.

... Andy upset Peter ... Peter left ...

Once the time of 'past in the past' has been established, the Past Simple can be used as long as there is no ambiguity.

Time clauses

1 We can use time conjunctions to talk about two actions that happen one after the other. Usually the Past Perfect is not necessary in these cases, although it can be used.
   After I'd had/had a bath, I went to bed.
   As soon as the guests left/had left, I started tidying up.
   I sat outside until the sun had gone/went down.

2 The Past Perfect can help to make the first action seem separate, independent of the second, or completed before the second action started.
   When I had read the paper, I threw it away.
   We stayed up until all the beer had gone.

3 Two verbs in the Past Simple can suggest that the first action led into the other, or that one caused the other to happen.
   When I heard the news, I burst out crying.
   As soon as the alarm went off, I got up.

4 The Past Perfect is more common with *when* because it is ambiguous. The other conjunctions are more specific, so the Past Perfect is not so essential.
   As soon as all the guests left, I tidied the house.
   Before I met you, I didn't know the meaning of happiness.
   When I opened the door, the cat jumped out.
   When I'd opened the mail, I made another cup of tea.

See Unit 11 for information on the Past Perfect used for hypothesis.

UNIT 4

🔊 4.1 Questions

Question forms

Notice these question forms.

- Subject questions with no auxiliary verb
  Who broke the window?
  What happens at the end of the book?

- Questions with prepositions at the end
  Who is your letter **from**?
  What are you talking **about**?

- Question words + noun/adjective/adverb
  What sort of music do you like?
  How big is their new house?
  How fast does your car go?

- Other ways of asking *Why?*
  What did you do that **for**?
  How come you got here before us?

  How come …? expresses surprise. Notice that there is no inversion in this question form.

what and which

1 *What* and *which* are used with nouns to make questions.
  What size shoes do you take?
  Which of these curries is the hottest?

2 Sometimes there is no difference between questions with *what* and *which*.
  What/which is the biggest city in your country?
  What/which channel is the match on?

3 We use *which* when the speaker has a limited number of choices in mind.
  There's a blue one and a red one. **Which** do you want?

  We use *what* when the speaker is not thinking of a limited number of choices.
  What car do you drive?

Asking for descriptions

1 *What is X like?* means Give me some information about X because I don't know anything about it.
  What's your capital city **like**?
  What are your parents **like**?

2 *How is X?* asks about a person's health and happiness.
  How's your mother these days?

  Sometimes both questions are possible. *What … like?* asks for objective information. *How … ?* asks for a more personal reaction.
  '**What** was the party **like**?' *'Noisy. Lots of people. It went on till 3.'*
  '**How** was the party?' *'Brilliant. I danced all night. Met loads of great people.'*
  How was your journey?
  How's your new job going?
  How's your meal?

Indirect questions

There is no inversion and no *do/does/did* in indirect questions.
I wonder what she's doing. **I wonder ~~what is she doing~~.*
I don't know where he lives. **I don't know ~~where does he live~~.*
Tell me when the train leaves.
Do you remember how she made the salad?
I didn't understand what she was saying.
I've no idea why he went to India.
I'm not sure where they live.
He doesn't know whether he's coming or going.

🔊 4.2 Negatives

Forming negatives

1 We make negatives by adding *not* after the auxiliary verb. If there is no auxiliary verb, we add *do/does/did*.
  *I **haven't** seen her for ages.*
  *It **wasn't** raining.*
  *You **shouldn't** have gone to so much trouble.*
  *We **don't** like big dogs.*
  *They **didn't** want to go out.*

2 The verb *have* has two forms in the present.
  *I **don't** have ⎫ any money.*
  *I **haven't** got ⎭*
  *But … I **didn't** have any money.*

3 Infinitives and *-ing* forms can be negative.
  *We decided **not to do** anything.*
  *I like **not working**. It suits me.*

4 *Not* can go with other parts of a sentence.
  *Ask him, **not me**.*
  *Buy me anything, but **not perfume**.*

5 When we introduce negative ideas with verbs such as *think, believe, suppose,* and *imagine,* we make the first verb negative, not the second.
  *I **don't think** you're right. *~~I think you aren't~~ …*
  *I **don't suppose** you want a game of tennis?*

6 In short answers, the following forms are possible.

  Are you coming? ⎧ *'I think so.'*
  ⎪ *'I believe so.'*
  ⎨ *'I hope so.'*
  ⎪ *'I don't think so.'*
  ⎩ *'I hope not.'*

  I think not is possible. *~~I don't hope so~~ is not possible.

Negative questions

1 Negative questions can express various ideas.
Haven't you **finished** school yet?	(surprise)
Don't you **think** we should wait for them?	(suggestion)
Wouldn't it be better to go tomorrow?	(persuasion)
Can't you **see** I'm busy? Go away!	(criticism)
Isn't it a lovely day!	(exclamation)

2 In the main use of negative questions, the speaker would normally expect a positive situation, but now expresses a negative situation. The speaker therefore is surprised.
  ***Don't** you **like** ice-cream? Everyone likes ice-cream!*
  ***Haven't** you **done** your homework yet? What have you been doing?*

3 Negative questions can also be used to mean *Confirm what I think is true.* In this use it refers to a positive situation.
  ***Haven't** I **met** you somewhere before? (I'm sure I have.)*
  ***Didn't** we **speak** about this yesterday? (I'm sure we did.)*

4 The difference between the two uses can be seen clearly if we change them into sentences with question tags.
  You haven't done your homework yet, have you? (negative sentence, positive tag)
  We've met before, haven't we? (positive sentence, negative tag)

UNIT 5

🔊 Introduction to future forms

There is no one future tense in English. Instead, there are several verb forms that can refer to future time. Sometimes, several forms are possible to express a similar meaning, but not always.

will for prediction

1 The most common use of *will* is as an auxiliary verb to show future time. It expresses a future fact or prediction – *at some time in the*

future this event will happen. This use is uncoloured by ideas such as intention, decision, arrangement, willingness, etc.

I'll be thirty in a few days' time.
It will be cold and wet tomorrow, I'm afraid.
Who do you think will win the match?
You'll feel better if you take this medicine.
I'll see you later.

This is the nearest English has to a neutral, pure future tense.

2 *Will* for a prediction can be based more on an opinion than a fact or evidence. It is often found with expressions such as *I think ..., I hope ..., I'm sure ... .*

I think Labour will win the next election.
I hope you'll come and visit me.
I'm sure you'll pass your exams.

3 *Will* is common in the main clause when there is a subordinate clause with *if, when, before*, etc. Note that we don't use *will* in the subordinate clause.

You'll break the glass if you aren't careful.
When you're ready, we'll start the meeting.
I won't go until you arrive.
As soon as Peter comes, we'll have lunch.

going to for prediction

Going to can express a prediction based on a present fact. There is evidence now that something is sure to happen. We can see the future from the present.

Careful! That glass is going to fall over. Too late!
Look at that blue sky! It's going to be a lovely day.

Notes

*   Sometimes there is little or no difference between *will* and *going to*.

    We'll | *run out of money if we aren't careful.*
    We're going to |

*   We use *going to* when we have physical evidence to support our prediction.

    She's going to have a baby. (Look at her bump.)
    Liverpool are going to win. (It's 4–0, and there are only five minutes left.)
    That glass is going to fall. (It's rolling to the edge of the table.)

*   We can use *will* when there is no such outside evidence. Our prediction is based on our own personal opinion. It can be more theoretical and abstract.

    I'm sure you'll have a good time at the party. (This is my opinion.)
    I reckon Liverpool will win. (Said the day before the match.)
    The glass will break if it falls. (This is what happens to glasses that fall.)

*   Compare the sentences.

    I bet John will be late home. The traffic is always bad at this time. (= my opinion)
    John's going to be late home. He left a message on the answerphone. (= a fact)
    Don't lend Keith your car. He'll crash it. (= a theoretical prediction)
    Look out! We're going to crash! (= a prediction based on evidence)

Decisions and intentions – *will* and *going to*

1 *Will* is used to express a decision or intention made at the moment of speaking.

I'll phone you back in a minute.
Give me a ring some time. We'll go out together.
'The phone's ringing.' 'I'll get it.'

2 *Going to* is used to express a future plan, decision, or intention made before the moment of speaking.

When she grows up, she's going to be a ballet dancer.
We're going to get married in the spring.

Other uses of *will* and *shall*

1 *Will* as a prediction is an auxiliary verb that simply shows future time. It has no real meaning.

Tomorrow will be cold and windy.

2 *Will* is also a modal auxiliary verb, and so it can express a variety of meanings. The meaning often depends on the meaning of the main verb.

I'll help you carry those bags. (= offer)
Will you marry me? (= willingness)
Will you open the window? (= request)
My car won't start. (= refusal)
I'll love you for ever. (= promise)   *'The phone's ringing.'*
                    'It'll be for me.' (= prediction about the present)

3 *Shall* is found mainly in questions. It is used with *I* and *we*.

Where shall I put your tea? (I'm asking for instructions.)
What shall we do tonight? (I'm asking for a decision.)
Shall I cook supper tonight? (I'm offering to help.)
Shall we eat out tonight? (I'm making a suggestion.)

Present Continuous for arrangements

1 The Present Continuous is used to express personal arrangements and fixed plans, especially when the time and place have been decided. A present tense is used because there is some reality in the present. The event is planned or decided, and we can see it coming. The event is usually in the near future.

I'm having lunch with Brian tomorrow.
What time are you meeting him?
Where are you having lunch?
What are you doing tonight?

2 The Present Continuous for future is often used with verbs of movement and activity.

Are you coming to the dance tonight?
I'm meeting the director tomorrow.
I'm just taking the dog for a walk.
We're playing tennis this afternoon.

3 The Present Continuous is used to refer to arrangements between people. It is not used to refer to events that people can't control.

It's going to rain this afternoon. *It's raining this afternoon.*
The sun rises at 5.30 tomorrow. *The sun is rising ...*

Notes

*   Sometimes there is little or no difference between the Present Continuous and *going to* to refer to the future.

    We're seeing | *Hamlet at the theatre tonight.*
    We're going to see |

*   When there is a difference, the Present Continuous emphasizes an arrangement with some reality in the present; *going to* expresses a person's intentions.

    I'm seeing my girlfriend tonight.
    I'm going to ask her to marry me. *I'm asking ...*
    What are you doing this weekend?
    What are you going to do about the broken toilet? (= What have you decided to do?)

Present Simple for timetables

1 The Present Simple refers to a future event that is seen as unalterable because it is based on a timetable or calendar.

My flight leaves at 10.00.
Term starts on 4 April.
What time does the film start?
It's my birthday tomorrow.

2 It is used in subordinate clauses introduced by conjunctions such as *if, when, before, as soon as, unless*, etc.

We'll have a picnic if the weather stays fine.
When I get home, I'll cook the dinner.
I'll leave as soon as it stops raining.

Future Continuous

1 The Future Continuous expresses an activity that will be in progress before and after a time in the future.
Don't phone at 8.00. We'll be having supper.
This time tomorrow I'll be flying to New York.

2 The Future Continuous is used to refer to a future event that will happen in the natural course of events. This use is uncoloured by ideas such as intention, decision, arrangement, or willingness. As time goes by, this event will occur.
Don't worry about our guests. They'll be arriving any minute now.
We'll be going right back to the football after the break. (said on television)

Future Perfect

The Future Perfect refers to an action that will be completed before a definite time in the future. It is not a very common verb form.
I'll have done all my work by this evening.

UNIT 6

Expressing quantity

Quantifiers

1 The following can be used before a noun.

some/any	much/many	each/every	more/most
a little/little	a few/few	both	fewer/less	several
all/no	enough		

With count nouns only	With uncount nouns only	With both count and uncount nouns
(not) many cigarettes a few cars very few trees fewer books several answers	(not) much luck a little cheese very little experience less time	some money some eggs (not) any water (not) any friends more/most wine more/most people all/no work all/no children enough food enough apples

With singular count nouns only	With plural count nouns only
each boy every time	both parents

2 Most of the quantifiers can be used without a noun. *No, all, every,* and *each* cannot.

Have you got any money?	**Not much/a little/enough.**
Are there any eggs?	**A few/not many.**
Have some wine.	*I don't want **any**.*
How many people came?	*Very **few**.*
Have some more tea.	*I've got **some**.*
Did Ann or Sam go?	**Both.**

3 Most of the quantifiers can be used with *of + the/my/those*, etc. + noun. *No* and *every* cannot.
*They took **all of my money**.*
*Take **a few of these tablets**.*
***Some of the people** at the party started dancing.*
*Were **any of my friends** at the party?*
*Very **few of my friends** smoke.*
*Not **much of the food** was left.*
*I've missed **too many of my French lessons**.*
*I couldn't answer **several of the questions**.*
*I'll have **a little of the strawberry cake**, please.*

Both of my children are clever.
*I feel tired **most of the time**.*
*I've had **enough of your jokes**.*

4 For *no* and *every*, we use *none* and *every one* or *all*.
***None of the audience** was listening.*
***All of the hotels** were booked.*
In formal, written English, *none* is followed by a singular form of the verb.
***None of the guests has** arrived yet.*
But in informal English, a plural verb is possible.
***None** of my friends **smoke**.*
***None** of the lights **are** working.*

Note
When we use *none* with a plural noun or pronoun, the verb can be singular or plural. Grammatically, it should be singular, but people often use the plural when they speak.
*None of my friends **is** coming.*
*None of my friends **are** coming.*

some, any, somebody, anything

1 The basic rule is that *some* and its compounds are used in affirmative sentences, and *any* and its compounds in negatives and questions.
*I need **some** help.*
*I need **somebody** to help me.*
*Give me **something** for my headache.*
*I don't need **any** shopping.*
*We can't go **anywhere** without being recognized.*
*Is there **any** sugar left?*
*Did **anyone** phone me last night?*

2 *Some* and its compounds are used in requests or invitations, or when we expect the answer 'yes'.
*Have you got **some** money you could lend me?*
*Would you like **something** to eat?*
*Did **someone** phone me last night?*
*Can we go **somewhere** quiet to talk?*

3 *Any* and its compounds are used in affirmative sentences that have a negative meaning.
*He **never** has **any** money.*
*You made **hardly any** mistakes.*
*I made the cake myself **without any** help.*

4 *Any* and its compounds are used to express *It doesn't matter which/who/where*.
*Take **any book** you like. I don't mind.*
***Anyone** will tell you 2 and 2 makes 4.*
*Sit **anywhere** you like.*
*I eat **anything**. I'm not fussy.*

nobody, no one, nowhere, nothing

1 These are more emphatic forms.
*I saw **nobody** all weekend.*
*I've eaten **nothing** all day.*

2 They can be used at the beginning of sentences.
***No one** was saved.*
***Nobody** understands me.*
***Nowhere** is safe any more.*

much, many, a lot of, lots of, a great deal of, a large number of, plenty of

1 *Much* and *many* are usually used in questions and negatives.
*How **much** does it cost?*
*How **many** people came to the party?*
*Is there **much** unemployment in your country?*
*I don't have **much** money.*
*Will there be **many** people there?*
*You don't see **many** snakes in England.*

2 We find *much* and *many* in affirmative sentences after *so, as,* and *too.*
   *He has **so much** money that he doesn't know what to do with it.*
   *She hasn't got **as many** friends as I have.*
   *You make **too many** mistakes. Be careful.*

3 In affirmative sentences, the following forms are found.

   Spoken/informal
   *There'll be **plenty of food/people**.* (uncount and count)
   *We've got **lots of time/friends**.* (uncount and count)
   *I lost **a lot of my furniture/things**.* (uncount and count)

   Written/more formal
   ***A great deal of money** was lost during the strike.* (uncount)
   ***A large number of strikes** are caused by bad management.* (count)
   ***Many world leaders** are quite young.* (count)
   ***Much time** is wasted in trivial pursuits.* (uncount)

4 These forms are found without nouns.
   *'Have you got enough socks?' '**Lots**.'*
   *'How many people were there?' '**A lot**.'*
   *Don't worry about food. We've got **plenty**.*

little/few/less/fewer

1 *A little* and *a few* express a small amount or number in a positive way. Although there is only a little, it is probably enough.
   *Can you lend me **a little sugar**?*
   ***A few friends** are coming round tonight.*

2 *Little* and *few* express a small amount in a negative way. There is not enough.
   ***Very few people** passed the exam.*
   *There's **very little milk** left.*

3 *Fewer* is the comparative of *few*; *less* is the comparative of *little*.
   ***Fewer people** go to church these days.* (= count noun)
   *I spend **less and less time** doing what I want to.* (= uncount noun)
   It is becoming more common to find *less* with a count noun. Many people think that this is incorrect and sounds terrible.
   *Less people go to church.
   *You should smoke less cigarettes.

all

1 We do not usually use *all* to mean *everybody/everyone/everything*.
   ***Everybody** had a good time.*
   ***Everything** was ruined in the fire.*
   *I said hello to **everyone**.*
   But if *all* is followed by a relative clause, it can mean *everything*.
   ***All** (that) I own is yours.*
   *I spend **all** I earn.*
   This structure can have a negative meaning, expressing ideas such as *nothing more* or *only this*.
   ***All I want** is a place to sleep.*
   ***All I had** was a couple of beers.*
   ***All that happened** was that he pushed her a bit, and she fell over.*

2 Before a noun with a determiner (for example *the, my, this*) both *all* and *all of* are possible.
   *You eat **all (of) the time**.*
   ***All (of) my friends** are coming tonight.*
   Before a noun with no determiner, we use *all*.
   ***All people** are born equal.*

3 With personal pronouns, we use *all of*.
   ***All of you** passed. Well done!*
   *I don't need these books. You can have **all of them**.*

UNIT 7

Introduction to modal auxiliary verbs

1 These are the modal auxiliary verbs.

can	could	may	might	shall should
will	would	must	ought to	

They are used with great frequency and with a wide range of meanings. They express ideas such as willingness and ability, permission and refusal, obligation and prohibition, suggestion, necessity, promise and intention. All modal auxiliary verbs can express degrees of certainty, probability, or possibility.

2 They have several characteristics.

- There is no *-s* in the third person.
  He can swim.
  She must go.

- There is no *do/does* in the question.
  May I ask a question?
  Shall we go?

- There is no *don't/doesn't* in the negative.
  You shouldn't tell lies.
  You won't believe this.

- They are followed by an infinitive without *to*. The exception is *ought to*.
  *It might **rain**.*
  *Could you **help**?*
  *We ought **to be** on our way.*

- They don't really have past forms or infinitives or *-ing* forms. Other verbs are used instead.
  *I **had** to work hard when I was young.*
  *I'd love **to be able to** ski.*
  *I hate **having** to get up in the morning.*

- They can be used with perfect infinitives to refer to the past. For more information, see Grammar Reference Unit 10 on p151.
  *You should **have told** me that you can't swim.*
  *You might **have drowned**!*
  *She must **have been** crazy to marry him.*

Modal auxiliary verbs of probability, present and future

The main modal auxiliary verbs that express probability are described here in order of certainty. *Will* is the most certain, and *might/could* are the least certain.

will

1 *Will* and *won't* are used to predict a future action. The truth or certainty of what is asserted is more or less taken for granted.
   *I'll **see** you later.*
   *His latest book **will be** out next month.*

2 *Will* and *won't* are also used to express what we believe or guess to be true about the present. They indicate an assumption based on our knowledge of people and things, their routines, character, and qualities.
   *'You've got a letter from Canada.' 'It'll **be** from my aunt Freda.'*
   *Leave the meat in the oven. It **won't be cooked** yet.*
   *'I wonder what Sarah's doing.' 'Well, it's Monday morning, so I guess that right now she'll **be taking** the children to school.'*

must and can't

1 *Must* is used to assert what we infer or conclude to be the most logical or rational interpretation of a situation. We do not have all the facts, so it is less certain than *will*.
   *You say he walked across the Sahara Desert! He **must be** mad!*
   *You **must be joking**! I simply don't believe you.*

2   The negative of this use is *can't*.
    She **can't have** a ten-year-old daughter! She's only twenty-one herself.
    'Whose is this coat?' 'It **can't be** Mary's. It's too small.'

should

1   *Should* expresses what may reasonably be expected to happen.
    Expectation means believing that things are or will be as we want
    them to be. This use of *should* has the idea of *if everything has gone
    according to plan*.
    Our guests **should be** here soon (if they haven't got lost).
    This homework **shouldn't take** you too long (if you've understood what
    you have to do).
    We **should be moving** into our new house soon (as long as nothing
    goes wrong).

2   *Should* in this use has the idea that we want the action to happen. It
    is not used to express negative or unpleasant ideas.
    You **should pass** the exam. You've worked hard.
    *~~*You should fail the exam*~~. You haven't done any work at all.
    We would say … I don't think you'll pass the exam.

may and might

1   *May* expresses the possibility that an event will happen or is
    happening.
    We **may go** to Greece this year. We haven't decided yet.
    'Where's Ann?' 'She **may be having** a bath, I don't know.'

2   *Might* is more tentative and slightly less certain than *may*.
    It **might rain**. Take your umbrella.
    'Where's Peter?' 'He **might be** upstairs. There's a light on.'

3   Learners of English often express these concepts of future possibility
    with *perhaps* or *maybe … will* and so avoid using *may* and *might*.
    However, these are widely used by native speakers, and you should
    try to use them.

could

1   *Could* has a similar meaning to *might*.
    You **could be** right. I'm not sure.
    That film **could be** worth seeing. It had a good review.

2   *Couldn't* is not used to express a future possibility. The negative of
    could in this use is *might not*.
    You **might not be** right.
    That film **might not be** any good.

3   *Couldn't* has a similar meaning to *can't* above, only slightly weaker.
    She **couldn't have** a ten-year-old daughter! She's only 21 herself.

Related verbs

Here are some related verb forms that express probability.
William's so brainy. He's **bound to pass** the exam.
We're having a picnic tomorrow, so it's **bound to rain**.
You're **likely to find** life very different when you live in China.
Are you likely to come across Judith while you're in Oxford?

Other uses of modal auxiliary verbs and related verbs

Here is some further information about modal auxiliary verbs, but it is
by no means complete. See a grammar book for more details.

Ability

1   *Can* expresses ability. The past is expressed by *could*.
    I can speak three languages.
    I could swim when I was three.

2   Other forms are provided by *be able to*.
    I've never **been able to** understand her. (Present Perfect)
    I'd love **to be able to** drive. (infinitive)
    Being able to drive has transformed my life. (-ing form)
    You'll **be able to** walk again soon. (future)

3   To express a fulfilled ability on one particular occasion in the past,
    could is not used. Instead, we use *was able to* or *managed to*.
    She **was able to** survive by clinging onto the wrecked boat.
    The prisoner **managed to** escape by climbing onto the roof.

Advice

1   *Should* and *ought* express mild obligation or advice. *Should* is much
    more common.
    You **should go** to bed. You look very tired.
    You **ought to** take things easier.

2   We use *had better* to give strong advice, or to tell people what to do.
    There can be an element of threat – 'If you don't do this, something
    bad will happen.'
    You'd **better get** a haircut before the interview. (If you don't, you won't
    get the job.)
    I'm late. I'd **better get** a move on. (If I don't, I'll be in trouble.)

Note
The form is always past (*had*), but it refers to the immediate future.
She'd **better start** revising. The exams are next week.

Obligation

1   *Must* expresses strong obligation. Other verb forms are provided by
    have to.
    You **must** try harder!
    You **mustn't** hit your baby brother.
    What time **do** you **have to** start work?
    I **had to** work hard to pass my exams. (Past Simple)
    You'll **have to** do this exercise again. (future)
    We might **have to** make some economies. (infinitive)
    She's **never had to** do a single day's work in her life. (Present Perfect)
    I hate **having to** get up early. (-ing form)

2   *Must* expresses the opinion of the speaker.
    I **must** get my hair cut. (I am telling myself.)
    You **must** do this again. (Teacher to student)
    Must is associated with a more formal, written style.
    Candidates **must** answer three questions. (On an exam paper)
    Books **must** be returned by the end of the week. (Instructions in a
    library)

3   *Have to* expresses a general obligation based on a law or rule, or
    based on the authority of another person.
    Children **have to** go to school until they're sixteen. (It's the law.)
    Mum says you **have to** tidy your room.

4   *Mustn't* expresses negative obligation. *Don't have to* expresses the
    absence of obligation.
    You **mustn't** steal. It's very naughty.
    You **don't have to** go to England if you want to learn English.

5   *Have got to* is common in British English. It is more informal than
    have to.
    I've **got to** go now. Cheerio!
    Don't have a late night. We've **got to** get up early tomorrow.

6   Here are some related verb forms that express obligation.
    Visitors **are required to** have a visa.
    When you're 18, you're **supposed to** take responsibility for yourself.
    You **aren't supposed to** park on double yellow lines.
    You **need to** think carefully before you make a decision.
    He **doesn't need to** work. He's a millionaire.

Permission

1   *May, can,* and *could* are used to ask for permission.
    May I ask you a question?
    May I use your phone?
    Can/Could I go home? I don't feel well.
    Can/Could I borrow your car tonight?

2 *May* is used to give permission, but it sounds very formal. *Can* and *can't* are more common.
   *You **can** use a dictionary in this exam.*
   *You **can't** stay up till midnight. You're only five.*
   *You **can't** smoke in here. It's forbidden.*

3 To talk about permission generally, or permission in the past, we use *can*, *could*, or *be allowed to*.
   *Children **can/are allowed to** do what they want these days.*

   | *I **couldn't** | | *go out on my own until I was sixteen.* |
   | ***wasn't allowed to*** | |

4 Here are some related verb forms that express permission.
   *Passengers **are not permitted to** use mobile phones.*
   *My parents **don't allow** me **to***
   *I'm **not allowed to** stay out late.*
   *My parents don't **let** me*
   Note that this sentence with *let* is not possible in the passive.
   *I'm not let ...

Willingness and refusal

1 *Will* expresses willingness. *Won't* expresses a refusal by either people or things. *Shall* is used in questions.
   *I'**ll** help you.*
   *She says she **won't** get up until she's had breakfast in bed.*
   *The car **won't** start.*
   ***Shall** I give you a hand?*

2 The past is expressed by *wouldn't*.
   *My mum said she **wouldn't** give me any more money. Isn't she mean?*

Requests

Several modal verbs express a request.
***Can/could/will/would** you do me a favour?*
***Can/could** I open the window?*
Modal verbs are also dealt with in Units 9, 10, and 11.

UNIT 8

8.1 Introduction to relative clauses

It is important to understand the difference between two kinds of relative clauses.

1 Defining relative (DR) clauses qualify a noun, and tell us exactly which person or thing is being referred to.
   *She likes people **who are good fun to be with**.*
   *Politicians **who tell lies** are odious.*
   *A corkscrew is a thing **you use to open a bottle of wine**.*
   She likes people on its own doesn't mean very much; we need to know which people she likes.
   who tell lies tells us exactly which politicians are odious. Without it, the speaker is saying that all politicians are odious.
   A corkscrew is a thing doesn't make sense on its own.

2 Non-defining relative (NDR) clauses add secondary information to a sentence, almost as an afterthought.
   *My friend Andrew, **who is Scottish**, plays the bagpipes.*
   *Politicians, **who tell lies**, are odious.*
   *My favourite building is Durham Cathedral, **which took over 200 years to build**.*
   My friend Andrew is clearly defined. We don't need to know which Andrew is being discussed. The clause *who is Scottish* gives us extra information about him.
   The clause *who tell lies* suggests that all politicians tell lies. It isn't necessary to identify only those that deceive – they all do!
   My favourite building is clearly defined. The following clause simply tells us something extra.

3 DR clauses are much more common in the spoken language, and NDR clauses are more common in the written language. In the spoken language, we can avoid a NDR clause.
   My friend Andrew plays the bagpipes. He's Scottish, by the way.

4 When we speak, there is no pause before or after a DR clause, and no commas when we write. With NDR clauses, there are commas before and after, and pauses when we speak.
   I like the things you say to me. (No commas, no pauses)
   My aunt (pause), *who has been a widow for twenty years* (pause), *loves travelling.*

Defining relative clauses

1 Notice how we can leave out the relative pronoun if it is the object of the relative clause. This is very common.
   Pronoun left out
   Did you like the present (   ) I gave you?
   Who was that man (   ) you were talking to?
   The thing (   ) I like about Dave is his sense of humour.

2 We cannot leave out the pronoun if it is the subject of the clause.
   Pronoun not left out
   *I met a man **who** works in advertising.*
   *I'll lend you the book **that** changed my life.*
   *The thing **that** helped me most was knowing I wasn't alone.*

3 Here are the possible pronouns. The words in brackets are possible, but not as common. ____ means 'nothing'.

	Person	Thing
Subject	who (that)	that (which)
Object	____ (that)	____ (that)

Notes

- *That* is preferred to *which* after superlatives, and words such as *all*, *every(thing)*, *some(thing)*, *any(thing)*, and *only*.
  *That's the **funniest** film **that** was ever made.*
  ***All that**'s left is a few slices of ham.*
  *Give me **something that**'ll take away the pain.*
  *He's good at **any** sport **that** is played with a ball.*
  *The **only** thing **that**'ll help you is rest.*

- *That* is also preferred after *it is ...*
  ***It is** a film **that** will be very popular.*

- Prepositions usually come at the end of the relative clause.
  *Come and meet the people I work **with**.*
  *This is the book I was telling you **about**.*
  *She's a friend I can always rely **on**.*

Non-defining relative clauses

1 Relative pronouns *cannot* be left out of NDR clauses.
   Relative pronoun as subject
   *Paul Jennings, **who** has written several books, addressed the meeting.*
   *His last book, **which** received a lot of praise, has been a great success.*
   Relative pronoun as object
   *Paul Jennings, **who** I knew at university, addressed the meeting.*
   *His last book, **which** I couldn't understand at all, has been a great success.*

2 Look at the possible pronouns. *Whom* is possible, but not as common.

	Person	Thing
Subject	... , who ... ,	... , which ... ,
Object	... , who (whom) ... ,	... , which ... ,

Note

Prepositions can come at the end of the clause.
*He talked about theories of market forces, which I'd never even heard **of**.*

In a more formal written style, prepositions come before the pronoun.
*The privatization of railways, **to which** the present government is committed, is not universally popular.*

which

Which can be used in NDR clauses to refer to the whole of the sentence before.
*She arrived on time, **which** amazed everybody.*
*He gambled away all his money, **which** I thought was ridiculous.*
*The coffee machine isn't working, **which** means we can't have any coffee.*

whose

Whose can be used in both DR clauses and NDR clauses.
*That's the woman **whose son was killed recently**.*
*My parents, **whose only interest is gardening**, never go away on holiday.*

what

What is used in DR clauses to mean *the thing that.*
*Has she told you **what**'s worrying her?*
***What** I need to know is where we're meeting.*

why, when, where

1 Why can be used in DR clauses to mean *the reason why.*
*I don't know **why** we're arguing.*

2 When and where can be used in DR clauses and NDR clauses.
*Tell me **when** you expect to arrive.*
*The hotel **where** we stayed was excellent.*
*We go walking on Mondays, **when** the rest of the world is working.*
*He works in Oxford, **where** my sister lives.*

8.2 Participles

1 When present participles (-*ing*) are used like adjectives or adverbs, they are active in meaning.
*Modern art is **interesting**.*
*Pour **boiling** water onto the pasta.*
*She sat in the corner **crying**.*

2 When past participles (-*ed*) are used like adjectives or adverbs, they are passive in meaning.
*I'm **interested** in modern art.*
*Look at that **broken** doll.*
*He sat in his chair, **filled** with horror at what he had just seen.*

3 Participles after a noun define and identify in the same way as relative clauses.
*I met a woman **riding** a donkey. (= who was riding ...)*
*The car **stolen** in the night was later found abandoned. (= that was stolen ...)*

4 Participles can be used as adverbs. They can describe:

• two actions happening at the same time.
*She sat by the fire **reading** a book.*

• two actions that happen one after another.
***Opening** his case, he took out a gun.*
If it is important to show that the first action is completed before the second action begins, we use the perfect participle.
***Having finished** lunch, we set off on our journey.*
***Having had** a shower, she got dressed.*

• two actions that happen one because of another.
***Being** mean, he never bought anyone a Christmas present.*
***Not knowing** what to do, I waited patiently.*

5 Many verbs are followed by -*ing* forms.
*I **spent** the holiday **reading**.*
*Don't **waste** time **thinking** about the past.*
*Let's **go swimming**.*
*He **keeps on asking** me to go out with him.*

UNIT 9

Expressing habit

Present Simple

1 Adverbs of frequency come before the main verb, but after the verb *to be*.
*We **hardly ever** go out.*
*She **frequently** forgets what she's doing.*
*We don't **usually** eat fish.*
*I **rarely** see Peter these days.*
*We are **seldom** at home in the evening.*
*Is he **normally** so bad-tempered?*

2 *Sometimes*, *usually*, and *occasionally* can come at the beginning or the end of a sentence.
***Sometimes** we play cards.*
*We go to the cinema **occasionally**.*
The other adverbs of frequency don't usually move in this way.
*~~*Always I have~~ tea in the morning.*

Present Continuous

1 The Present Continuous can be used to express a habit which happens often and perhaps unexpectedly. It happens more than is usual.
*I like Peter. He's always **smiling**.*
*She's always **giving** people presents.*

2 However, there is often an element of criticism with this structure. Compare these sentences said by a teacher.
*Pedro always **asks** questions in class. (This is a fact.)*
*Pedro is always **asking** questions in class. (This annoys the teacher.)*

3 There is usually an adverb of frequency with this use.
*I'm always **losing** my keys.*
*She's **forever leaving** the bath taps running.*

will and would

1 *Will* and *would* express typical behaviour. They describe both pleasant and unpleasant habits.
He'll sit in his chair for hours on end.
She'd spend all day long gossiping with the neighbours.
Would cannot be used to express a state.
*~~*He'd live in a large house.~~*

2 *Will* and *would*, when decontracted and stressed, express an annoying habit.
*He **WILL** come into the house with his muddy boots on.*
*She **WOULD** make us wash in ice-cold water.*

used to + infinitive

1 This structure expresses a past action and/or a state. It has no present equivalent.
*When I was a child, we **used to go** on holiday to the seaside. (action)*
*He **used to live** in a large house. (state)*

2 Notice the negative and the question.
*Where **did** you **use to** go?*
*We **didn't use to** do anything interesting.*

3 We cannot use *used to* with a time reference + a number.
*~~*We used to have a holiday there for 10 years/three times~~.*
But ...
*We **used to** go there every year.*

In a narrative, when expressing a series of past actions, it is common to begin with *used to*, then continue with *would*, for reasons of style.
*When I was a child, we **used to go** on holiday to the seaside. We'd **play** on the beach, then we'd **eat** at a small café at lunchtime*

be/get used to + noun + -ing form

1 This is totally different from *used to* + infinitive. It expresses an action that was difficult, strange, or unusual before, but is no longer so. Here, *used* is an adjective, and it means *familiar with*.
I found it difficult to get around London when I first came, but I'm used to it now.
I'm used to getting around London by tube.

2 Notice the use of *get* to express the process of change.
I'm getting used to the climate.
Don't worry. You'll get used to eating with chopsticks.

UNIT 10

Modal auxiliary verbs 2

Modal auxiliary verbs of probability in the past

1 All modal auxiliary verbs can be used with the perfect infinitive. They express the same varying degrees of certainty as explained on pp147–149. Again, *will have done* is the most certain, and *might/may/could have done* is the least certain.
'I met a girl at your party. Tall. Very attractive.' 'That'll have been Sonya.'
It must have been a good party. Everyone stayed till dawn.
The music can't have been any good. Nobody danced.
Where's Pete? He should have been here ages ago!
He may have got lost.
He might have decided not to come.
He could have had an accident.

2 *Would have thought* is common to express an assumption or supposition.
I'd have thought they'd be here by now. Where are they?
You'd have thought she'd remember my birthday, wouldn't you?
Wouldn't you have thought they'd ring if there was a problem?

Other uses of modal verbs in the past

should have done

1 *Should have done* can express advice or criticism about a past event. The sentence expresses what is contrary to the facts.
You should have listened to my advice. (You didn't listen.)
I shouldn't have lied to you. I'm sorry. (I did lie.)
You shouldn't have told her you hated her. (You did tell her.)

2 Look at these sentences.
You should have been here yesterday!
You should have seen his face!
Should have done is used here for comic effect. The suggestion is *because it was so funny!*

could have done

1 *Could have done* is used to express an unrealized past ability. Someone was able to do something in the past, but didn't do it.
I could have gone to university, but I didn't want to.
We could have won the match. We didn't try hard enough.
I could have told you that Chris wouldn't come. He hates parties.
I was so angry with her, I could have killed her!

2 It is used to express a past possibility that didn't happen.
You fool! You could have killed yourself!
We were lucky. We could have been caught in that traffic jam.
When I took the burnt meal out of the oven, I could have cried!

3 It is used to criticize people for not doing things.
You could have told me that Sue and Jim had split up!
I've been cleaning the house for hours. You could at least have done your bedroom!

might have done

1 The above use of *should have done* can also be expressed with *might have done*.
You might have helped instead of just sitting on your backside!

2 *I might have known/guessed that …* is used to introduce a typical action of someone or something.
I might have known that Peter would be late. He's always late.
The car won't start. I might have guessed that would happen.

needn't have

Needn't have done expresses an action that was done, but it wasn't necessary. It was a waste of time.
I needn't have got up so early. The train was delayed.
'I've bought you a new pen, because I lost yours.' 'You needn't have bothered. I've got hundreds.'

UNIT 11

Hypothesizing

First and second conditionals

1 First conditional sentences are based on fact in real time. They express a possible condition and its probable result in the present or future.
If you pass your exams, I'll buy you a car.

2 Second conditional sentences are not based on fact. They express a situation which is contrary to reality in the present and future. This unreality is shown by a tense shift from present to past. They express a hypothetical condition and its probable result.
If I were taller, I'd join the police force.
What would you do if you won the lottery?

Notes

- The difference between first and second conditional sentences is not about time. Both can refer to the present and future. By using past tense forms in the second conditional, the speaker suggests the situation is less probable, or impossible, or imaginary. Compare the pairs of sentences.
  If it rains this weekend, we'll … (said in England where it often rains)
  If it rained in the Sahara, it would … (this would be most unusual)
  If global warming continues, we'll … (I'm a pessimist.)
  If global warming continued, we'd … (I'm an optimist.)
  If you come to my country, you'll have a good time. (possible)
  If you came from my country, you'd understand us better. (impossible)
  If I am elected as a member of Parliament, I'll … (said by a candidate)
  If I ruled the world, I'd … (imaginary)

- We can use *were* instead of *was*, especially in a formal style.
  If the situation were the opposite, would you feel obliged to help?
  I'd willingly help if it were possible.

Third conditional

1 Third conditional sentences are not based on fact. They express a situation which is contrary to reality in the past. This unreality is shown by a tense shift from past to Past Perfect.
If you'd come to the party, you'd have had a great time.
I wouldn't have met my wife if I hadn't gone to France.

2 It is possible for each of the clauses in a conditional sentence to have a different time reference, and the result is a mixed conditional.
If we had brought a map (we didn't), we would know where we are (we don't).
I wouldn't have married her (I did) if I didn't love her (I do).

Other structures that express hypothesis

1 The tense usage with *wish, if only,* and *I'd rather* is similar to the second and third conditionals. Unreality is expressed by a tense shift.
*I wish I **were** taller.* (But I'm not.)
*If only you **hadn't said** that!* (But you did.)
*I'd rather you **didn't wear** lots of make-up.* (But you do.)
I'd rather you … is often used as a polite way to tell someone to do something differently. The negative form *I'd rather you didn't …* is especially useful as a polite way to say 'no'.
*'I'll come in with you.' '**I'd rather you waited** outside.'*
*'Can I smoke in here?' '**I'd rather you didn't.**'*

Notes

• *wish … would* can express regret, dissatisfaction, impatience, or irritation because someone WILL keep doing something.
*I wish you'**d** stop smoking.*
*I wish you'**d** do more to help in the house.*
*I wish it **would** stop raining.*

• If we are not talking about willingness, *wish … would* is not used.
*I wish my birthday **wasn't** in December.* (*~~I wish it would be …~~*)
*I wish I **could** stop smoking.* (*~~I wish I would~~* is strange because you should have control over what you are willing to do.)
*I wish **he** would stop smoking.*
This is correct because it means *I wish he were willing to …*

UNIT 12

🔊 Determiners

There are two kinds of determiners.

1 The first kind identifies things.
articles – *a/an, the*
possessives – *my, your, our …*
demonstratives – *this, that, these, those*

2 The second kind are quantifiers, expressing *how much* or *how many.*
some, any, no
each, every, either, neither
much, many, more, most
(a) little, less, least
(a) few, fewer, fewest
enough, several
all, both, half
another, other
Determiners that express quantity are dealt with in Unit 6.

each and every

1 *Each* and *every* are used with singular nouns. *Each* can be used to talk about two or more people or things. *Every* is used to talk about three or more.
Every/each time I come to your house it looks different.
Each/every bedroom in our hotel is decorated differently.

2 In many cases, *each* and *every* can both be used with little difference in meaning.
We prefer *each* if we are thinking of people or things separately, one at a time. We use *every* if we are thinking of the things or people all together as a group.
Each student gave the teacher a present.
Every policeman in the country is looking for the killer.

enough

1 When *enough* is used as a determiner, it comes before the noun.
*We haven't got **enough food**.*

2 When it is used as an adverb, it comes after the adjective, adverb, or verb.
*Your homework isn't **good enough**.*
*I couldn't run **fast enough**.*
*You don't **exercise enough**.*

Articles

The use of articles is complex as there are a lot of 'small' rules and exceptions. Here are the basic rules.

a/an

1 We use *a/an* to refer to a singular countable noun which is indefinite. Either we don't know which one, or it doesn't matter which one.
*They live in **a** lovely house.*
*I'm reading **a** good book.*
*She's expecting **a** baby.*

2 We use *a/an* with professions.
*She's **a** lawyer.*

the

1 We use *the* before a singular or plural noun, when both the speaker and the listener know which noun is being referred to.
*They live in **the** green house opposite **the** library.*
***The** book was recommended by a friend.*
*Mind **the** baby! She's near **the** fire.*
*I'm going to **the** shops. Do you want anything?*
*I'll see you in **the** pub later.*
*'Where's Dad?' 'In **the** garden.'*

2 We use *the* when there is only one.
***the** world*   ***the** River Thames*   ***the** Atlantic*

3 We use *the* for certain places which are institutions. Which particular place isn't important.
*We went to **the cinema/theatre** last night.*
*We're going to **the seaside**.*

a followed by the

We use *a* to introduce something for the first time. When we refer to it again, we use *the.*
*I saw **a** man walking **a** dog in the park today. **The** man was tiny and **the** dog was huge!*

Zero article

1 We use no article with plural and uncountable nouns when talking about things in general.
***Computers** have changed our lives.*
***Love** is eternal.*
***Dogs** need a lot of exercise.*
*I hate **hamburgers**.*

2 We use no article with meals.
*Have you had **lunch** yet?*
*Come round for **dinner** tonight.*
*But … We had **a lovely lunch** in an Italian restaurant.*

Extra material

UNIT 1 *p15*

EVERYDAY ENGLISH
Social expressions and the music of English

T 1.12

A Excuse me, is this yours?
B Let me see. Yes, it is. Thank you. I must have dropped it.
A Are you going far?
B Yeah, all the way to London. What about you?
A I'm getting off at Bristol.
B Oh, d'you live there?
A Actually, no. I work in Bristol but I live in Bath.
B Lucky you! I think Bath's a beautiful city!
A Yeah, you and thousands of others!
B What d'you mean?
A Well, you know, the tourists. There are just so many, all year round.
B Ah yes, that's a drag. You don't like tourists then?
A Well, I shouldn't really complain.
B How come? You can complain if you want.
A Not really – you see I'm a travel agent, so I make a living from tourists.

UNIT 2 *p18*

PRACTICE
Exchanging information

Student A
Ask and answer questions to complete the information about Tony and Maureen Wheeler.

> How many people does it employ?
> Five hundred. Where does it have offices?
> In the USA, France, England, and Australia.

Lonely Planet is one of the outstanding publishing successes of the past three decades. It employs more than . . . people (*How many?*), and has offices in the USA, France, England, with its headquarters in Melbourne, Australia.

Tony and Maureen Wheeler have been writing *Lonely Planet* guide books for . . . (*How long?*). They have written more than 650 guides. They sell . . . copies a year (*How many?*) in 118 countries. The books have been translated into 17 languages.

Tony lived . . . (*Where?*) when he was young because his father's job took him all over the world. He studied . . . at Warwick University (*What?*), then business studies at the London Business School.

Maureen was born in . . . (*Where?*). She went to London at the age of 20 because she wanted to see the world. Three days later she met Tony . . . (*Where?*). In 1972 they travelled overland across Europe, through Asia, and on to Australia. The trip took six months. They wrote their first book, called . . . (*What?*), on their kitchen table in Melbourne. They have lived in Melbourne on and off for over thirty years.

Together they have been to . . . countries (*How many?*). Tony says that the most amazing place he has ever visited is a remote hilltop city called Tsaparang, in Tibet.

Venture to a higher plain

They are currently travelling in . . . (*Where?*), researching a new edition of their guide to the country.

He is thinking of selling . . . (*What?*). He said, 'I've had a wonderful time, it's been terrific, but it has now got too much like a business.'

PRACTICE
Exchanging information

Student B
Ask and answer questions to complete the information about Tony and Maureen Wheeler.

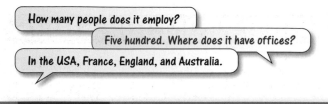

How many people does it employ?

Five hundred. Where does it have offices?

In the USA, France, England, and Australia.

lonely planet

Lonely Planet is one of the outstanding publishing successes of the past three decades. It employs more than 500 people, and has offices in . . . *(Where?)*, with its headquarters in Melbourne, Australia.

Tony and Maureen Wheeler have been writing *Lonely Planet* guide books for over thirty years. They have written . . . guides *(How many?)*. They sell around 5.5 millions copies a year in 118 countries. The books have been translated into . . . languages *(How many?)*.

Tony lived in many different countries when he was young because . . . *(Why?)*. He studied engineering at Warwick University, then business studies at . . . *(Where?)*.

Maureen was born in Belfast. She went to London at the age of 20 because . . . *(Why?)*. Three days later she met Tony on a bench in Regent's Park. In 1972 they travelled overland across Europe, through Asia, and on to Australia. The trip took . . . *(How long?)*. They wrote their first book, called *Across Asia on the cheap*,

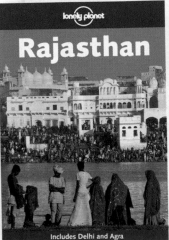

Rajasthan

Includes Delhi and Agra

on their kitchen table in Melbourne. They have lived in Melbourne on and off for over . . . *(How long?)*.

Together they have been to more than 100 countries. Tony says that the most amazing place he has ever visited is . . . *(What?)*.

They are currently travelling in India, . . . *(What ... doing ... ?)*

He is thinking of selling his shares in the company. He said, '. . .' *(What?)*.

PRACTICE
Exchanging information

Information for Tony Wheeler

BACKGROUND
- Father worked for British Airways
- Lived in Pakistan, Bahamas, USA
- Lived overseas for most of my school days

EDUCATION
- Educated mainly in Britain and the USA, most of my secondary education was in the States
- Came back to England to do my A-levels when I was 16
- Went to Warwick University to study engineering

WORK
- Started a career in engineering, did this for a couple of years in Coventry
- Went to do an MBA in business studies in London

LONELY PLANET GUIDES
- First one came out in 1973
- Idea came because a lot of people were asking us questions about our trip across Asia
- Worst moment was when we first started the business. We didn't have enough money
- Best moment was doing something that no one had done before. Our guides were the first of their kind
- The secret of our success is that people can rely on us, so they keep coming back to us.
- If you want to get into travel writing, you have to have travelled a lot. You have to be able to write well. You have to believe in what you're doing. Wanting to do it is far more important than wanting to make money

FAMILY
- Two children, a girl and a boy

HOLIDAYS
- Like walking and diving

FUTURE
- Would like to go back to Nepal.
- Am looking forward to spending a long time in Australia. In my opinion, there's no better place in the world to be alone

SPEAKING AND LISTENING

Dreams come true

These are the top 15 things that people most wanted to do before they die.

1 swim with dolphins
2 go scuba diving on the Great Barrier Reef
3 go whale-watching
4 dive with sharks
5 go skydiving
6 fly in a hot air balloon
7 fly in a fighter jet
8 go on safari
9 see the Northern Lights
10 visit Machu Picchu
11 climb Sydney Harbour Bridge
12 escape to a paradise island
13 drive a Formula-1 car
14 go white-water rafting
15 walk the Great Wall of China

PRACTICE

News and responses

Student A
Read the newspaper story. Then tell the story to your partner. Show him/her the photo.

GIRL BARRED FROM TOP STORE

As fashion-conscious GILLY WOODWARD left Harrods last Friday, she felt proud of the £120 designer jeans that she had just bought. But when Gilly, 31, returned to the store the next day to do some more shopping, she was barred from entry because she was wearing the same jeans.

Gilly, now back home in Liverpool, had been staying with friends in London for a few days. She explained what had happened.

'I was walking through the swing doors, when suddenly I was stopped by a large, uniformed security guard. He pointed at my knees, and said that my jeans were torn and I couldn't enter. I tried to tell him that I had bought them in Harrods the day before, and that the torn bits were fashionable. But he didn't listen. He told me to get out. By this time, a crowd of people had gathered. I left immediately because I had never felt so embarrassed in my life.'

A spokesperson from Harrods said that the dress code had been introduced in 1989, and it states: no beachwear, no backpacks, no torn denims.

PRACTICE

Quiztime!

Group A

Music
1 Louis Armstrong played <u>jazz</u> music. (*What sort?*)
2 A violin has <u>four</u> strings. (*How many?*)

Sports
3 <u>A bronze medal</u> is given to the person who comes third in the Olympic Games. (*What?*)
4 Golf was first played in <u>Scotland</u>. (*In which?*)

Science
5 <u>The sun</u> is the nearest star to the earth? (*Which?*)
6 <u>Albert Einstein</u> developed the theory of relativity. (*Who?*)

Geography
7 The capital of <u>New Zealand</u> is Wellington. (*Which country?*)
8 The 'Richter Scale' measures <u>earthquakes</u>. (*What?*)

History
9 President John F. Kennedy was assassinated in <u>1963</u>. (*Which year?*)
10 Nelson Mandela was in prison for <u>twenty-eight</u> years. (*How long ... for?*)

PRACTICE
News and responses

Student B
Read the newspaper story. Then tell the story to your partner. Show him/her the photo.

Man fined for keeping tiger in apartment

A MAN WHO kept a 400-pound tiger in his apartment in Harlem, New York, has been fined $2,500, and forbidden from keeping animals for ten years.

Brian Jackson, 31, had bought the Bengal tiger, named Ming, when it was just a three-month-old cub. It had been living in his fourth-floor apartment for three years, eating raw meat provided by Jackson, who worked as a butcher. Neighbours had often complained of strange smells and loud noises.

Jackson's unusual pet came to light because he had had to go to hospital with cuts and bites to his arm. The tiger had attacked him in an apparent attempt to capture and kill a cat that he also kept in the apartment.

Police officers scaled down the outside of the building and fired tranquilizer darts through an open fourth-floor window. They removed the tiger, and also an alligator, to a New York animal shelter.

A neighbour said, 'We liked having Ming here. He was cool. My worry is that he won't like the country. He's a city cat, and likes jazz and hip-hop.'

 UNIT 4 *p35*

PRACTICE

Quiztime!

Group B

Music
1 Eminem sings <u>rap</u> music. *(What kind?)*
2 <u>Michael Jackson's</u> brothers formed the pop group 'The Jackson Five.' *(Whose?)*

Sports
3 <u>The Marathon</u> is the longest running race in the Olympic Games. *(What ... called?)*
4 Baseball was first played in <u>the United States</u> in the <u>19th century</u>. *(Where and when?)*

Science
5 A butterfly has <u>six</u> legs. *(How many?)*
6 Charles Darwin developed <u>the theory of evolution</u>. *(Which theory?)*

Geography
7 <u>Alaska</u> is the biggest state in the US. *(Which state?)*
8 <u>The Atlantic and Pacific Oceans</u> are linked by the Panama Canal. *(Which oceans?)*

History
9 President John F. Kennedy was assassinated in <u>Dallas, Texas</u>. *(Which town and state?)*
10 The last Concorde flew to New York in <u>2003</u>. *(In which year?)*

EVERYDAY ENGLISH
Roleplay

A = Anna **B** = Ben **H** = Henry **K** = Kim

B Kim! Hello! Great to see you. Come on in. Let me take your coat.

K Thanks very much. Oh, these are for you.

A What lovely flowers! How kind of you! Thank you so much. Now, I don't think you know Henry? Let me introduce you. Henry, this is Kim.

H Hello, Kim. Nice to meet you. I've heard a lot about you.

K …

H Where exactly are you from, Kim?

K …

H That's interesting. And what are you doing in London?

K …

H And how do you find London, Kim? Is it like home, or is it very different?

K …

B Now, Kim. What would you like to drink?

K …

B Right. I'll just get that for you.

K …

A Right, everybody. Dinner's ready. Come and sit down. Kim, can you sit next to Henry?

K …

B Has everyone got a drink? Cheers, everybody!

K …

A Kim, help yourself. Would you like some Parmesan parsnips?

K …

A Well, they're parsnips coated in Parmesan cheese and roasted. Would you like to try some?

K …

B Another glass of wine, perhaps?

K …

B Yes, of course. Sparkling or still?

K …

A Well, *bon appétit* everyone!

READING AND SPEAKING
Nobody listens to us

These are the ten social issues that the group of 18–24 year-olds cared about, in order of importance.

1 Improving the NHS
2 Ensuring equal rights and protections for everyone, regardless of gender, sexual orientation, colour, or religion
3 Reducing crime levels
4 Raising standards in schools
5 Improving public transport
6 Ending the arms trade
7 Addressing the causes of global warming
8 Redistributing wealth from the richest to the poorest
9 Increasing the amount of aid we give to developing countries
10 Ending globalization

 **UNIT 10** *p87*

ÖTZI THE ICEMAN

He died 5,300 years ago. He was 46 years old and 5ft 2in tall. He had a beard.

His last meal was goat steak and bread baked in charcoal.

He wore goatskin leggings, a deerskin jacket, a thick grass cape, and a bearskin hat.

He stuffed his leather shoes with grass to keep out the cold.

He lived his entire life in a world just 50 kilometres across.

He knew how to look after himself. He had over seventy items in his possession, including flints for skinning animals and sharpening tools. In his backpack he carried herbs with pharmaceutical properties, dried fruit, and flint and tinder for starting fires.

He was probably a herdsman or hunter, but on this day he was a warrior. He had an axe and a longbow, and arrows tipped with a flint. No one knows how the battle started. Perhaps Ötzi and his companions deliberately entered enemy territory, or perhaps they were ambushed, or attacked one another.

From the DNA on his clothing and weapons, and the injuries to his body, Ötzi's last and fatal fight can be reconstructed with some precision.

Ötzi stabbed one of his enemies with his flint dagger. He shot an arrow into another and managed to retrieve the valuable weapon before shooting it again. He killed or wounded at least three men, but the hand-to-hand fighting was ferocious. Ötzi tried to hold off one assailant and suffered a deep wound in one hand that left three fingers useless.

Ötzi put up a fierce fight until an arrow, fired from behind, entered his shoulder and penetrated close to his lung. Ötzi retreated into the mountains, but not before lifting a wounded companion on to his back. The blood of the injured man mixed with Ötzi's, soaking into his deerskin jacket.

Finally, high in the Ötzal Alps, Ötzi staggered into a small ravine, and collapsed. It took two more days before he died, and the ice closed over him.

VOCABULARY AND PRONUNCIATION
Word pairs

T 11.6

A Are you going to have a holiday this year?

B I'd love to – but we'll have to wait and see. We're a bit hard up at the moment.

A We're hoping to go to that farmhouse in the South of France, but it's touch and go whether we will.

B Why's that?

A Well, I don't know if I can get the time off work.

B But I thought they were good about giving you time off.

A Yeah, they are, by and large, but we're a small firm and we have to cover for each other, so it's always a case of give and take.

B Yeah, I can see that. At least *you* got away last year. I'm sick and tired of not being able to go anywhere.

A You get away now and then, don't you?

B More 'then' than 'now'. We used to get the odd weekends in the country but since the kids came along it's more difficult. Oh for the peace and quiet of the countryside – uh, but I don't suppose we'd get much peace or quiet, even if we *could* afford to go, what with three kids and two dogs.

A Is Chris fed up too?

B You know Chris. Never complains, just grins and bears it.

A I tell you what. If we do manage to get that farmhouse, why don't you all join us? It's huge.

B Oh – that's so kind …er but I don't know. Wouldn't we be spoiling your holiday? What would Pat think? What if …

A Look, no ifs or buts. The offer's there – you can take it or leave it!

B I can't tell you how much I appreciate it. It would be brilliant, but can I talk to Chris about it first?

A Of course, of course. I'm sure you'll want to go through all the pros and cons together.

B I can't think of many cons. It's just too good to be true. Thank you so much.

A Well, as I said, the offer's there. Let's hope I get the time off work – we'll have a great time together.

LISTENING AND SPEAKING
The interpretation of dreams

a Buildings and houses are symbols of yourself. The upstairs represents your conscious mind and the lower floors and cellar your hidden self. The cramped feeling of the cellar indicates frustration and a need to expand your activities or thinking. Decayed or crumbling buildings indicate that your self-image has suffered. Treat yourself to a few activities that make you feel good about yourself.

b This dream symbolizes rediscovering a part of yourself. There may be something that you have neglected or repressed. It could be that you had an ambition in life and only now have found the opportunity to try again.

The dream may also have a literal interpretation. If you're worried about finances, now may be the time to start a new venture.

c This dream highlights a loss of self-control. It may represent your insecurity, a lack of self-confidence, a fear of failure, or an inability to cope with a situation. There could also be a literal interpretation. You may have noticed something unsafe – a loose stair rail, wobbly ladder, or insecure window. Check it out. The dream may be a warning.

THE PACE OF LIFE
How well do you use your time?

Answers to quiz

Mostly a answers
You're a daydreamer. Did you actually manage to finish the quiz? You have little control over your life. Chaos surrounds you. Perhaps you tell yourself that you are being creative, but the truth is you are frightened of failure so you don't try. Your abilities remain untested and your dreams unfulfilled.

Mostly b answers
You represent balance and common sense. Your ability to manage your life is impressive, and you know when to relax. You understand that the best decisions are never made in an atmosphere of pressure. You are able to meet deadlines and look ahead to make sure crises don't happen.

Mostly c answers
You live in hope that something or somebody will make everything in life come right for you. I'll get round to it you tell yourself. What you don't tell yourself is that you alone can manage your life. You are expert at putting things off till later and finding excuses when you do so. Forget these excuses. The right time is now.

Mostly d answers
You are certainly an achiever. Superman or superwoman. You know how to get a job done and you are proud of the way you manage your life. You are obsessive about using every second of the day to best effect and get irritated by people who are not like you and prefer to take life at a slower pace. Learn to relax a little. Remember, stress kills.

Phonetic symbols

Consonants

1	/p/	as in	**pen**	/pen/
2	/b/	as in	**big**	/bɪg/
3	/t/	as in	**tea**	/tiː/
4	/d/	as in	**do**	/duː/
5	/k/	as in	**cat**	/kæt/
6	/g/	as in	**go**	/gəʊ/
7	/f/	as in	**four**	/fɔː/
8	/v/	as in	**very**	/ˈveri/
9	/s/	as in	**son**	/sʌn/
10	/z/	as in	**zoo**	/zuː/
11	/l/	as in	**live**	/lɪv/
12	/m/	as in	**my**	/maɪ/
13	/n/	as in	**near**	/nɪə/
14	/h/	as in	**happy**	/ˈhæpi/
15	/r/	as in	**red**	/red/
16	/j/	as in	**yes**	/jes/
17	/w/	as in	**want**	/wɒnt/
18	/θ/	as in	**thanks**	/θæŋks/
19	/ð/	as in	**the**	/ðə/
20	/ʃ/	as in	**she**	/ʃiː/
21	/ʒ/	as in	**television**	/ˈtelɪvɪʒn/
22	/tʃ/	as in	**child**	/tʃaɪld/
23	/dʒ/	as in	**German**	/ˈdʒɜːmən/
24	/ŋ/	as in	**English**	/ˈɪŋglɪʃ/

Vowels

25	/iː/	as in	**see**	/siː/
26	/ɪ/	as in	**his**	/hɪz/
27	/i/	as in	**twenty**	/ˈtwenti/
28	/e/	as in	**ten**	/ten/
29	/æ/	as in	**stamp**	/stæmp/
30	/ɑː/	as in	**father**	/ˈfɑːðə/
31	/ɒ/	as in	**hot**	/hɒt/
32	/ɔː/	as in	**morning**	/ˈmɔːnɪŋ/
33	/ʊ/	as in	**football**	/ˈfʊtbɔːl/
34	/uː/	as in	**you**	/juː/
35	/ʌ/	as in	**sun**	/sʌn/
36	/ɜː/	as in	**learn**	/lɜːn/
37	/ə/	as in	**letter**	/ˈletə/

Diphthongs (two vowels together)

38	/eɪ/	as in	**name**	/neɪm/
39	/əʊ/	as in	**no**	/nəʊ/
40	/aɪ/	as in	**my**	/maɪ/
41	/aʊ/	as in	**how**	/haʊ/
42	/ɔɪ/	as in	**boy**	/bɔɪ/
43	/ɪə/	as in	**hear**	/hɪə/
44	/eə/	as in	**where**	/weə/
45	/ʊə/	as in	**tour**	/tʊə/

OXFORD
UNIVERSITY PRESS

Great Clarendon Street, Oxford OX2 6DP

Oxford University Press is a department of the University of Oxford.
It furthers the University's objective of excellence in research, scholarship,
and education by publishing worldwide in

Oxford New York

Auckland Cape Town Dar es Salaam Hong Kong Karachi
Kuala Lumpur Madrid Melbourne Mexico City Nairobi
New Delhi Shanghai Taipei Toronto

With offices in

Argentina Austria Brazil Chile Czech Republic France Greece
Guatemala Hungary Italy Japan Poland Portugal Singapore
South Korea Switzerland Thailand Turkey Ukraine Vietnam

OXFORD and OXFORD ENGLISH are registered trade marks of
Oxford University Press in the UK and in certain other countries

ISBN-13: 978 0 19 439299 0 (International edition)
ISBN-10: 0 19 439299 6
First published 2005
2009 2008 2007 2006 2005
10 9 8 7 6 5 4 3 2 1

ISBN-13: 978 0 19 439326 3 (German edition)
ISBN-10: 0 19 439326 7
First published 2005
2009 2008 2007 2006 2005
10 9 8 7 6 5 4 3 2

Bestellnummer 375625

Printed and bound by Grafiasa S.A. Portugal

ACKNOWLEDGEMENTS

The authors would like to thank charles Lowe for his valuable contribution
to the development of this project, and in particular for his ideas on the
Music of English.

*The authors and publisher are grateful to those who have given permission to reproduce
the following extracts and adaptations of copyright material:* p10 'Expat e-mail:
Chile' by Ian Walker-Smith, BBC News, 11 February 2003. Reproduced by
permission of BBC. pp30-31 from *The Blind Assassin* by Margaret Atwood.
Copyright © O. W. Toad Ltd., 2000. Reproduced with permission of Curtis
Brown Group Ltd.; Doubleday, a division of Random House, Inc.; and
McClelland & Stewart Ltd., The Canadian Publishers. p48 'Nobody Listens to
Us' by Damian Whitworth & Carol Midgley, *The Times*, 30 October 2003
© D Whitworth and C Midgley. Reproduced by permission of NI Syndication.
p67 'Meet the Kippers' by Ray Connolly, *Daily Mail*, 18 November 2003.
Reproduced by permission of Atlantic Syndication. pp74-75 'Fall asleep and
you'll freeze to death' by Sarah Oliver, *Mail on Sunday*, 23 November 2003.
Reproduced by permission of Atlantic Syndication. pp90-91 The American
West 1840-1895 by Mike Mellor © Cambridge University Press, 1998.
Reproduced by permission of Cambridge University Press. p92 *Jim And The
Lion* from *Cautionary Verses* by Hilaire Belloc. Reprinted by permission of PFD
on behalf of The Estate of Hilaire Belloc © The Estate of Hilaire Belloc, 1930.
p106-107 'A Life in the Day of Mary Hobson' by Caroline Scott, *The Sunday
Times Magazine*, 30 November 2003. Reproduced by permission of NI
Syndication. p108 *That's Life* Words & Music by Dean Kay & Kelly Gordon
© Copyright 1964 Bibo Music Publishers, USA. Universal Music Publishing
Limited. All Rights Reserved. International Copyright Secured. p122 'A
Darwin Award, Larry was a Truck Driver' from www.tech-sol.net as shown on
14 June 2004. Reproduced by permission of Mike Guenther, Techsol.

Sources: pp102-103 Based on copyright material 'How's your timing' by Celia
Brayfield.

Location art directors: Sally Smith and Mags Robertson

Art editing by: Pictureresearch.co.uk

Illustrations by: Derek Brazell p 72; Gill Button p 93; Stuart Briers p 31;
CartoonBank p 61 (Thursday's out/© The New Yorker collection 1993 Robert
Mankoff from cartoonbank.com. All rights reserved); Cartoon Stock pp 13
(homework/Vahan Shirvanian), (home made/Chris Patterson), 23 (Carroll
Zahn), 42 (Mike Baldwin), 51 (Roy Nixon), 68 (snake/Grizelda), (TV/Tony Hall),
81 (Timmy/Aaron Bacall), 101 (John Morris); Stefan Chabluk pp 10, 12, 16, 17,
74, 86; Mark Duffin p 122; Paul Gilligan/Getty Images p 34 & 35; Illustrations
from "Jim" in Cautionary Tales for Children by Hilaire Belloc, illustrations
copyright © 2002 by The Estate of Edward Gorey, reproduced by permission
of Harcourt Inc & Donadio & Olson Inc pp 92 & 93; Andy Hammond pp 8, 84;
John Holder p 89; Tim Maars pp 100, 158

Commissioned Photography by: Dennis Kitchen Studio p 6; Gareth Boden pp 43,
44 (Mickey), 45 (Janine), 52 (Students), 67 (Martin), 77 (all except Tattoo), 94,
95 (football); MM Studios pp 14 (pillow, wallet, teabags, straighteners, coffee,
newspapers), 26 (mobile), 29, 32 (banknotes) 77 (Tattoo), 113 (mobile), 117
(Fair Trade produce);

We are grateful to the following for providing locations and props: Roger Noel & the
children's football club, Forest Side Sports Ground p 95; Oselli Ltd, Witney
p 94; Oxford United Football Club p 44; Annie Price, Traffic Warden p 94;
Travelcare Travel Agents, Thame p 94

*We would also like to thank the following for permission to reproduce the following
photographs:* The Advertising Archives p 47 (India), (Côte D'Azur), (Chamonix);
AKG-Images p 16 (manuscript illumination, Paris, studio of the Boucicaut
master, c.1412. Paris, Bibliotheque Nationale); Alamy pp 19 (Uluru/D. &
J.Heaton/SC Photos), 22 (northern lights/D.Tipling/ImageState), 22 (rafting/
G.Pearl/StockShot), (jet/R.Cooke), (Great Wall/View Stock China), (Shark/
J.Rotman), 26 (falls/J.Agarwal/SCPhotos), 41 (funeral/Popperfoto), 46
(Wagner), 54 (J.Angerson), 60 (acestock), 64 (Miranda/J.Morgan), (Central
Park/F.Skold), 111 (Van Hilversum), 113 (J.Cleare/Worldwide Picture Library),
116 (J.Greenberg), 117 (burger/Wildmann/f1online), 155 (shark/J.Rotman),
(jet/R.Cooke); Alamy royalty free pp 14 (radio/Ablestock/Hemera
Technologies), 81 (teacher/SuperStock), 95 (student/D.Hammond/Design Pics
Inc.), 121 (Iwish); Associated Press pp 26 (man/T.McMullen) 156; BBC Photo
Library p 28; Capital Pictures p 83 all; Central News p 27 (schoolboy/
E. Wilcox); John Cleare Mountain Camera pp 26 (mountain), 113 (mountain);
John Connor Press Associates p 32 (S.Dennett); Corbis pp 11 (R.Ressmeyer), 16
(camels/K.Su), 19 (Thailand/C.Lisle), (Kilimanjaro/T.Davis), (Venice/S.Pitamitz),
20 (A.Cooper), 22 (dolphin/B.Krist), 24, 37 (biscuits/R.Faris), (boy looking up at
mother/N.Schaefer), (boy with report/J-L. Pelaez Inc.), 38 (Bettmann), 39
(Diana/Tim Graham/Sygma), Newspapers/Tim Graham), 41 (JFK Jr/Reuters), 45
(Katrina/J.Woodcock/Reflections Photolibrary), 50 (H.King), 52 (cathedral/
A.Woolfitt), 53 (Barry - red tie/S.Prezant), (Andy – blue shirt/T.McGuire), 57
(D.H.Wells), 59 (B. Ward), 63 (women in bar/LWA- S.Welstead), 65 (Indian
wedding/J.Wishnetsky), 69 (Bettmann), 73 (Russia/S.Sherbell/SABA), 74
(M.Finn-Kelcey), 75 (Chukotka/N.Fobes), 80 (H. Armstrong Roberts), 86
(snow/Corbis Sygma), 90 (Seth Eastman, The Buffalo Hunter/G.Clements), 112
(S.Maze), 114 (Bettmann), 123 (detail from The Creation of Adam by
Michelangelo Buonarroti/World Films Enterprises), 155 (dolphin/B.Krist);
Empics p 74 (ChelseaFC/EPA); pp 7 (Sophie & Catherine/J.Slater), 7 (tourists/
D.Hiser), 9 (Tokyo/Adastra), 14 (motorbike/E.Fitkau), 14 (cats/W.Eastep), 19
(Greece/G.Hellier), 22 (racing car/P.Rondeau), 25 (eating/S.Stickler), 33
(S.Krouglikoff), 36 (D.Durfee), 37 (girl in coat/T.Corney), 44 (Elsie/A.Upitis), 45
(Gavin/Chabruken), 53 (woman/S.Cohen), 56 (D.Sacks), 58 (S.Chernin/
Stringer), 61 (businessmen/D.Lees), 63 (forgive & forget/H. Grey), 63
(boys/T.Vine), 65 (wedding line-up/B.Thomas), 66 (Vicki & father/K.Webster),
67 (Bill & Judy/T.Schmidt), 76 (crowd/M.Powell), 79 (Hulton Archive), 81 (30's
teacher/W.Vanderson/Stringer/Hulton Archive), 85 (Chabruken), 88 (G.&M-
D.de Lossy), 89 (painter/A.Roberts), 103 (R.Daly), 105 (couple/D.Pizzi), 105
(bench/Creaps), 105 (guitar/N.Daly), 110 (J-L.Batt), 119 (theatres/A.Lyon), 120
(S.Justice); Pal Hansen p 107; JoongAng Ilbo, Seoul with special thanks to
Chun Su-jin p 12; Courtesy of Maureen, Tony & Tashi Wheeler and Lonely
Planet Guides pp 18, 19, 24, 153, 154; NASA p 40 (astronauts); National
Pictures p 27 (Rachel de Kelsey); NI Syndication p 49 (The Times/R.Cannon);
Peter Newark pp 16 (Marco Polo), 91; Punchstock pp 9 (Kirsty/Photodisc), 15
(Photodisc Green), 17 (Digital Vision), 44 (Tony/Thinkstock), 62 (Comstock),
65 (drive-in wedding/Brand X Pictures), 65 (Pratima/Comstock), 67 (Sandra/
Thinkstock), 96 (Photodisc Green), 98 (Photodisc Red), 115 (Dynamic
Graphics Group / Creatas), 119 (Soho), 119 (Piccadilly/Goodshoot), 153 (on
train); Jacket cover of The Blind Assassin by Margaret Atwood. Used by
permission of Doubleday, a division of Random House Inc; Redferns p 108
(BBC); Rex Features pp 55 (T.Buckingham), 70 (Silver Image), 76 (S.Cook), 76
(Oscar/D.Lewis); Robin Scagell/Galaxy Picture Library p 40 (moon rock/
Johnson Space Centre); Science Photo Library pp 10 (Observatory/D.Nunuk),
40 (Moon/NASA), 105 (grandfather and child/Maximilian Stock Ltd); Liz Soars
p 105 (sea tractor); South Tyrol Museum of Archaeology, Bolzano
www.iceman.it pp 86 (Iceman model), 87, 157; Still Pictures p 73
(pyramids/H.Schwarzbach)